Border Lives

Border Lives

*Fronterizos, Transnational Migrants,
and Commuters in Tijuana*

SERGIO CHÁVEZ

OXFORD
UNIVERSITY PRESS

Oxford University Press is a department of the University of Oxford. It furthers the University's objective of excellence in research, scholarship, and education by publishing worldwide.Oxford is a registered trade mark of Oxford University Press in the UK and certain other countries.

Published in the United States of America by Oxford University Press
198 Madison Avenue, New York, NY 10016, United States of America.

Chávez, Sergio R., author.Border lives : fronterizos, transnational migrants and commuters in Tijuana / Sergio Chavez.
pages cm
Includes bibliographical references and index.
ISBN 978–0–19–938057–2 (hardcover : alk. paper) — ISBN 978–0–19–938058–9 (pbk. : alk. paper)
1. Tijuana (Baja California, Mexico)—Emigration and immigration—Social aspects. 2. San Diego (Calif.)—Emigration and immigration—Social aspects. 3. Immigrants—Mexico—Baja California (Peninsula)—Social conditions. 4. Mexican-American Border Region—Social conditions. 5. Mexican-American Border Region--Economic conditions. 6. Transnationalism. I. Title.
JV7409.Z6T5534 2016
305.9'0691097223—dc23
2015027797

In memory of my abuelitos, José Refugio Chávez Lara (1923–1991) and Isidro Ramírez Ramos (1919–2007), both ex-braceros from Las Jícamas, Guanajuato, and my abuelitas, Guadalupe Pantoja Zavala and Paulina Ramírez Lara. For my parents, Trinidad and Aurelia Chávez.

CONTENTS

FIGURES AND TABLES

Figure

Tables

ACKNOWLEDGMENTS

As a first-generation college student, I grew up with limited resources, which made college especially challenging and often a very lonely place. However, I was blessed with having a strong social support system of people who cared about me and wanted to see me succeed at every stage of the way. Despite all of the obstacles that I faced, I believe that it was worth it, not just because I was able to eventually become a professor but because I have met some wonderful people whom I would not have otherwise met. My life would have been very different had I decided to become an automobile mechanic and remained in the Salinas Valley, which was what I wanted to pursue before I decided to enroll in Hartnell Community College. Let me thank and introduce you to all those wonderful people who helped to cultivate the scholar that I am today.

I want to start by thanking Max J. Pfeffer, David Brown, and María Cristina García, who all played an integral role in my early development as a migration scholar. Whenever I encountered roadblocks in graduate school, Angela Gonzales always made time to meet with me, whether it be over coffee or lunch. Becky Márquez provided important emotional support and believed in the project from its very early stages. While in Tijuana, the Instituto de Investigaciones Históricas at the Universidad Autónoma de Baja California provided workspace during my field research. I would like to also thank Elizabeth Maier from El Colegio de La Frontera Norte (Colef) and Ariel Mojica (El Colegio de Michoacán), who sparked and nurtured my love for "lo fronterizo." I also thank Magalí Muría for being a great friend and colleague and adopting me into her family. Finally, I would like to thank Karen Ann Watson-Gegeo who first inspired me to become an ethnographer through her own research with people from the

Solomon Islands. I am also really grateful that she was willing to write letters of recommendation at every stage in my academic career that ultimately made it possible to write this book.

I thank places that provided much-needed nourishment during my stay in Tijuana, including: Panadería La Sonrisa, Casa del Mole (the one in Colonia Libertad), Paleteria Michoacana, Tacos El Ruso and Tacos La Glorietta in El Soler, Tacos Chávez, Yogurt Place in Playas, Tortillería Grano de Oro and "el paisa," who sells coconuts in Mercado Hidalgo, and the one street vendor who sold the best burritos for only $1.00 each in La Revu out of a styrofoam cooler. Additionally, I thank all of the hard-working taxi and bus drivers who moved to Tijuana to provide better futures for their families, who took care of me and made me feel at home through my conversations with them while I was away from my family.

I never would be where I am today had it not been for the generous funding that I have received, including the Ford Foundation, which provided generous support to help me finish coursework and the fieldwork. Finally, the Woodrow Wilson National Foundation Career Enhancement Fellowship for 2013 allowed me to complete the book by giving me the time. As a Postdoctoral Fellow at the Carolina Population Center and the Sociology Department, I met many great colleagues who were influential in the early stages of the book. I want to thank Jackie Hagan and Ted Mouw for forcing me to work on my book even when I wanted to work on other projects. I would also like to thank Liana Richardson and Heather Edelblute who provided much-needed emotion work during the early writing stages.

I will forever be grateful to my colleagues at the Sociology Department at Rice University, who provided an environment that allowed me to grow as an independent scholar. I am especially thankful to Elizabeth Long and Elaine Howard Ecklund for reading the first draft of the book and encouraging me to publish it. Sarah Damaske, thank you for encouraging me to consider Oxford University Press. I also want to thank my awesome colleagues Jenifer Bratter, Rachel Kimbro, Ruth López Turley, Justin Denney, Bridget Gorman, Steve Murdock, Steve Klineberg, and Michael Emerson. Most importantly, I am grateful to the Culture Writing Group, which comprises Elizabeth Long, Robin Paige, Erin Cech, and myself. They read multiple drafts of my chapters and provided very constructive feedback on everything from honing my argument to expanding the implications of the study to larger sociological issues. I would also like to thank Claire Altman for forcing me to finish the last round of reviews and my undergraduate students who helped me on this project, including Lilly Yu, Rocio

Rosa-Lebrón (especially her work on the index), Tyler Woods, and graduate students Elizabeth Korver-Glenn, Irina Chukhray, MacKenzie Brewer, Laura Freeman, and Ellen Whitehead, who helped edit various sections of the book. I also thank Juan Manuel Avalos González and Maribel Campos Muñuzuri, who helped to conduct in-depth interviews, and Gretchen Rivero, who helped transcribe them. One person whom I cannot forget because he has helped to provide so much research assistance over the years is "el famoso" Erick Zamora Mendoza; gracias amigo.

I would also like to thank Rubén Hernández-León for inviting me to give a talk at UCLA's International Migration seminar that ultimately helped provide the much-needed push to complete the final book. I would like to especially thank James Cook, editor at Oxford University Press, for taking a chance on my book and providing much-needed guidance during the entire process. He was an incredible editor and I plan on working with him in the near future. I thank Amy Klopfenstein, editorial assistant at OUP, for helping move the book forward in the production process. I also thank Jessica Cobb, who made many of the stories in the book come alive and who helped me to strengthen the argument. Finally, I especially want to thank the anonymous reviewers at OUP for taking time to review my book and provide constructive feedback that ultimately made the book much stronger. Thank you for taking time out of your busy schedules to review my manuscript.

Finally, this book is dedicated to my family, Trinidad and Aurelia (a.k.a. Cleme) and my siblings, Angélica, Trinidad, Adriana, and Christopher, for being supportive of me throughout my life. I thank my parents for teaching me about the power of stories, something that I hope to teach to our new third-generation family members: Abriel Chávez, Evan and Elise Villegas. I could not have completed the book had it not been for Robin Paige, who not only spent an enormous time listening to and helping me formulate my argument but also did a lot of emotion work during the difficult writing times. You are the best. And to Abriel for waiting until the book was done before you decided to arrive.

Despite the vast array of social and financial support that I received, any final errors are strictly my own doing. I hope that by producing the scholarship that I have produced and, I have repaid some of the generosity for those who gave it to me.

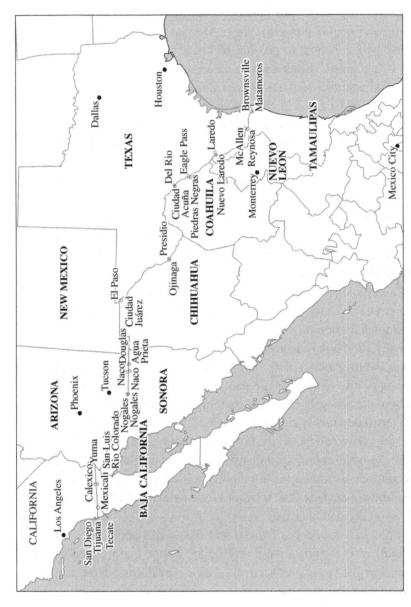

MAP 1 Map of the US-Mexico borderlands

FIGURE 0.1 The San Ysidro–Tijuana border, before and after Operation Gatekeeper.

Left: People crossing clandestinely through Tijuana in 1991, about one mile west of the port of entry in San Ysidro, California. People on the left side of the fence are hanging around on the US side and waiting for the opportune time to cross when the Border Patrol does not detect them. Right: The identical location, taken in 1999 after the implementation of Operation Gatekeeper, shows how increased border enforcement curtailed clandestine crossings. (Courtesy of the US Border Patrol)

FIGURE 0.2 Border commuters crossing into Tijuana, 2013.

Tijuana residents returning from shopping and working in the United States. (Author's collection)

Border Lives

CHAPTER 1 | Crafting Border Livelihoods

RAMÓN'S LIFE IS A border life. In 1968, at the age of eighteen, Ramón García left the small community of Jocotepec, Jalisco, because he had trouble finding work.[1] He went to the rapidly growing border city of Tijuana and never returned to his hometown. Soon after arriving in Tijuana, he found construction work at the home of a radio station owner who later hired him as an office assistant. This job provided Ramón with the stable employment he needed to apply for a Border Crossing Card (BCC), a permit that allows residents of border communities to legally cross to the United States to shop or visit family. In 1982, when the peso plummeted and he lost his job, Ramón used his BCC to work in Los Angeles at a distribution warehouse under the pretense of crossing to shop. Ramón spent the workweek in Los Angeles and returned to Tijuana every Friday night to spend time with his wife and their four children.

During one of his crossings, Ramón was involved in a verbal altercation with an immigration official who had mistreated an elderly border crosser. When Ramón questioned the US Customs and Border Protection (CBP) agent, the angry agent confiscated Ramón's BCC, leaving him unable to cross into Los Angeles. A few days later, Ramón returned to the San Ysidro port of entry and with the help of several family members, he jumped the fence. He boarded a Mexican bus line and moved to Los Angeles. Fortuitously, Ramón's border crossing took place just before the enactment of the Immigration Reform and Control Act of 1986 (IRCA), which granted legal residency to almost three million formerly unauthorized immigrants. A few years after obtaining his Green Card through IRCA, Ramón returned to Tijuana, where he settled permanently and became a daily border commuter. For the past seventeen years, Ramón has crossed into San Diego each day to work in construction, returning to Tijuana at the end of the workday.

Over the course of his life, Ramón has crossed numerous internal and international boundaries to secure a livelihood for himself and his family. Life histories like Ramón's are common in Mexican border cities. Previous migration and border scholars have long noted the distinct migration and labor market practices of border residents in comparison to their rural unauthorized Mexican counterparts.[2] *Border Lives* describes the strategies that people like Ramón employ to navigate the US-Mexico border and reveals the resources that US border and immigration policy offers to borderland residents that they utilize to construct their livelihoods. The book follows the lives of Tijuana residents as they establish roots in the borderlands, find work in the United States and Mexico, develop family and friendship ties that aid in the settlement process, and cross the border using legal and extralegal means across distinct historical periods.

The book is filled with the narratives of people who migrate to craft livelihood strategies in Tijuana, the United States, or both in an era of globalization and increased border enforcement. The border presents challenges to people on a daily basis but it also provides economic opportunities that extend beyond the confines of the nation-state. As large-scale historical and contemporary political-economic changes alter the structures and opportunities, border residents must adapt their livelihoods to survive. In particular, the book focuses on border residents' adaptation at a time when the political economy of the Mexico-US border was undergoing major changes, including: the displacement of peasants from Mexico's countryside that pushed men into the Bracero Program then to the borderlands; the Mexican economic crisis of the 1980s that created further unauthorized migration and led to the enactment of IRCA in 1986; and the contemporary era of escalating border policing and immigration restrictions through Operation Gatekeeper in 1994 that attempted to curtail unauthorized migration into the United States. In addition to looking at these immigration and border policy changes, the book also follows the working lives of migrants during a historical period of precarious employment in the United States, characterized by the rise in nonstandard work practices such as subcontracting, part-time work, and informal work arrangements, that have forced migrants and their families to find creative ways to survive in an increasingly globalized world marked by rising social and economic inequalities.[3]

Unpacking Agency

Border Lives also engages with a fundamental sociological question regarding border residents: do they exercise agency, living on their own terms? Or are they merely products of social, political, and economic structures? In the case of unauthorized immigrants, these questions are difficult to answer. Their legal status renders them vulnerable in the labor market, limiting their power and resources to make choices. But sociologists agree that although structures constrain human action they also "make possible a whole range of choices in everyday life."[4] That is, though political-economic structures constrain human action, they also provide new courses of action that people may take to live according to their needs and desires. By examining the strategies that people such as Ramón employ to cross the border, find work, and settle in the borderlands across time and space, this book provides a nuanced picture of how people reproduce social structure and challenge—successfully and unsuccessfully—the very system which restricts their mobility and livelihood options. While the book focuses on the lives of savvy border residents who were able to turn the border into a source of opportunity, it also documents the tremendous toll that these strategies exact on the everyday lives of border residents. The life stories in this book highlight border residents' actions and choices in the face of the considerable obstacles posed by restrictive border enforcement and immigration policies intended to limit workers' mobility in a region long known for cross-border trade. Their actions must be investigated ethnographically, by describing people's everyday lived experiences, and historically, to capture how those lived experiences change as people navigate the shifting context of the border.

Mustafa Emirbayer and Ann Mische assert the need to study "historical changes in agentic orientations" to show how "actors formulate new temporally constructed understandings of their own abilities to engage in individual and collective change, as well as how these micro level processes intersect with longer-term social, political and economic trajectories."[5] What better way to understand these processes than by studying the ultimate structural constraint on opportunity, choice, and social action: the physical border? A focus on the border reveals that structures are not always "virtual," existing only as traces of memory "orienting the conduct of knowledgeable human agents" as Anthony Giddens describes them.[6] Rather, as William Sewell points out, material resources like factories and land are also resources that define possibilities for human agency.[7] This book focuses on both physical and symbolic changes in the structure of the border and the immigration policies that separate Mexico and the United States to examine related changes in people's livelihood strategies as the physical and symbolic border itself changes. By studying agency and structure at the US-Mexico border, I am able to examine changes not only in human action but also in border residents' goals and desires. By describing the strategies that people employ to navigate the US-Mexico border, I reveal the resources that US economic and integration policy offer to borderland residents that they may utilize to construct their livelihoods.

Theorizing the Border

Thomas M. Wilson and Hastings Donnan argue that "the anthropological study of the everyday lives of border communities is simultaneously the study of the daily life of the state, whose agents there must take an active role in the implementation of policy and the intrusion of the state's structures into its people's lives."[8] A study about the border must then take into consideration how the border has been refashioned on a continual basis as a result of the efforts by lawmakers and law enforcers to regulate the political economy of the borderlands region. According to the historian George Sánchez, during the early part of the twentieth century, the border in El Paso–Juárez was continually remade by the US and Mexican governments to "suit the new and social economic realities of the region."[9] For example, the expansion of Mexican railroad lines helped to facilitate the mobility of Mexicans first to northern Mexican cities and eventually into Los Angeles and other southwest destinations. Furthermore, Sánchez argues that US immigration officials in the early 1900s did little to regulate the entry of Mexicans so as to not disrupt the flow of migrant labor into the US economy. The constant crossing of the border by Mexicans helped recreate the border on a continual basis and forced crossers to reinvent their strategies for gaining access to US labor markets.

In the contemporary period, Peter Andreas describes the theatrics of boundary enforcement at the US-Mexico border in an era of globalization marked by economic integration and market changes. He argues that border policing has been "less about achieving the stated instrumental goal of deterring illegal border crossers and more about politically recrafting the image of the border and symbolically reaffirming the state's territorial authority."[10] In fact, he asserts that unauthorized crossings have long been an integral part of the border and US-Mexico migration, yet the labeling of unauthorized immigration as a social problem only recently emerged as central to political discourse. Beginning with IRCA 1986 and accelerating during the mid-1990s, lawmakers and law enforcers enacted a series of immigration reforms and border enforcement tactics to demonstrate to their US constituents that the border was secure and orderly. However, the image of a "secure" and "orderly" border fails on two fronts according to Peter Andreas. First, it fails to address the unintended consequences of previous immigration policies, which have only exacerbated future unauthorized migration that then requires more policing of the boundary and newly constructed fences. Second, this image does not take into consideration the social and economic integration (through trade, tourism, and labor migration) that has long existed between Mexico and the United States that produces the steady flow of people and goods across the border.

These previous studies suggest that lawmakers and law enforcers have regulated the movement of populations through the creation of borders. They have executed this by establishing borders in the form of a fence to mark the geographical limits of each nation-state. At ports of entry, the CBP further regulates borders by screening travelers, charging duties, and enforcing US import and export laws. The US government further regulates migration through the disbursement of documents such as passports, BCCs, Green Cards, and visas that visitors use to verify their identity and enter the United States. Thus, the story of the border is a story of state power, and how the exertion of power, whether through immigration policy, border enforcement, or the allocation of passports and identification cards, shapes the movement of people and their livelihood options. John Torpey argues that the implementation of passports and identification cards—like border crossing or tourist cards—enabled "[t]he state monopolization of the means of legitimate movement" and "rendered individual travelers dependent on the state."[11] The implementation of passports, identification cards, and borders fostered what sociologist Max Weber terms "social closure," or the exclusive access to resources based on elements of social status such as race, social origin, and residence.[12] The lives of border residents reflect the state's mechanisms for regulating and controlling cross-border movement as well as crossers' strategies of adapting to increased surveillance at the border.[13]

Tijuana: City of Migrants

Tijuana provides a fertile ground to study how a constantly changing border restricts the workers' movement and how workers respond to the structural barriers they face on a daily basis. This book addresses the following questions: How do people adapt to social structures to make their livelihoods? How is the border both a barrier and a source of opportunity for people who reside in the borderlands? How do people craft a diverse set of livelihoods in the borderlands? What are the strategies which people use to settle in the borderlands to secure livelihoods? How do these strategies change as individuals encounter structural obstacles and personal issues?

Tijuanenses' livelihood strategies are dynamic, changing as they navigate shifting immigration policies, growing border restrictions, and declining economic opportunities in Mexico and the United States, as well as personal issues. By locating borderlanders' changing strategies in both place and time through the use of life-history narratives, this book shows that the border is both a barrier that limits possibilities and a resource that people tap into to form a diverse set of livelihood strategies and residential choices. Indeed, northern Mexico has historically been presented as a site of opportunity for migrants due to the complex economies that flourish in the borderlands and as a site of constraint because the border creates inequality between crossers and noncrossers.[14] This book expands on existing border scholarship by demonstrating how borderlanders negotiate the particular constraints and opportunities that they encounter as they leave their places of origin and arrive in Tijuana. It does not treat structures and strategies as static but rather looks at how a change in political or economic structures leads to changes in strategies by migrants and border commuters.

Tijuanenses make choices that are not limited to employment on one side of the border or the other or to a single migration event. Instead, they use the border to develop full social, emotional, and economic lives in Tijuana. Border commuters and migrants employ a variety of migration, border crossing, and labor market strategies to deal with growing economic insecurity in Mexico and in the United States and also to achieve social mobility. Some people substitute border commuting for international migration, which allows them to live in Mexico while crossing the border only to work for the day. This cross-border practice is an attractive livelihood strategy for migrants to Tijuana as well as for locals, providing the best of both worlds: higher wages in the United States and the cultural comforts of living in Mexico. For others, relocating to the border allows them to recraft their livelihood strategies by developing new contacts, obtaining job opportunities, and gaining access to legal documents to cross the border. In an era of increasing border enforcement, gaining access to legal documents, whether to become a border commuter or for international migration, becomes a key strategy that savvy residents use to turn structural barriers into a potential source of opportunity.

This study focuses on a subpopulation of crossers in Tijuana, but their experiences resonate with thousands of other border commuters and migrants. Along the entire US-Mexico border, including Calexico-Mexicali, El Paso–Ciudad Juárez, and Laredo–Nuevo Laredo, commuters and migrants cross to work in agriculture, construction, and the service sector industry. Because border commuters are a hard-to-find population, it is difficult to know the exact number of people who cross daily. Border commuting is also an experience that extends beyond the US-Mexico border: a 2010 study of the European Union (EU) labor force found that seven of every 1000 people surveyed lived in one country but were employed in another.[15] Although border commuting may exist in the EU, the frequency of return to primary residence for cross-border commuters like Irish commuters is less, given the long and costly commutes across EU states.[16]

Along the Mexico-US border, border commuting emerged historically from the Bracero Program (a guest-worker treaty between Mexico and the United States, 1942–1964) and is shaped by contemporary immigration, tourism, and trade policies. This study of border commuters will detail how these policies shape cross-border labor flows. The Pew Hispanic Center estimates that about half of the twelve million unauthorized immigrants currently residing in the United States entered through the port of entry and subject to immigration and customs inspection but joined the unauthorized population as either Non-Immigrant Visa overstayers or BCC violators.[17] The experiences of unauthorized migrants with legal documents to cross the border reveal important insights about an unauthorized population in the United States with regard to how they obtain documents that allow them to live in Mexico and cross the border. Their experiences also reveal the importance of social interaction at the border with regard to how border residents engage in strategic interaction to gain access to the US labor market and to prevent their documents from being confiscated by US state agents. The study also reveals the stresses associated with living a binational life as residents establish roots in the borderlands.

Borderland Strategies

Internal, International, and "Stepwise" Migration Trajectories

For Mexican rural families, migration represents an alternative to traditional livelihood strategies. For almost a century, development in Mexico has spurred rural Mexicans to migrate within and beyond national borders.

The entry of capital-intensive agricultural production and market-oriented farming practices displaced working people from traditional livelihoods like subsistence farming.[18] To obtain credit and income, rural inhabitants migrated domestically to work in urban industrial occupations or internationally to work in agriculture and construction.[19] Much of our knowledge about Mexican migration comes from these rural inhabitants whose main resource for migrating has been their tight, home-based kinship, friendship, and paisano (fellow countrymen) ties that help them cross the border, get a job, and mitigate emotional hardships when living abroad.[20] The study of Mexican rural migrants has yielded theoretical insights on how poor unauthorized migrants from Mexico's heartland utilize social ties to navigate constantly changing border and immigration policies.[21]

Recently a growing body of literature has begun to address labor migration flows emanating from Mexican border cities[22] and urban areas.[23] These studies highlight rural and urban differences in international migration strategies. In her research on Tijuana, Elizabeth Fussell identified four migration streams in Mexico. The first traditional rural migration stream was composed of young men with limited skills who relied on social networks to find low-skilled jobs in the United States. The second stream consisted of urban migrants, who had more human capital than their rural counterparts. The third stream was a small group of internal migrants who settled in Tijuana after finding employment opportunities in the border economy. Fussell also identified a fourth stream of internal migrants who used the city as a base to plan documented and undocumented trips.[24]

Rubén Hernández-León also studied urban migrants, and in particular, how the structural transformation of Monterrey's industrial sector displaced skilled workers who were forced to turn to international migration as a livelihood strategy.[25] To enter the US labor market, the metropolitan migrants that he studied turned to neighborhood and workplace friendships, strong family ties, and migration entrepreneurs to obtain the necessary knowledge and resources to enter the United States. Andrés Villareal and Erin Hamilton, meanwhile, found that cities with high levels of foreign investment and employment in the maquiladora (foreign factory) industry in Mexico were magnets that lured migrants—many from rural backgrounds—to border cities. The border cities also served as "staging sites" for some migrants before they moved abroad.[26] Thus, current migration scholarship highlights the diversity of migration strategies including internal, international, and also "stepwise" migration. These strategies are employed by rural and urban migrants as they search for new labor market opportunities.

Another strategy that transnational scholars have identified is that of transnationalism. This migration strategy consists of some migrants establishing roots abroad while others circulate back and forth, never preferring one place over another. Nina Glick Schiller and her colleagues developed the concept of "transnationalism" to show how poor migrants from Latin American and the Caribbean adapt to new environments.[27] Migrants and their descendants are not totally uprooted in their destinations but instead remain connected to their places of origin in part to escape racism and other forms of inequality that they face in the United States. Transnational migration scholars categorize this livelihood strategy as one in "which borders and boundaries are being contested and transgressed."[28] "Transmigrants" engage in cross-border exchanges and activities, such as sending remittances, traveling home, and engaging in telephone communication, that connect origin and destination.[29] These exchanges constitute a "transnational social field" where migrants can seek to expand notions of community, challenge gender relations, and overcome poverty.[30]

Skeptical of the durability of transnational ties, Roger Waldinger argues that "transnationalism is a rare condition of being" and that "transmigrants are an uncommon class of persons."[31] This is because immigration policies and border enforcement restrict back-and-forth movement across borders and with it, people's ability to be transmigrants. As migrants prolong their stay in the United States, they are more likely to call the destination their new home. While this may be the case for long-distance migrants who settle over time in the United States, Waldinger's assertion does not seem to hold in the borderlands. To live in the borderlands and to negotiate its boundaries means having two cell phones—one for engaging in transactions in each country—being bilingual and bicultural, knowing how to count change in dollars and in pesos, having friends with ties to Mexico and the United States, and having economic ties to Mexico and the United States. This book contributes to the literature on transnationalism by showing how Tijuanenses navigate social and economic relations on both sides of the border to fulfill their social and economic needs. Additionally, even when people do not cross, their close proximity to the United States means that they come in contact on a regular basis with people who bring back goods, ideas, and money as a result of their ties to the United States.

This book contributes to the literature on Mexico-US migration by highlighting the ways in which border residents engaged in internal, international, and "stepwise" migration as a means to become a border commuter.

Expanding Social Ties

Migrants all over the world are no longer moving simply from point A to point B but rather are utilizing a variety of strategies including internal, international, and "stepwise" in an effort to obtain contacts and information and to diversify livelihood strategies. In her study of Filipino domestic workers, Anju Mary Paul found that migrants engaged in a "stepwise migration" trajectory, moving from country to country until reaching their preferred location.[32] The Filipino domestic migrants resided in multiple locations across Asia and the Middle East in an effort to obtain money, knowledge, documents, and social connections that they could then use to reach a "dream destination" in the West.

In the Mexico-US case, previous studies demonstrate that when families relocate to the border, they form new ties based on the migration experience, regional affiliation, and settlement on the border.[33] Relocating to the border allows migrants to form new social ties that provide access to diverse social networks and migration information that facilitates entry into the US labor market that the migrants would not have access to otherwise in their hometowns.[34] Migrating to the border is a process that expands notions of family and community as people establish roots in northern Mexico. In sum, a relocation to the border allows migrants to form relationships that provide the necessary information and contacts and aids in their decision to migrate internationally. This study highlights how border residents form social ties in Tijuana as a means to obtain employment in Mexico or the United States. It also shows the ways in which border residents utilize contacts in deciding whether to migrate to the United States or to become a border commuter. Finally, it also investigates how social ties are also utilized to establish roots in Tijuana.

Diversifying Economic Opportunities

While demographers, sociologists, and anthropologists examine the experiences of long-distance migrants who utilize a variety of migration trajectories, border studies scholars look at the large-scale historical forces that bring residents to border cities and how residents establish new social ties in these cities. Josiah Heyman studied laborers along the Sonora-Arizona border and found that these labor migrants settled in the borderlands following a series of major life events.[35] The people in his study first migrated from their homes in rural Sonora to jobs in the state's copper mining industry. They then left for the United States to work in agriculture and finally went to the maquiladoras in northern Mexico as a result of political-economic forces and personal reasons. Heyman's research thus demonstrates that migration for northern border residents is a continuous process across the life course that entails a series of moves across internal and international labor markets.

Laura Velasco Ortiz and Oscar F. Contreras, meanwhile, investigated how the border and its unique economy impacted the daily lives of those who crossed the border and those who did not. On the one hand, they found that the border is a source of opportunity that allows Mexican border residents to gain access to money, employment, housing, and government assistance in Mexico and, for a select few, to take advantage of US employment opportunities. On the other hand, they were critical of the social inequalities that the border produces through "differentiation and social hierarchization" between crossers and noncrossers and through those who restrict entry (such as immigration officials) for Tijuana residents.[36] These scholars provide an alternative to the dominant view that all Mexicans want to live in the United States, showing that even when they don't cross, they can earn dollars, and when they do cross to work, they return to their homes at the end of the workday. The border then becomes a source of opportunity because it allows residents access to a diverse pool of income-generating activities in both the formal and the informal labor market on both sides of the border. As such, it is not surprising when research studies find that migrants are no longer returning to their communities of origin but, given the opportunities that exist there, are instead relocating to border cities, either by migrating domestically or settling there after returning from the United States.[37]

Border studies are characterized by the themes of opportunity (whether economic or social) and constraint. Oscar Martínez argues that borderlanders have access to opportunities including "human relationships, and access to a foreign economy [that] increases employment possibilities and consumer choices."[38] According to one study, the informal economy in the borderlands is an important source of income for many border residents; one-third of economic transactions in the South Texas border occur outside of the formal economy.[39] These and other authors contend that Mexican residents are able to cross the border and "work off the books" in domestic work, construction, and gardening.[40] They can also generate income by crossing the border to buy used clothing, appliances, electronics, construction materials, and automobiles, which are then resold for profit in Mexico to those unable to cross.[41] Elizabeth Fussell notes that Tijuana is an attractive destination to many domestic migrants because of its complex urban labor market, which provides stable and year-round employment and also provides the opportunity to work in the United States for those willing to cross the border.[42]

Opportunity and constraint are relevant themes because sister cities like San Diego–Tijuana, El Paso–Ciudad Juárez, and Laredo–Nuevo Laredo form transborder metropolises.[43] Despite being separated by an international border, these urbanized regions of Mexico and the United States form unified systems whose binational levels of activity like shopping and working "[integrate] settlements on either side of the border."[44] For example, in addition to the Mexican residents of Tijuana who work in the United States, the region also hosts a "much smaller" group of "highly qualified workers . . . who live north of the border but work for transnational companies . . . with subsidiaries in Mexico."[45] Consumerism also works both ways, allowing Mexican residents access to a broad range of commodities in the United States and US residents access to goods and services in Mexico.[46] Some scholars argue that the idea that this type of interaction leads to integration is problematic. This is because the border acts as a powerful institutional constraint that shapes mobility for residents who live on its southern side. Tito Alegría argues that a transborder metropolis will exist when the economies of both countries are equal and people from the south can circulate as freely as their northern counterparts across international boundaries.[47]

One unique opportunity that the US-Mexico border offers is the ability to become border commuters or transmigrants.[48] Border commuters reside in one country but cross the border on a daily basis to work in another country.[49] Border commuters are neither migrants nor immigrants per se, but some may previously have lived as immigrants in the United States before becoming border commuters[50] or they may reside in the United States during the workweek and return to Mexico on weekends.[51] Border commuters form a unique cross-border labor force, and their opportunities to cross are produced by US immigration policies such as the Bracero Program or IRCA[52] and other policies aimed at stimulating tourism.[53] Studies of border commuters largely emphasize border commuting as a US-Mexico phenomenon. Border commuting is a work-family arrangement in which internal migrants relocate to the border, settle on the Mexican side, and cross the border to work in immigrant jobs, including landscaping, agriculture, construction, restaurants, and as domestic workers.[54] Studies find that only half of border commuters enter the United States with legal work authorization while the rest enter the country legally using tourist visas or BCCs.[55] BCCs allow border residents to enter the United States for a period of seventy-two hours for the purposes of shopping and visiting relatives. BCCs also allow border residents to return to Tijuana as non-immigrants rather than as authorized or unauthorized immigrants. BCCs are a resource for border residents, who use them not only to shop and visit relatives in the United States but also to generate income through unauthorized employment or the purchasing of goods in the United States for resale in Mexico.[56] Tijuana residents are more likely to use legal documents when they first migrate to the United States in comparison with migrants in the rural and urban migration streams, who are more likely to cross the border without documents.[57]

What the above studies show is that border commuting is a strategy used by *fronterizos* (northern Mexican border residents) to minimize the costs of reproduction by taking advantage of the social and economic benefits of each country.[58] Michael Burawoy long ago characterized the system of migrant labor in California as one in which the processes of production and reproduction of the labor force were separated by international borders.[59] This arrangement allowed migrant laborers to survive on low wages from their work in the United States because the Mexican economy lowered the costs of day-to-day subsistence and the Mexican state provided resources such as healthcare and education.[60] The case of border commuters provides important theoretical insights on how residents who live in the borderlands negotiate this form of binational work-life by crossing borders to take advantage of the resources found in both nation-states. Additionally, it shows that the benefits derived from each country vary historically and across a person's life history.

Why Study Tijuana?

Tijuana is an ideal location to study livelihood strategies in the borderlands. Known by locals as "*la ciudad de los migrantes* [the city of migrants]" or "*la ciudad del brinco* [jumping-point city]," Tijuana is characterized by a vibrant economy and by complex migration and border commuting practices. The municipality of Tijuana had a population of 1,210,820 residents in 2000 and 1,559,682 in 2010,[61] most whom were born in another state.[62] Some Mexicans migrate internally to Tijuana with the intention of "jumping to the other side," but as they spend time in the city, they establish roots and decide to stay on the Mexican side of the border. Others are lured to Tijuana by the promise of employment in manufacturing, commerce, and construction, and the fact that wages tend to be higher than in other regions of Mexico.[63]

In the early 1960s, the Mexican government began to develop northern Mexico's economy by instituting the Programa Nacional Fronterizo (National Border Program: PRONAF) and the Border Industrialization Program (BIP), which created many employment opportunities. Magalí Muriá argues that prior to the implementation of PRONAF in 1961, Tijuana's economy was more tied to the United States, but the program integrated the city into Mexico's national economy.[64] PRONAF sought "economic, political, and cultural integration at the *fronterizo* level" with the primary goal of raising the living standards of fronterizos.[65] To accomplish this, PRONAF engaged in a series of infrastructure projects to enhance the physical appearance of the ports of entry in hope of attracting US tourists. The Mexican government also altered the landscape of Mexican northern cities through the construction of sports fields, parks, theaters, museums, and other public spaces.[66] These development projects transformed border cities into economically active markets.[67] The program also eliminated taxes and provided discounts to Mexican producers who imported products to Tijuana. PRONAF also created jobs and services in Mexican border cities,[68] transforming places like Tijuana into attractive destinations for domestic and international migrants.

Following the implementation of PRONAF, the Mexican government also instituted BIP in 1965, shortly after the termination of the Bracero Program, as a way of integrating returning braceros into Mexico's economy. This program allowed the establishment of foreign factories, known as maquiladoras, in Mexico. Maquiladoras operated duty-free as long as the finished products were exported. In Mexican northern border cities like Tijuana, maquiladoras generated manufacturing jobs that required large labor pools that were filled by either locals or migrants from Mexico's heartland. These jobs are a source of employment for women who fill them because they provide stable employment despite poor wages.[69]

Sociologist John A. Price conducted a community study of Tijuana in 1969, a few years after the implementation of PRONAF and BIP.[70] He documented how these policy changes shaped the consumer practices of US residents, who crossed into Mexico to take advantage of services provided by mechanics, barbers and hairstylists, photographers, and tailors 50–60 percent cheaper than in the United States.[71] The growth of service jobs provided employment opportunities for fronterizos and domestic migrants. Price also observed that hundreds of people crossed the border to work in the United States or stayed in Tijuana to work in a factory producing televisions for the US-based Sears, Roebuck & Company. Border residents who lived in close proximity to the United States were also able to access discarded and used US goods, producing economies based on the sale of used electronics, clothing, and even automobiles.[72] Thus, Tijuana presents a unique context to study the border as a site for economic opportunity and access to new contacts and legal documents to cross the border that were unavailable in migrants' communities of origin.

As a result of cross-border trade, Tijuana is home to one of the largest populations of border commuters (people who live in Mexico but cross the border to work in the United States), at 35,943, followed by Mexicali, with 16,013, and Ciudad Juárez, with 15,164. Even though border commuters make up only a small proportion of the overall labor force in Tijuana (8 percent), their earnings make a significant contribution to the city.[73] According to one estimate, border commuters earn about one-fifth of all Tijuana resident wages.[74]

Because of the presence of migrant and commuter populations who move across national and international lines, Tijuana was one of the first Mexican border cities to experience intense US border controls. In 1994, Operation Gatekeeper was instituted in San Ysidro, California, increasing the number of Border Patrol agents who watched the international line while extending and reinforcing the fence separating Mexico and the United States.[75] This approach reduced clandestine crossings in Tijuana and forced migrants and smugglers to find pathways through the dangerous Sonoran desert terrain or South Texas landscape where hundreds of migrants die each year.[76] The United States' effort to keep out "undesirables" mirrors a global trend toward the proliferation of barricades designed for human containment. The Israeli border that runs through the West Bank, Saudia Arabia's construction of a ten-foot-high fence along the Yemen border, and the Zimbabwe–South African border are other examples of prohibitive barriers to human mobility.[77]

As a "city of migrants," Tijuana provides an interesting site to study how people build their lives in the borderlands amid rising border enforcement. In addition to its being home to the largest population of border commuters and a "jumping point" for international migration, Claudia Masferrer and Bryan R. Roberts find that Tijuana, in addition to Guadalajara, Ciudad Juárez, and Mexicali, is emerging as a preferred destination for return migrants who opt out of returning to their place of birth.[78] Finally, though they are not the focus of this study, the researchers also found that Tijuana is home to many repatriated deportees.[79] According to the Department of Homeland Security, 438,000 aliens were removed during 2003; of these, 72 percent were from Mexico.[80] These demographic trends highlight the growing importance of border cities that house diverse populations who constitute an international labor force. What remains to be understood is how individuals integrate socially and economically into a borderland society where they must learn to construct their lives binationally.

Ethnography at the Border

From September 2004 to January 2006, I lived continuously in Tijuana, Baja California, Mexico in the working-class community of Infonavit Lomas del Porvenir. I also conducted a number of short revisits to the field (ranging from a weekend to a week) in 2007, 2009, and 2010–11. I conducted a final trip in October 2013, when I returned to understand how the lives of respondents had changed in the intervening years, and I document these changes in the epilogue.

The study consisted of ethnography and in-depth interviewing. During the first month of fieldwork, I engaged in participant observation in an effort to become familiar with Tijuana and to develop key contacts. I conducted in-depth interviews with respondents and collected their complete labor histories in Mexico and the United States; I also recorded the stories of their migration and border crossing, their social networks, and their consumption practices. All interviews were conducted in Spanish. The recordings were transcribed verbatim, and coded and analyzed for common themes and patterns. I read and reread each interview until I was deeply familiar with the individual stories. I also crossed the port of entry several times a week to document people's border-crossing experiences and encounters with CBP agents.

In total, I conducted 158 interviews with border residents, 118 with commuters and forty with non-commuters (the methodological appendix describes the methods in greater detail). Though the focus of the book is primarily on border commuters, I also interviewed noncommuters to understand how people who relocate to the border obtain information, contacts, and BCCs to navigate the border economy. For example, to get a comprehensive overview of ex-braceros' labor market histories, I interviewed both ex-braceros who became border commuters after the termination of the Bracero Program and those who chose the Mexican labor market. A purposive nonrandom selection process was utilized to sample a diverse set of respondents distinct with regard to migration and labor market backgrounds, and also with regard to age, family composition, education, homeownership, years living in Tijuana, and region of origin.

In my research, I was unable to explore the experiences of women as deeply as I would have liked. Because my research dealt with a highly sensitive topic—legal status—it was difficult for me to establish a rapport across a second layer of sensitivity—gender dynamics. While previous scholars report few problems in conducting their research with unauthorized populations after establishing a rapport, my research faced high barriers to rapport building.[81] People who used BCCs valued this key to their livelihoods and feared that by talking to me they might be identified as a violator and lose this precious resource. For many, it was too much of a gamble to share stories with a stranger. I surmounted this barrier in many cases by forming friendships with other men who included me in their networks of trust. However, these networks rarely included women. In the *machista* society of early 2000s Tijuana, it was not culturally appropriate for me to sit down alone with women who were married or in long-term partnerships.[82] When I asked some men if I could talk to their wives or girlfriends who were also crossers, they told me that they could relay the experiences of their partners. I was able to conduct some interviews with women, who were in relationships with those men with whom I had established a close rapport. However, this book focuses primarily on the experiences of men because I was able to gather rich data for comparison based on their stories. This indicates that positionality matters in the field, especially in qualitative sociology; in my case, gender was a constraint.

Table 1.1 provides an overview of the entire sample broken down by the categories of noncommuters and border commuters. The majority of participants were male (70 percent) with a mean age of about forty-six years (high due the presence of ex-braceros in the sample). Most respondents were married or cohabited (75 percent), had completed about eight years of education, and were born in the historic region of Mexico (primarily Guanajuato, Jalisco, and Michoacan) or in border states (Baja California). Border commuters were slightly younger at 41.5 years and had a bit more education (9.5 years). The border residents I interviewed had lived in Tijuana an average of twenty-five years and had employed a diverse range of migration and labor market strategies including: domestic migration (46 percent), international migration (63 percent), stepwise migration (23 percent), and border commuting (75 percent).

Table 1.2, meanwhile, presents demographic trends for border commuters by cohort. Drawing on the work of Douglas Massey, Jorge Durand, and Nolan Malone, I grouped my respondents by broad periods of Mexican migration. These periods capture the major economic transitions and immigration policy changes that were underway when people began to cross the border on a daily basis to work in neighboring San Diego County.[83] Six of my respondents became border commuters after

TABLE 1.1 Sociodemographic characteristics of border commuters and noncommuters (N = 158)

VARIABLES	OVERALL MEAN OR %	NONCOMMUTERS MEAN OR % (N = 40)	COMMUTERS MEAN OR % (N = 118)
Background			
Age	45.8	58.4	41.5
Male	69.6%	77.5%	66.9%
Ever married or cohabitating	75.3%	90%	70.3%
Has children	62.7%	85%	55.1%
Education (years)	8.1	4.0	9.5
Owns home	47.5%	45%	48.3%
Years lived in Tijuana*	24.8	21.3	26.5
Region Born**			
Historic	34.8%	70.0%	22.9%
Border	39.9%	7.5%	50.9%
Center	11.4%	22.5%	7.6%
USA	13.9%	0	18.6%
Lifetime migratory and commuting experience**			
Domestic migrant	45.6%	87.5%	31.3%
International migrant	63.3%	92.5%	53.4%
Stepwise migrant	23.4%	35.0%	19.5%
Border commuter	74.7%	0	100%

* Calculations exclude residents born in Tijuana.
** Historic region: Aguascalientes, Colima, Durango, Guanajuato, Jalisco, Michoacan, Nayarit, San Luis Potosi, and Zacatecas; Border region: Baja California, Chihuahua, Coahuila, Nuevo Leon, Sinaloa, Sonora, and Tamaulipas; Center region: Mexico City (DF), Guerrero, Hidalgo, Mexico, Morelos, Oaxaca, Puebla, Queretaro, and Tlaxcala. USA refers to people born there.
*** Each migratory and commuting experience is treated as a different life-course event. The migrations are not mutually exclusive and a person can experience more than one type of migration. For this reason, the column percentages do not add up to 100 percent.

their participation in the Bracero Program (1942–1964) which provided them with Green Cards; eight respondents became border commuters crossing without documents or with BCCs or Green Cards during the open-border period (1965–1985), when unauthorized migrants were largely undeterred from entering the United States; twenty-four respondents became border commuters during the post-IRCA period (1987–1993), when the US government closely monitored the US-Mexico boundary and when formerly unauthorized immigrants were able to obtain Green Cards that they used to cross the border on a daily basis; finally, eighty respondents

TABLE 1.2 Border-commuter demographics by cohort* (N = 118)

VARIABLES	BRACERO PERIOD (1942–1964) MEAN OR % (N = 6)	OPEN-BORDER PSERIOD (1965–1985) MEAN OR % (N = 8)	POST-IRCA PERIOD (1987–1993) MEAN OR % (N = 24)	POST-GATEKEEPER (1994–) MEAN OR % (N = 80)
Background				
Age	73.0	66.6	46	35.3
Male	100%	75.0%	79.2%	60.0%
Ever married or cohabitating	100%	87.5%	91.7%	60.0%
Has children	100%	87.5%	70.8%	43.8%
Education (years)	0.83	4.5	10.6	10.4
Owns home	66.7%	37.5%	66.7%	42.5%
Years lived in Tijuana**	45.5	27.3	27.1	23.7
Lifetime migratory behavior*				
Domestic migrant	83.3%	62.5%	29.2%	25.0%
International migrant	100%	87.5%	66.7%	42.5%
Stepwise migrant	66.7%	50%	20.8%	12.5%
Mexican occupation before first commute				
Agriculture	100%	37.5%	0	2.5%
Professional	0	0	8.3%	5.0%
Manufacturing	0	25.0%	25.0%	20.0%
Service	0	37.5%	25.0%	41.2%
Unemployed / Not in labor force	0	0	33.3%	23.8%
Other	0	0	8.3%	7.5%
Primary US occupation as commuter				
Agriculture	100%	50.0%	0	0
Professional	0	0	4.2%	5.0%
Manufacturing	0	25.0%	50.0%	23.8%
Service	0	25.0%	29.2%	62.5%
Unemployed / Not in labor force	0	0	0	0
Other	0	0	16.7%	8.8%
Location of employment (at time of interview)				
Mexico	0	25.0%	16.7%	22.5%
United States	0	25.0%	83.3%	63.8%
Unemployed / Not in labor force	83.3%	50.0%	0	5%
Both countries	16.7%	0	0	8.8%

* Each cohort represents the initiation of commuting.

** Calculations exclude residents born in Tijuana.

*** Each migratory and commuting experience is treated as a different life-course event. Migrations are not mutually exclusive and a person can experience more than one type of migration. For this reason, the column percentages do not add up to 100 percent.

became border commuters during the post–Operation Gatekeeper period (from 1994), a time when the border was fortified with fence construction, increased Border Patrol, and more port inspectors.[84] During the post–Operation Gatekeeper period, people crossed the border with BCCs, Green Cards, and also US citizenship.

Though I divide the overall sample into four groups based on the period of their initiation into border commuting, my analysis is mainly focused on two key events: the enactment of IRCA in 1986 and Operation Gatekeeper in 1994. These are defining events in the history of Mexico-US migration that altered how border commuters were able to cross the US-Mexico border. Table 1.2 shows that the oldest cohorts were more likely to have employed a diversity of migration strategies including domestic migration, international migration, and stepwise migration to seek new livelihoods in comparison to new cohorts of border commuters such as those in the post-Gatekeeper era. The table also reveals that people who crossed the border during the Bracero period and the open-border period were more likely to have worked in agriculture in comparison to later cohorts who were more likely to work in services.

In addition to in-depth interviews, I also conducted observations throughout Tijuana's urban space in an effort to locate people's behaviors in their social settings. One key site for my observations was the port of entry in San Ysidro, California, where I documented interactions among daily crossers and between crossers and immigration officials. Nearly every morning for the first year, I awoke before dawn to join the thousands of men and women who lined up in cars and by foot and waited at the port of entry to get to their jobs. Some border crossers arrived as early as 4:00 a.m. to get to work or to get their children to school on the US side. Crossers who commuted to work in San Diego County woke early to leave their homes in such neighborhoods as Colonia Libertad (one of the first neighborhoods established within walking distance of the United States), El Florido (located in an industrial area), El Soler, Francisco Villa, or Playas de Tijuana (located along the Pacific Ocean).

I observed border commuters arriving at the San Ysidro port of entry by car, taxi, motorcycle, bicycle, or bus. After they were dropped off at *La Linea*, as locals refer to it, crossers walked past pharmacies, convenience stores selling Mexican candies and cold bottles of water, and street vendors who ran a brisk business during the commuter rush hour. These vendors provided early morning crossers with the calories that they needed to make it through the morning. On their way to the pedestrian check point, these crossers grabbed *tamales, tortas* (Mexican sandwiches), *champurrado* (Mexican hot chocolate made with corn flour), *arroz con leche* (warm rice pudding), and burritos. The vendors who sold these goods adopted border names like *Tacos La Linea* or *Tamales La Linea*. Once in line, Mexican commuters from all occupational sectors waited together to cross the border. This included cooks, construction workers, janitors, engineers, mechanics, landscapers, hotel workers, and even a US Postal Service worker. Only professional occupations were not well represented among crossers.

Some mornings, I simply observed border crossers as they interacted with others or purchased burritos, fish tacos, and coffee; other times, I struck up conversations as we awaited inspection. During these informal conversations, I asked crossers which neighborhoods they came from, what jobs they were headed to in the United States, and how long they had been crossing the border to work. I also asked commuters about their experiences crossing through the port of entry, especially with regard to interactions with CBP officials and fellow border crossers. People were generally quite receptive to talking about their experiences of crossing the border informally, but they were less receptive to being interviewed, a topic of discussion I deal with in greater depth in the appendix. In addition, I documented commuters' consumption practices by visiting shopping centers and recording specific observations about crossers who returned with purchases from the United States. I also asked participants about their shopping behaviors on both sides of the border, such as where they preferred to put gas in their car or buy groceries and clothes, and their reasons for these choices. By crossing the border daily, I was able to get a better sense of how people who work and shop in the United States navigate one of the most heavily policed points along the border. I carried a small notebook and took notes in fast-food restaurants in the United States as soon as I crossed the border.

I also established close relationships with border commuters and migrants by visiting them at their homes and neighborhoods on a regular basis, joining them in crossing the border to shop and work, and shadowing them as they socialized with family and friends. I observed them as they fought, reflected, worried, laughed, cried, and celebrated everyday events one-on-one or with friends and family. I drove with people to Los Angeles and San Diego to meet extended family members who had offered commuters a place to live at various points in their migration history. During these daily interactions, I conducted informal and formal interviews with border residents about how they navigated the constantly changing social and economic structures in the borderlands. By focusing on their daily lives, I was able to document not only how these migrants used the various resources at their disposal but also how the choices they made determined the location of their jobs and homes on either side of the border.

During my time in Tijuana, I also visited the neighborhoods and homes of respondents. For example, Ramón, whose narrative opened this chapter, moved to Tijuana before migrating to the United States but eventually returned to build a life in Tijuana. When I met Ramón, he was crossing the US-Mexico border daily to work in San Diego. Despite having a Green Card that allowed him to live in the United States, he decided to settle in Tijuana to escape a more hurried US lifestyle. Together, Ramón and his wife Chelo built a nine-bedroom home with the hope that their four children would move in after they got married. Two of their children, however, moved to the United States because they found better employment opportunities across the border. When Ramón and Chelo were not working, they enjoyed visiting Playas de Tijuana, where they ate fresh fruit and listened to the waves or watched movies at the local theater. They also hosted family parties to entice their US-based children back to visit.

In addition, I conducted participant observation of city life in general and with border commuters and migrants in particular as they constructed livelihoods in their homes, neighborhoods, workplaces, and at the port of entry. I also observed the emotions that border crossers felt when they witnessed the arrest of other Mexican nationals crossing the port of entry. I took photographs and collected photographs and employment documents from respondents' archives to provide context about living in the US-Mexico borderlands. My selection of research participants and places to observe emerged through a process of ethnographic discovery and selection of participants who represented the complex and varied border commuting experience. I also developed networks of informants and honed my interview questions as I learned to navigate the urban landscape and as I began to understand how border commuters and migrants planted roots in the borderlands. At each stage of the research process, my access broadened to a diverse group of border residents who provided a unique perspective on the border crossing experience.

During one of my return trips from the United States, I stopped at a local ice cream shop where I met Rubén and his father, Aurelio Nava, a former bracero and undocumented migrant. Aurelio had worked in Stockton, California, as a bracero picking tomatoes in 1963 and as an ice cream street vendor in Los Angeles in the 1980s. After I explained my project to Aurelio, he suggested that any study about Tijuana would be incomplete without interviewing the ex-braceros who were key actors in the making of northern Mexico's economy. A few days after our conversation, I joined him and his friends at Parque Teniente Guerrero (Tijuana's first public park), where ex-braceros congregated weekly. At these Sunday gatherings, I spoke with ex-braceros about their US work experiences. I also observed these men as they met in groups and talked about the process of forming relationships in Tijuana. They often argued passionately about whether migrating to the United States had been worth the sacrifice of abandoning their birthplaces.

I eventually interviewed the ex-braceros formally and conducted hundreds of informal interviews with others. I also interviewed many of their family members who were internal migrants, commuters, and return migrants. Many scholars consider these ex-braceros to be pioneer migrants who changed the face of large-scale international migration from Mexico to the United States.[85] Thus, I integrated the experiences of ex-braceros into my book on the border to understand their role in the making of a cross-border resident population both as internal migrants and as border commuters. After all, border cities were initially targeted by the Mexican government for economic development to help absorb the thousands of returning, underemployed braceros after their contracts ended in the United States I was fortunate to access this pioneer group of migrants who played an intricate role in Mexico-US migration and the economic development of northern Mexico.

During the field research process, I developed rapport with several key informants and interviewed a variety of people who represent different border lives. One such key informant was again Ramón. I attended various soccer matches, birthday parties, and dinners with him. I interviewed Ramón, his wife Chelo, and other members of their family. By developing close rapport with Ramón, I was able to document how he helped integrate his sons into the cross-border labor market in the United States but was unable to help them find work in Mexico when they lost their BCCs. In addition, through an informal group of mountain bike riders, I met Jorge, a former daily border crosser. Jorge invited me to his neighborhood and allowed me to "hang out" at a garage sale he organized on Sunday afternoons. He introduced me to his childhood friends, all of whom had international migration experience and ultimately participated in this study. It was through one of Jorge's friends that I met Cesar, who then introduced me to a *coyote* (smuggler). I was initially worried about my personal safety, but I agreed that without access to clandestine border crossers, my work would not be complete. So one Sunday afternoon, I agreed to meet with a lifelong friend of Cesar's who worked smuggling migrants across the border. In stark contrast to my fears, the man looked like he could be my uncle, in a white t-shirt, faded blue jeans, sandals, and a baseball cap. He kindly shared his story with me, as did two other ex-smugglers who provided their insights on the dynamic of border crossings in Tijuana.

One of the difficulties of conducting research in urban settings as opposed to rural communities is the anonymous nature of social relations. As an ethnographer studying the US-Mexico border, I wanted to get to know as many people as possible to learn about life in the borderlands. I spoke with residents from all walks of life, including migrants, street vendors, factory workers, teachers, students, taxi drivers, current and former smugglers, and even drug dealers. Contrary to most popular depictions of border cities as dangerous and chaotic, I developed close relationships with people from a wide variety of backgrounds, including some I was warned not to meet. Through my formal and informal interviews, I provide readers with depictions of the people who make Tijuana into a border city and how they negotiate their cross-border lives.

While most ethnographers have tended to limit their analysis to present-day conditions, I follow the work of contemporary ethnographers who have begun to integrate history into ethnography to understand how global forces and larger structures shape the behaviors of individuals and groups. Mario Luis Small argues that history allows ethnographers to "interpret the observed present conditions in light of continuously invoked elements of the past."[86] As a result, I examine the past of Tijuana and its residents to make sense of how the current state of affairs came into being. How the border is defined, how it has changed, and how people draw resources from it are central themes that I study through life histories and everyday lives as people make their living in the borderlands. The border is a reflection not only of the state actors who construct it, but also of the individuals who uphold or challenge it in their daily lives. As I show throughout the book, the border is made and remade on an everyday basis, not only through theatrics between law makers and enforcers and their US audience, as Peter Andreas describes, but also through daily face-to-face interactions between border crossers and state officials.[87]

A Note on Terminology

To better understand transborder interactions, I employ several key terms. First, the term *border residents* refers specifically to people in Tijuana who made the decision to reside permanently in the borderlands, though this decision can change from one day to another. Border residents include two main groups: border commuters and migrants (both internal and return), categories that are not mutually exclusive. "Border commuters" refers to people who live in Mexico and cross the border on a daily, weekly, or monthly basis to work in the United States. For these crossers, their place of residence is Mexico while their place of employment is the United States. "Migrants" refers to people who settled in Tijuana through domestic or international routes. Migrants can settle in Tijuana either as a domestic migrant (for example, a person who relocated from Guanajuato to Tijuana) or as an international migrant (for example, a person who moved to Tijuana after having lived in Los Angeles, California). It is important to note that a person may occupy one or more categories throughout their migratory and border commuting life history. I also employ "fronterizos" to refer to people of northern Mexico including those with and without US experience.

Second, the term *borderlands* refers to the geographic region that encompasses Tijuana in Mexico and southern San Diego County in the United States. The borderlands comprise the political and economic structures that inhibit human action and that provide resources to migrants, such as access to social networks, crossing cards, and access to diverse employment opportunities on either side of the border. These structures, and their attendant constraints and resources, are place-specific and unlike what migrants would find in the interior of Mexico.[88]

Organization of the Book

The book examines how people construct their livelihoods in Tijuana, Baja California, Mexico within the context of large-scale social forces, including border enforcement, immigration policies, and the restructuring of the US and Mexican labor markets. These forces have created a precarious situation for Mexicans and their families. Tijuanenses construct livelihoods using the resources they are able to obtain from the political and economic structures at the US-Mexico border.

In chapter 2, I trace the return migration and labor market reintegration of ex-braceros who left their homes in western central Mexico or the United States and resettled as fronterizos. These men settled in Tijuana after the Mexican government instituted the 1965 Border Industrialization Program in northern Mexico with the intention of providing employment to return migrants. The men entered the border economy through two labor market pathways. First, economic reshuffling in northern Mexico provided ex-braceros with access to jobs in construction, small business, and transportation that were unavailable in their places of origin, allowing former peasants to reinvent themselves as urban workers in the borderlands. Second, US farmers cultivated a cross-border commuter labor force stationed in Tijuana but economically active in San Diego after the end of the Bracero Program. These US farmers constructed a reserve army of labor by protecting their workforce from Border Patrol agents and legalizing workers. Ex-braceros continued to cross the border to work for US farmers because agriculture provided stable jobs with some benefits. By focusing on these two distinct labor market pathways, I show how migrants built careers that were not restricted to one side of the border or the other.

In chapter 3, I examine the contemporary experiences of border commuters in Tijuana. I describe how border residents obtain legal documents that allow them to cross the border to work in the United States in two different historical periods. First, I detail the ways in which border residents strategized to obtain Green Cards through the Immigration Reform and Control Act in 1986 to become border commuters. Second, I turn to the experiences of crossers in the post–Operation Gatekeeper era who cross the border to work in the United States using Border Crossing Cards that allow them to cross but not to work. BCCs were integral to multiple labor and migration strategies, allowing holders to join the cross-border labor force or to become stepwise or even return migrants. Finally, the chapter describes how border residents use Green Cards and BCCs to seek livelihoods that span nation-state boundaries.

Chapter 4 focuses specifically on how people cross the border to obtain unauthorized work. It compares the border-crossing strategies of migrants before and after 1994, when Operation Gatekeeper rerouted migration patterns in the borderlands. I argue that the shift from a fluid to a closed border did not end cross-border migration but instead reinvented crossing practices. I also discuss the border-crossing strategies of clandestine crossers bound for interior labor markets in the United States and daily undocumented commuters who crossed clandestinely to work in regional agricultural labor markets. In particular, I examine their use of interpersonal networks, smugglers, and employers to evade inspection and successfully gain access to unauthorized employment. In this chapter, I also examine the experiences of border commuters who use BCCs to work without authorization. The chapter catalogues the various strategies that BCC commuters use to get past CBP officials. I find that present-day crossers employ Goffmanian strategies of impression management to outwit U.S. Customs and Border Patrol agents. At the US-Mexico border, the state continues to be a powerful player in regulating labor migration, but a select group of crossers is able to pursue employment opportunities by challenging the political structure that attempts to restrict borderland residents to the Mexican labor market.

In chapter 5, I provide an ethnography of social networks as they are formed, used, and reconfigured by border migrants through face-to-face interaction in occupational settings, in the streets and neighborhoods, and at the international port of entry. Despite social ties to current and former migrants as well as border commuters, fronterizos are prevented from capitalizing on these resources to work in the United States by the physical border and by immigration and border policies that govern mobility. Thus, the chapter illustrates how networks both enable and constrain human action along one of the most guarded borders in the world.

The final chapter addresses the implications of the empirical evidence presented throughout the book. Here, I revisit the question of structure versus agency to consider how border crossers challenge existing social structures and the institutions that attempt to regulate human action. I show that the relationship between agency and structure should be studied historically and contextually. In particular, I discuss how border residents who encountered blocked trajectories reconstructed their contexts of action.[89] Studying how migrants alter their agency as they encounter barriers becomes critical in a rapidly changing society, as the meaning of agency can change across different historical periods. As such, I illustrate how border residents navigate domestic and international labor markets, formal and informal employment, and legal and illegal activities in ways that vary with changes in the economic and political landscape of northern Mexico. To truly locate the agentic actions of border residents in their structural context, one must understand how their daily lives are conditioned by the porous and dynamic nature of the border itself.

Following the conclusion, I provide an epilogue and methodological appendix. The epilogue checks in on the lives of several key actors almost ten years after the initial fieldwork to ask whether their border livelihoods were sustainable over a long period of time. Finally, the methodological appendix presents the "story behind the story," providing a detailed discussion of my approach to the study. In particular, I describe methodological successes and failures in my study of migration and border-crossing behaviors in the large city of Tijuana.

CHAPTER 2 | The Occupational Careers
of Ex-Braceros

IN 1956, A DROUGHT devastated the corn harvest in Mesilla de Sombrerete, Zacatecas, prompting twenty-two-year-old Agustín Méndez to enroll in a guest-worker program and leave for the United States. Between 1942 and 1964, the US government issued nearly five million temporary labor contracts to Mexican workers under the Bracero Program. Two of these contracts went to Agustín to work picking strawberries, first in northern San Diego County and then in Santa Cruz County. Previous studies have described how, after finishing their contracts, braceros returned to their previous agrarian lives in their origin communities, became circular migrants, or obtained legal permanent residence and settled in communities throughout the United States.[1] Yet Agustín and many other former braceros like him chose an alternate life path, relocating to Mexican border cities to build occupational careers that were not restricted to one side of the border. At the border, these former peasants, with few resources and limited work experience outside of agriculture, recrafted themselves as Mexican urban workers or continued to labor as US farmworkers in a rapidly changing economy in the years following the end of the Bracero Program.

Why did these men decide to relocate to the border? Why did some men decide to work in Mexico while others continued to cross the border to work in the United States? What economic and noneconomic factors shaped their decisions of where to live and work? In this chapter, I demonstrate that ex-braceros were not just rational actors seeking to maximize wages as they moved from origin to destination and back. To build livelihoods in the borderlands, ex-braceros dug into their pasts as peasants in

Mexico and as bracero field hands in the rural southwest United States. Many scholars describe how US-based migrants navigate primary and secondary labor markets and how they acquire English skills, obtain higher wages, and become entrepreneurs as they adapt to US life.[2] However, we know very little about what happens to return migrants in border contexts. Focusing on the stories of braceros, this chapter fills this void by unpacking the agency of ex-braceros to understand why they chose to relocate to the border from Mexico's heartland and how they recrafted a variety of livelihood strategies as an emerging population of fronterizos.

This chapter describes ex-braceros' strategies to navigate a dynamic border economy following the termination of the Bracero Program through the open-border period (1965–1985). This was a time of major economic changes in the borderlands as the Mexican government instituted the 1965 Border Industrialization Program (BIP), which created jobs in manufacturing and services. After the demise of the guest-worker program, US farmers also sought new methods for recruiting migrant farmworkers. In this rapidly changing economy, ex-braceros utilized the border as a source of opportunity to fulfill their occupational needs.

Specifically, the ex-braceros I met pursued two labor market trajectories in Tijuana. One group retrained themselves as urban workers and played important roles during the modernization of Tijuana's labor market. Another continued to cross the border to work in a low-wage US agricultural labor market. All of these migrants made strategic labor market decisions in a rapidly changing border economy based on both economic and noneconomic factors. Those who chose to labor in Tijuana did so because they found urban jobs that provided stability for most of their working career. Some ex-braceros who worked in Tijuana reported earning wages that were equal to or higher than what they had earned in the United States. The complex division of labor in the city exposed ex-braceros to newfound jobs and skills that brought an end to their US migration careers. Those who continued to cross the border identified access to higher wages through US employment and the opportunity to live in Mexico as determining factors. Their previous exposure to agriculture brought them into contact with key employers who provided access to legal documents to cross the border. In some cases, their US jobs even provided lifelong relationships with employers and the ability to experience occupational mobility within US agriculture. This latter group became border commuters, who straddled the border in an effort to take advantage of higher wages in the United States but cheaper costs of living in Mexico. Though ex-braceros chose to labor in Mexico and in the United States for different reasons, they had in common the desire to find jobs that provided economic stability and a sense of personal fulfillment.

In this chapter, I present the life stories of ex-braceros living in the borderlands to provide a deeper understanding of the social, cultural, and economic contexts that shaped their working lives in the borderlands. During the post-bracero and open-border period, broad political and economic forces in the borderlands created dynamic contexts for these men to carve out their livelihoods. Though ex-braceros encountered many of the same structural constraints and opportunities, their varied life experiences evidence the multifaceted ways in which individuals encountered, navigated, and utilized the border to pursue diverse livelihood strategies.

Becoming Braceros

The ex-braceros that I interviewed were born into large families in rural Mexico. Their parents struggled on a daily basis to provide adequate food, education, and medicine. As a result, many respondents began to work as children rather than attend school (most ex-bracero respondents had less than a year of formal education). This was not unusual in their agrarian communities, where young boys and girls cared for farm plots and tended goats, sheep, cattle, and donkeys and women worked alongside men in the fields, weeding and harvesting beans and also preparing food. Pedro Pantoja, a native of La Mojonera, Michoacán, recalled helping his family by gathering and reselling wood during the winter and by selling his labor to landowning families, the only employment opportunity in rural Michoacán at the time. This was sporadic work that barely provided his family with enough income to buy basic necessities.

In rural communities, the main source of economic sustenance was small-scale farming, either on family land or as sharecroppers. Most families farmed nonirrigated land. Seventy-one-year-old Agustín, whose story introduced this chapter, spent the first part of his life in Mesilla de Sombrerete, Zacatecas, growing and harvesting corn and beans. As a young man, he loved working outdoors, but each year, he worried that he would be unable to grow his crops because he depended on rain to water his fields. The day Agustín departed from Zacatecas to the United States, after the corn he had planted did not sprout due to drought, was ingrained in his memory: November 6, 1956. Even though the event occurred some fifty years before our interview at Parque Teniente Guerrero, he remembered well the distraught feeling of leaving behind the fruits of his labor, as well as his wife, parents, and siblings. With the exception of brief revisits to Zacatecas, he would ultimately settle in Tijuana, where he found better job opportunities.

Other families survived by working as sharecroppers, earning a percentage of what they grew rather than wages. Florentino Vargas, who eventually became a taxi driver in Tijuana, recalled that the large landowner whose land he farmed paid in sacks of corn and beans. This provided only enough to eat and nothing more. Other ex-braceros attempted to provide for their families by leasing out their labor, and their childhoods were similarly painful to recall. Guillermo Lara, for example, complained that his father rented him out to a hacendado (the owner of a hacienda, or large-scale farmer) as a child. Decades later, shortly before his father's death, Guillermo asked why he had been rented out. His father responded, "I had to rent you so that I could give schooling to the older children."

Though ex-braceros like Agustín, Florentino, and Guillermo engaged in different kinds of work as children to help support their family, their lives in agrarian communities were quite similar. They told me that few jobs existed outside of subsistence farming, and even when they did find work, it was seasonal. Ex-braceros lived childhoods of rural poverty. Their communities often lacked schools and, combined with the need for children to work to support their families, this meant that few young men and women were able to get an education in their communities, further restricting their life chances.

Prior to the implementation of the Bracero Program, much of the Mexican countryside was filled with unemployed and underemployed young men, eager to work and earn money. This reserve army of campesinos became an ideal labor force for the US government, who together with the Mexican government implemented the Bracero Program, which brought temporary workers to the United States to labor in agriculture and, to a lesser extent, in the railroad industry. Over its twenty-two years of existence, the program granted millions of contracts to young Mexican migrants. These migrants worked on a temporary basis in fields picking tomatoes, cotton, lemons, strawberries, asparagus, grapes, and other fruits and vegetables. In one small town in Michoacán, nine out of every ten "first-time" migrants entered the United States by enrolling in the Bracero Program during those years.[3] Because rural migrants were a source of cheap, temporary labor for US growers, reducing labor costs for growers by as much as 50 percent in some regions,[4] US-Mexico migration became vital to the development of large-scale agriculture in the American southwest.[5] Although only about 4,200 men participated in the program in its first year, studies estimate that guest workers made up anywhere from about a quarter to one-third of the overall seasonal agricultural labor force in California though in some counties it was much higher.[6]

The Bracero Program was originally meant to be temporary, but it was extended to last twenty-two years, with the US government issuing nearly five million total temporary work contracts. During the same period, there were also five million *arrests* of unauthorized migrants who crossed the border without authorization because they were unable to participate in the program.[7] The state-sanctioned Bracero Program would play a vital role in the development of labor migration streams before social networks came to play a dominant role in the migration process of both authorized and unauthorized border crossings.

When the Bracero Program ended, unauthorized migration flows intensified, and the mode of entry into the labor market changed. Some braceros became legal permanent residents in the United States while others became "Green Card commuters," who continued to migrate to work in the US agricultural labor market on a seasonal basis. Still other braceros returned to the border region where they settled in closer proximity to US farms, as was the case in the cities of Tijuana and Mexicali, Baja California. Though one of the goals of the Bracero Program was to modernize Mexico's agriculture industry with the newfound knowledge braceros brought back from the United States, historian Deborah Cohen found that few braceros returned to farming; instead, they migrated to Mexican cities, opened up businesses in Mexico, or continued to migrate to the United States.[8] And some of these ex-braceros formed their livelihoods in the borderlands, settling in cities like Tijuana, just as major structural changes were unfolding in northern Mexican cities that provided ex-braceros with newfound urban employment opportunities.

Reskilled Urban Workers

Ex-braceros were lured to the border economy during a period of urban expansion. The ex-braceros who chose to find jobs in emerging urban industries reinvented themselves from rural migrants into urban workers, shedding their agrarian backgrounds and substituting US wage labor for urban employment in Mexico. For this group of men, the border economy offered the opportunity to start a new life as retrained urban workers who provided important labor such as building homes and transporting workers between their homes and factories, which was essential as Tijuana was modernizing.

These men settled in the borderlands at a time when large-scale political-economic changes were unfolding in Tijuana. First, the Programa Nacional Fronterizo (PRONAF) created employment opportunities in Mexican border cities, particularly through construction projects and support services aimed at luring US tourists. After the termination of the Bracero Program, ex-braceros migrated to Tijuana because the city's economy and fronterizo population were expanding, offering a diverse array of employment opportunities. Tijuana's population soared from 16,486 before the start of the Bracero Program in 1940 to 277,306 in 1970 as a result of the BIP.[9] BIP was instituted in 1965 to curtail high unemployment rates in northern Mexican border cities, which were as high as 50 percent in some areas.[10] It was enacted the year following the termination of the Bracero Program, which transformed northern Mexico into an export-processing zone for foreign factories and established it as a duty-free zone. The BIP allowed foreign-owned factories to import manufacturing equipment and export finished goods while capitalizing on cheap labor. In the BIP's first year, twelve maquiladoras employed some 3,000 workers in border cities. By 1971, the maquiladora industry had grown rapidly to include 200 plants and 29,000 workers. Ten years later, the sector had mushroomed to 669 plants that employed 700,000 workers.[11] Although BIP came late to Tijuana, by 1975 there were 101 maquiladora plants in the city that employed 9,276 workers.[12]

Though one goal of BIP was to provide returning braceros with employment in industrial settings, studies show that most factory jobs were not filled by returnees. Sociologist Patricia Fernández-Kelly argues that the maquiladoras did not reduce unemployment rates because they did not target working-age males such as ex-braceros.[13] Instead, factory owners targeted those who were not in the labor force, such as the daughters and wives of border residents or internal migrants; as sociologist Jane Collins notes about employment patterns in Mexico, "Many firms prefer to employ workers with fewer labor market options and little exposure to organizing traditions."[14] In Tijuana, factory owners most likely targeted young women to increase the labor pool without providing infrastructure for migrant workers, such as housing and transportation.[15]

Though BIP did not provide direct employment for returning braceros in maquiladoras, the modernization of Tijuana's economy, with the introduction of export-processing firms in combination with the arrival of internal migrants to the city, provided returning braceros with employment opportunities. For some ex-braceros, these employment opportunities effectively ended their migration careers and allowed them to exit agricultural work. The restructuring of northern Mexico's industrial base expanded Tijuana's growth. Newly arrived urbanites needed housing, food, and other services. They also needed transportation to and from their homes and worksites. As the population of Tijuana soared, ex-braceros found their niche in the expanding border economy as mechanics, taxi drivers, and construction workers.

Mónico Paredes, a blue-eyed sixty-eight-year-old ex-bracero who worked five contracts between 1959 and 1962 picking fruit in California and cotton in Texas, migrated to Tijuana's urban labor market after his return to Mexico. There, he found employment opportunities that allowed him to reinvent himself as a worker. He originally left his hometown in San Marcos, Jalisco, because there were few jobs and no schools beyond sixth grade. After Mónico returned from the United States and married his childhood sweetheart, he became desperate because he could not find work in rural Jalisco. As a result, in 1969, at the age of thirty-six, he migrated to Tijuana with the intention of obtaining a Border Crossing Card (BCC) that he could use to migrate north. However, while waiting to obtain the BCC, Mónico ran into a paisano from Jalisco who was a bus driver. The paisano invited Mónico to ride along with him and collect money from passengers. With nothing else to do, Mónico agreed and was surprised to find that he enjoyed the job, especially when he saw the money he could earn. After the day ended, Mónico asked his friend to help him get a job, and his friend recommended Mónico to his employer. When he got the job, Mónico "lost the eagerness of going to the other side." He had more work than he could handle. In fact, it took nearly a month to schedule an interview with Mónico because he worked very long hours as a bus mechanic while also performing side jobs repairing his friends' and neighbors' vehicles.

When Mónico first started working in the city, he worked as many as sixteen hours a day driving a rented bus. His goal was to pick up as many passengers as possible each day and transport them to their workplaces or to the port of entry. Mónico was so busy that he sometimes ate lunch with one hand and drove with the other. Becoming a bus driver not only provided Mónico with a steady income but also gave him the opportunity to experience occupational mobility. With training, Mónico moved from the position of driver, whose earnings depended on passengers, to the position of mechanic, where he worked for a fixed salary. Mónico began training as a bus mechanic shortly after becoming a driver by assisting the company mechanic whenever he took his bus out for maintenance. He was soon able to transfer his newfound skills to his own bus. This allowed him to cut maintenance costs and develop his skills. He returned to Jalisco and announced to his family that they would relocate to Tijuana.

Over time, Mónico began to earn additional income fixing his neighbors' vehicles. Every time I passed by his home, he had a different vehicle in the front yard with the hood propped open. He had so much work that he even hired a local youth to help him with side jobs. Eventually, a friend notified him of an opening at the company's garage. Because he was well known in the company and viewed as a hard worker, Mónico received a one-week trial to prove that he could perform as a diesel mechanic. The trial proved successful and he worked as a mechanic until his retirement in 2002.

Despite completing only a second-grade education and working primarily in agriculture, the move to Tijuana allowed Mónico to retrain himself in the urban economy first by working as a bus driver and later as a mechanic.[16] In Tijuana, Mónico was making about $50 per day; this was a high wage considering that some of his neighbors who were commuters earned even less in the United States (at the time, the minimum wage in Tijuana was 42 pesos, or roughly $4, per day). By moving from the country to the city, he abandoned his previous agricultural livelihood and earned enough money as an urban worker to pay for his own car, a modest two-bedroom home, and the education of all three of his children. Thanks in part to his steady employment, Mónico was able to obtain credit in Tijuana that allowed him to buy furniture for his house and tools that he used to repair vehicles. All of his children grew up to assume professional occupations in Mexico, and two of the three lived and worked in Tijuana as adults.

Mónico took pride in the fact that he never returned to work in the United States even though he lived only a ten-minute taxi ride from the border. He held onto an expired BCC to remind him that he chose to remain in Mexico, where he had everything he needed. Mónico had only one complaint—that his eldest son succumbed to life in "El Norte" (the United States). Mónico was especially disappointed that he had paid for his son's education in Mexico but his son was "just" a *lavatrastes* (dishwasher), who used his BCC to make a life north of the border. To Mónico, relocating to Tijuana represented upward mobility because it allowed him to acquire new skills and to achieve socioeconomic advancement in Mexico.

All ex-braceros I spoke with, particularly those who retooled themselves as urban workers, mentioned their peasant backgrounds and experiences as US farmworkers as reasons for their relocation to Tijuana. As peasants and as farmworkers, they had labored under the hot sun in back-breaking agricultural jobs that provided limited occupational mobility. Juanillo Vásquez, a seventy-one-year-old migrant, remembered skipping school to start working as a goat herder in Durango, Mexico, at the age of five. While agriculture provided limited opportunities, Juanillo saw the automobile as an avenue for social mobility. As a young child he marveled when he saw an automobile or bus and became especially excited when he heard and smelled the fumes from a passing diesel engine. Eventually, Juanillo became friends with his pueblo's only mechanic, who introduced him to engine repair. However, during the 1950s, few families owned automobiles in Gómez Palacio, Durango. Although he was eager to become a mechanic, his parents did not have money to send him to technical school. Ironically, it was not until he was a bracero field hand that he developed his mechanical skills while working for one of his US employers:

> I used to see that mechanics made more money [compared to farm workers]; so, I asked to become an assistant and began by bringing them [auto] parts. I did this until one time the boss saw that I had a lot of potential so one day he told me, "Flaco [Juanillo's nickname], the güero [white American mechanic] did not come. Can you make the Caterpillar run?" . . . I got the Caterpillar running. . . . He said, ". . . So tomorrow when you come, instead of hoeing, you are going to work on tractors."

What is important to note about this passage is that Juanillo's bracero contract specified that he was to harvest and plant fruits and vegetables, not to operate heavy machinery or perform mechanic services. At the time, those jobs were reserved for US citizens or Mexicans with legal residency. However, Juanillo impressed his employer by successfully starting up a recalcitrant Caterpillar machine. After returning from his stint as a bracero, Juanillo recalled using his US earnings to pay for specialized training on diesel engines that provided newfound employment opportunities. Juanillo first landed a job as a mechanic's assistant for the Chihuahuenses, a national bus line in Ciudad Juárez, Chihuahua. He eventually became a full-time mechanic in the company. One day, an African American bus driver who drove a Greyhound bus between Texas and Ciudad Juárez told him about a job opening in the United States. Juanillo worked for

Greyhound from 1974 to 1979 but quit his job when he decided he wanted to see the world.

After returning from his travels in the 1980s, Juanillo settled in Tijuana and began to cross the border daily to the United States, where he held jobs on both sides of the border fixing diesel engines and transmissions. After improving his skills as a mechanic and receiving specialized training in other areas such as welding, he became one of the most sought-after mechanics for farm equipment. Juanillo repaired heavy equipment primarily for agricultural-based companies in the San Quintín Valley in Baja California, and he claimed that US-based mechanics in San Diego County called on him when they could not diagnose a problem. During his career, Tijuana provided Juanillo with abundant employment opportunities on both sides of the border. He was able to save money and invest in real estate in Tijuana, buying a small apartment complex. His monthly income of $800 was enough for Juanillo to live a comfortable lifestyle in Mexico.

Juanillo represents an exceptional case of a former subsistence farmer who became a highly skilled mechanic. Yet together, Mónico's and Juanillo's stories illustrate that rural-based migrants who moved to Tijuana found diverse employment opportunities in the expanding urban border economy. These two men worked repairing the thousands of cars and public transportation vehicles that were needed to transport factory employees to and from work. Migrants like Mónico and Juanillo were thus drawn to the border because the region provided them with avenues of employment that gave them a newfound identity as urban workers.

Braceros and the Modernization of Tijuana

Ex-braceros also found work as taxi drivers, construction workers, and entrepreneurs who helped transport, house, and feed the growing number of domestic migrants who were relocating to Tijuana. By taking on urban jobs, ex-braceros found personal fulfillment and steady employment with wages that were enough for them to abandon their previous careers as migrant farmworkers. For example, the ex-braceros who worked in the taxi industry found their work liberating—for the first time in their adult working lives, they were no longer obligated to respond to the white American and Mexican American bosses who had denigrated them. In Marxian terms, a transition out of agriculture meant that workers felt less alienated and had greater control of their labor.[17] As taxi drivers, they did not have fixed schedules or have to punch time clocks. They worked when they wanted, for as few or as many hours as they wished, because in Tijuana they owned their own taxis.[18]

As taxi drivers, ex-braceros earned wages that sometimes exceeded their previous earnings in the United States. In their rural communities, ex-braceros would not have been able to work as taxi drivers because people either walked or took a bus. In contrast, in Tijuana, people were constantly moving across homes, shopping districts, and work, which were all scattered throughout the city. Moreover, in their home communities, automobiles were expensive and scarce, while the borderlands provided them with access to cars imported from the United States.

Florentino, who shuffled back and forth across the border between 1956 and 1980, chose to become a taxi driver over US farm work. Although he was now seventy-two, he would still be a taxi driver if his vision had not deteriorated with age. He recounted his reasons for becoming a taxi driver one afternoon as we drank coffee at his home in Mesa de Otay.

> The thing is that you didn't work. You just rode around and transported young women. . . . You made more than if you were working [as a farmworker] because you would earn $30 in one day, in one day! And working, I would sometimes make $40 or $50 for the whole week [as a farmworker in the United States]. But in the taxi, I could make that much in one day . . . that is why I went into it.

As Florentino explained, he did not see taxi driving as "work" because his job allowed him to act as an urban explorer who got to know the city intimately and to socialize with people from all regions of Mexico. It was also as a taxi driver that he met his current wife. Moreover, he claimed that the wages were especially favorable when compared with the wages he earned as a migrant farm worker. Florentino told me that some passengers even paid him in American dollars, so he did not have the desire to migrate in search of the American dollar because he earned it in Tijuana.

Florentino decided to settle in Tijuana after spending more than two decades following the crops along US West Coast states. One month, he found himself picking avocados northeast of San Diego one month and the next, picking apples in Washington State. Despite traveling in the United States for more than two decades, Florentino's migrant career came to an abrupt end in 1980 when he was deported. He decided to settle in the outskirts of Tijuana near Mesa de Otay as the population grew with the introduction of maquiladoras, taking odd jobs to support himself before he eventually found work in a small shop that made and repaired shoes and jewelry. In Tijuana, he was separated from his family members and from the community in his hometown of Tepatitlán, Jalisco, but Florentino explained that he made friendships with coworkers who exposed him to new employment opportunities. He recounted:

> I used to work in a small shop that made shoes and *huaraches* [sandals] and belts. . . . [The boss] had a friend who was a taxi driver. He would bring him the materials. And he also became our friend. Then one day I asked him [the taxi driver] what we needed to become a *taxista* and he told me, "Well, you only need $30 and your license and when a [taxi driver position] opens up, I will come and tell you." When one opened up, he came and told me, "There is one car, if you want it, come and get it." That is how I got started.

Most of Florentino's family and friends back in Tepatitlán had labored as farmworkers along the US West Coast, picking crops like apples or strawberries. However, by relocating to the border, Florentino's social circles grew to encompass coworkers who provided him information about alternative job opportunities. As a young man with limited city life and occupational experience outside of agriculture, his newfound relations provided him with the necessary information and connections to obtain his first taxi. Once he chose to become a taxi driver, Florentino drove for the next thirty years and never returned to wage labor in the United States. For more than two decades, he worked the Mesa de Otay route transporting young factory workers in a 1976 Ford station wagon that seated seven passengers. He drove these workers to maquiladoras that produced electronic goods for companies like Panasonic, JVC, and Sony. Florentino's case illustrates that although maquiladoras did not necessarily provide direct employment, they did generate occupations that provided less-educated workers with employment opportunities in the borderlands. Taxi driving was so profitable, Florentino recalled at the time of the interview, that his Monday earnings alone were enough to pay for the entire week's transportation expenses. Any earnings after Monday, he pocketed. Florentino was able to purchase a home and a taxi during the three decades he worked as a driver. When I visited his home in Mesa de Otay, he was in the process of building three additional rooms that he planned to rent out to earn extra income.

The growth of northern Mexico's population not only necessitated the creation of a transportation industry to move workers to jobs but also led to other types of jobs as well. As the city of Tijuana grew, ex-braceros sought occupations in construction. They chose this line of work because it provided them with year-round employment and higher wages as their trade skills improved over time. Moreover, they also experienced occupational mobility from *peones* (unskilled workers) to *maestros* (skilled workers) who hired and supervised their own crews. Like the ex-braceros who labored in the transportation services, the ex-braceros who worked in construction earned enough money to provide an education for their children.

Seventy-two-year-old Pepe worked a total of five bracero contracts before he settled in Tijuana in 1964. Prior to establishing ties in Tijuana, Pepe had lived in various places in both the United States and northern Mexico. He claimed that what drew him most to Tijuana was "the beautiful weather," and that there were no "aggressive mosquitos," which were rampant in Romita, Guanajuato, and caused him to have many sleepless nights. In Tijuana, he found work in the vibrant construction industry, building homes for the newly arriving domestic migrants seeking jobs in the city.

Throughout his career, Pepe was able to move his way up the construction ladder from *peon* to *maestro*. Pepe said that for him, the United States had not been a land of opportunity. On his last visit to the United States, he ended up owing his employer money for room and board because the vegetable harvest was so sporadic. In contrast, the borderlands economy provided newfound employment opportunities.

> Look, here there is much that one can do to earn a living. Even better than the US. . . . I did not want to go to the US because I had many opportunities in Tijuana. Actually, where I am currently living, they used to give land away for free. They used to give land away for free, but some people did not even want it. It is possible to live better here more than any other place.

By "free land," Pepe referred to the extremely low land prices in Tijuana when he first arrived at a time when the city was not yet a haven for people who lived in Mexico but worked in the United States or a destination for retirees who wanted to live along the Pacific. In the United States, ex-braceros had limited opportunity for occupational mobility, but in Tijuana, Pepe believed that hard work would produce new opportunities. Pepe explained how even selling ice cream bars in the streets of Tijuana for two months was a means to a better occupation:

> To be able to survive here, at first I did not have any equipment to become a construction worker. And for that I had to sell ice cream bars. Then I began to sell ice cream bars and then I made enough money to buy my equipment, and I bought what I needed.

Like other ex-braceros who chose to settle in Tijuana, Pepe argued that the border economy provided him with abundant opportunities to earn an income, whether as an independent entrepreneur, a skilled worker, or a wage worker. These ex-braceros argued that employment in Mexico did not provide the same "dead-end jobs" they had been exposed to in US agriculture. Instead, they believed that all jobs in Tijuana had the potential to lead to other opportunities. As Pepe sold ice cream bars,

> I bought new equipment every eight days. I would buy a level, plumbing equipment, a cement trowel, and a hammer until I had all of the equipment. Then I went to a company and I helped build INFONAVIT homes [government-funded homes for salaried workers].

Pepe found an abundance of employment opportunities in Mexico as a result of his retraining in Tijuana. Pepe considered INFONAVIT a good employer because the program offered a full-time job at more than just a living wage. When Pepe was coming of age in Romita, there were few construction-related occupations. Most people either built their own homes or hired family members of close friends. Yet in Tijuana, construction work enabled Pepe to accumulate enough money to buy four different homes, and he claimed to own more than $100,000 worth of assets. Despite his agricultural background, the move to Tijuana provided the opportunity to seek new occupations.

Guillermo, the sixty-six-year-old migrant from Zacatecas whose father had rented him out in his youth, also landed a salaried job with the city government. After returning from the United States in 1971, Guillermo felt that as a Mexican, he had been "humiliated" in the United States by working in deplorable conditions. In contrast, in Mexico, he felt more "free" to express his athletic and creative capabilities by becoming a marathon runner and impersonating famous Mexican musicians in bars during his free time. When I interviewed Guillermo, he spoke passionately about the moment that would forever transform his life. Shortly after returning to Zacatecas in the early 1960s, he received a phone call from his brother who told him about the benefits of living in the borderlands, and he soon migrated to Tijuana. After arriving, he slowly worked his way up the occupational ladder:

> My first job was as an ice cream seller. I remember well that I said, "Well, what do I do now?" . . . I began to sell ice cream and when no ice cream would sell, I would go to First Street and sell guayabas, mangos, and

vegetables. And I made enough money. That is how I maintained myself. And every day I used to come to the city government offices to see if they would give me work but they would not. . . . You get a job in government and you get every type of benefit. Then I said, "I am going to get a job in city government."

Though Guillermo made many unsuccessful attempts to become a city maintenance worker, his persistence eventually paid off, and he landed a job cleaning street gutters, where he earned about $1,000 a month until his retirement. Guillermo was able to purchase a home and a new car, take family vacations, and provide educational opportunities to his children who grew up to become professionals in Tijuana. He knew that to avoid working in the fields again, he needed to reinvent himself in the Mexican economy. With hard work, he believed that it was possible to achieve occupational mobility in Tijuana beyond his previous status as a peasant in Mexico and a farmworker in the United States.

In addition to income, another benefit of working for the city government was that Guillermo and his wife were able to apply as a couple and obtain BCCs. They both use BCCs to cross the border occasionally to shop and work. Guillermo crossed the border to assist his friends in landscaping and painting work. Meanwhile, his wife used her BCC to cross the border to clean houses and earn money to pay for her daughter's education. Thus, by relocating to the border Guillermo was able to reinvent himself as a municipal worker and to access a BCC that allowed him to obtain work in the United States on a periodic basis.

Some ex-braceros became independent entrepreneurs and opened small businesses that catered to border commuters who earned a living in the United States. For example, sixty-three-year-old Aurelio Nava, who relocated to Tijuana with his two sons and wife with the intention of eventually crossing to the United States, opened an ice cream parlor very close to the US-Mexico border. When people left the port of entry and walked toward downtown Tijuana, they often stopped at his ice cream parlor. He sold ice cream and fruit drinks to tourists for eight years until he sold his business for $35,000 and purchased two taxis for $10,000 dollars each.

Isidro also became an independent entrepreneur, opening a taco vending business in Zona Norte. He sold tacos to the thousands of transient migrants who passed through Tijuana en route to the United States. Independent entrepreneurs like Aurelio and Isidro found a niche in the urban economy that brought in enough income to end their migrant careers.

Both Aurelio and Isidro continued to work in their respective businesses until their younger children took over. Even then, they continued to work for the family business on a part-time basis.

Why Ex-Braceros Became Urban Workers

This group of ex-braceros was able to adapt to the border economy, and they managed to secure employment and achieve social mobility after the termination of the Bracero Program. They transitioned from US farm work to urban work in Tijuana, starting at the bottom rungs of the border economy. Many of these ex-braceros started by selling ice cream bars or fruit before finding jobs that provided them with secure employment for the remainder of their working years. The border economy allowed these men to remain close to friends and family in Mexico and to purchase homes, cars, and education for their children without having to migrate on a seasonal basis like other ex-braceros.

These ex-braceros were able to achieve economic mobility only after reinventing themselves in the borderlands. As urban workers, they developed an occupational identity that they carried into their retirement years. These border residents and former migrants, now in their sixties, seventies, and eighties continued to identify as ex-braceros, or *migrantes*. However, because they had lived for so many years in the borderlands building their occupational careers, their identity expanded over time to include their region of origin (as transnational scholars have found) and their occupational identity, which they developed as *taxistas* (taxi drivers), *maestros* (master construction workers), *mecánicos* (mechanics), *paleteros* (ice cream vendors), and *taqueros* (taco vendors) in the Mexican economy. Additionally, the work that the braceros did in the city was significant, as northern Mexico was modernizing by providing important services to the masses of internal migrants who were working in factories or crossing the border to work in the United States.

In sum, returning to the question posed at the beginning of the section, of what attracted internal migrants to the border, we find that the move to the border expanded ex-braceros' networks that then introduced them to the borderlands way of making a living. "Making a living" included a diversity of occupations, some of which consisted of ex-braceros retraining themselves by learning new skills. These jobs provided full-time employment that brought an end to their need to continue to cross the border. These braceros found their niche by catering to domestic migrants who were also attempting to integrate themselves into a rapidly growing border economy. The dynamic border economy allowed these ex-braceros to find their niche in Mexico while their counterparts, as we shall see, continued to cross the border to work for US employers.

Cross-Border Farmworkers

Unlike the ex-braceros who retrained themselves in the urban economy of Tijuana, there was another group of ex-braceros whose livelihoods consisted of crossing the border daily to work in San Diego County. This group of migrants continued crossing the border for the remainder of their occupational careers to work in low-wage agricultural jobs as border commuters. However, rather than relocate to the United States, these workers became part of a cross-border labor force that preferred to live in Mexico but labor in the United States. These migrants crossed the border during what economist Philip Martin terms the "golden era" of US farm labor from 1964 to about 1980.[19] During that time, migrant farmworkers saw wage increases greater than even construction workers. Some workers experienced wage increases as high as 40 percent because of the termination of the guest-worker program, a drop in undocumented migration, and the unionization of the farm labor industry, which meant that farmworkers had more bargaining power in the workplace.[20] These ex-braceros chose to settle in Tijuana and continued to work in US agriculture during the golden era because they obtained legal residency through employer sponsorship, and some even found year-round employment. Working in farm labor also allowed workers to integrate their family and friends into the agricultural labor force.

A study by the Immigration and Naturalization Service on two different days in January 1966 found that roughly 40,000 commuters crossed through ports of entry such as Brownsville, Hidalgo, and Fabens, Texas; San Luis, Arizona; and Calexico and San Ysidro, California.[21] About 40 percent of these people crossed to work in agriculture. Thus, the experiences of ex-braceros who continued to work in San Diego County reflect a much larger cross-border labor force. These major changes in California agriculture provided a niche for braceros to find work in the fields. Yet what is interesting about the Tijuana case study is that braceros were able to reside in Tijuana, where the cost of living was cheaper, and cross daily to work in California. Thus, Tijuana became a home base for a binational labor force of farmworkers.

The Bracero Program in the Borderlands

During the Bracero Program, San Diego County farms incorporated Mexican workers into the labor force differently than did other farms throughout California. When braceros were brought to work on most California farms between 1942 and 1964, they were imported as guest workers with contracts ranging anywhere from forty-five days to six months. Once contracts were completed, braceros were sent back to Mexico. US growers in California and other regions of the United States provided housing and transportation to braceros for the duration of the contract, although the costs were deducted from the braceros' paychecks.[22] Farm labor associations generally contracted migrants, and growers hired these associations to supply the picking season's labor.[23] As a result, workers outside of San Diego County were alienated from employers during the Bracero Program.

One ex-bracero best summarized the typical experience of working as a bracero: "I never got to know my employer." This man recalled living in barracks that contained hundreds of bunk beds: "there were thousands of braceros where I worked. Sometimes I could not even find my bed." The living and working situation of most migrants during the Bracero Program was organized as what Erving Goffman calls a total institution, in which workers spent their entire day in the totalizing space of the farm. They were required to live in segregated camps removed from mainstream society and separated from their families during the harvest season.[24] As such, outside the labor camp and the bracero program, migrant workers had very little opportunity to expand their occupational opportunities. They were bound to their employers and bound to their work as field hands.

In comparison to large-scale growers that operated in other regions of California, the structure of farm labor in San Diego County was quite different. Farms in San Diego tended to be medium-sized and employed the same workers year after year. Most farm operators in San Diego County were also involved in the day-to-day farm operations, unlike the absentee farmers who owned many large-scale farms in other parts of the state. These operators made regular appearances on their farms and interacted with crew leaders, according to respondents. For example, in 1958, San Diego farms employed only 4,416 braceros. This was a low number compared to Imperial Valley's 14,042 and San Joaquin County's 15,576 braceros.[25] Although the number of braceros employed by San Diego farms was small, they still represented a large percentage of the agricultural workforce. In the late 1950s, 97 percent of San Diego County's hired workers were braceros and only 3 percent were US-born workers.[26] In San Diego County, the Bracero Program was managed by the San Diego County Farmers Association (SDCFA), whose sole purpose was to recruit workers. Unlike other farm labor associations, the SDCFA focused less on amassing a large labor pool and more on promoting worker quality that could be circulated within a tightly knit network of employers. The following letter of recommendation written in November 1961 illustrates the role of labor associations in San Diego County:

To Whom It May Concern:

Lázaro Jaramillo is known to us to be an excellent farm worker having been previously employed by Highland Ranch. . . . If contracted to San Diego County Farmers Inc., we will guarantee employment for the term of his contract. Any consideration to the above worker will be much appreciated.

This letter was shared by Lázaro himself, who kept it as a reminder of his first occupational experience in San Diego County. He explained that he carried the letter with him to prove that he was an "excellent worker" to potential employers he did not know. Now approaching eighty, he kept it as a memento of his working years as a bracero and of his days as a daily border commuter who crossed to work in the United States.

What especially differentiated the Bracero Program in San Diego County from other regions of the United States was that workers were allowed to live in Mexico but commute to work in the United States. The formation of this cross-border labor force was likely not unique to Tijuana–San Diego but also other Mexican border cities like Mexicali, Baja California–Calexico, California, and San Luis, Arizona–San Luis Rio Colorado, Sonora.[27] Seventy-eight-year-old Juan Nieves explained San Diego County growers' economic motive to encourage workers to reside in Tijuana:

It was worth it for the companies. You know why? Because they no longer had to have a [labor camp]. . . . [In a labor camp] they had to have electricity and water and have a place to make food. But here [in the borderlands] there were no labor camps. In the company that I worked for, they had homes so we could be there. So we could cook. But then they told us, "Whoever wants to and has family in Tijuana can go to Tijuana. You can cross with your bracero passport." So I came to Tijuana.

Juan was contracted several times to work for San Diego County farmers as a bracero. With encouragement from his employer, Juan relocated his family to Tijuana and used his bracero identification card to cross the border every weekday morning. After the end of the Bracero Program, from 1964 until the late 1980s, men like Juan and their wives crossed the border to harvest tomatoes, celery, and beans in San Diego County's agricultural fields. These men became part of a cross-border labor force when their employers integrated them into the US labor market after the end of the Bracero Program, providing legal status to key workers and their families. They then encouraged the key workers and their families to recruit other workers with and without legal status to work in the United States.

Though the evidence suggests that the primary beneficiaries of this labor market arrangement were growers who saved on labor costs, workers also felt they had benefited from their long-term ties to US growers. These relationships provided them with legal documents to cross the border and obtain full-time employment that lasted throughout their occupational careers.

Obtaining Legal Status from Employers

From oral histories with ex-braceros and their families, it is apparent that San Diego County growers were actively involved in the creation of a unique farmworker commuter labor force. Anthropologist Fred Krissman notes that US employers who hire immigrant workers generally used "their socioeconomic power to get others to recruit for them, whether it be agents of the State, subordinate personnel, or contractor staff" to replenish the labor force on a periodic basis.[28] Growers in the region replenished their labor force in the same manner. Interviewees frequently mentioned the Edwards and Smith Company as one of the most important agricultural employers in the borderlands that supported workers to make the transition from temporary guest-worker status to permanent Green Card commuters. Edwards and Smith Co. was a family-operated farm business located near the US-Mexican border from the 1940s until the mid-1980s. According to Jesús, a former crew supervisor, the firm owned some 400 acres in southern San Diego County that were used to farm labor-intensive commodities such as celery, beans, and tomatoes. He recalled that the company's workforce ranged from 175 to 300 workers during the peak picking season. Because Edwards and Smith Co. was a family-operated business, it played an active role in ensuring that workers could cross freely between Mexico and the United States. Being a small business allowed them to have closer connections with their workers, whom they could then draw on when they needed labor. Many of the ex-braceros claimed that the company worked in conjunction with US immigration officials to allow clandestine crossers to cross freely. They negotiated with officials and got them to look the other way when groups were crossing to work.

Previous scholars have pointed out the contradictory nature of border enforcement by showing how growers pressured US government officials to keep an open-border policy during harvest season.[29] Sociologist Julian Samora long ago noted that "it appears that the transition from a relative open border to a relative closed border occurs in *cycles* depending on the demands of the US economy, particularly as such demands affect the Southwest."[30] Ex-braceros explained that San Diego County growers developed close bonds with Border Patrol agents because their farms were located next to the US-Mexico divide. Thus, during the open-border period of 1965–1985, ex-braceros recalled large numbers of Tijuanenses crossing the border daily as documented workers through the port of entry and as clandestine crossers who evaded border inspection. Ex-braceros believed that growers established a tacit agreement with the state agents managing the border to allow undocumented workers to cross clandestinely as long as they stayed at farms located along the borderlands. Thus, rather than police all migrants, Border Patrol agents in this region worked to differentiate unauthorized workers heading for the interior of California from unauthorized workers allowed to circulate freely in the borderlands. Jesús, an undocumented border crosser for over thirty years, recalled how border enforcement operated in the Tijuana region before the implementation of Operation Gatekeeper in 1994, which eventually curtailed all forms of clandestine crossing:

> There was no fence by the immigration [port of entry]. They [undocumented commuters] used to enter and leave every day. The Border Patrol told them nothing. They used to let them enter. There was no fence—only a piece of wire that was on the floor. And my boss used to have his fields close to the airport [that runs along the US-Mexico border]. There, they [commuters] worked picking tomatoes.

As Jesús noted, the Border Patrol did little to curtail clandestine commuters who crossed to work roughly from the mid-1960s, when he began working for his employer, until 1986, when the employer closed operations. Jesús provided a mock exchange between a border patrol agent and an undocumented crosser to illustrate the typical interactions that he observed as a young worker:

BORDER PATROL: What's up? Where are you going?
UNDOCUMENTED CROSSER: I'm going to work!
BORDER PATROL: Who do you work with?
UNDOCUMENTED CROSSER: With Edwards and Smith.
BORDER PATROL: Oh, with Bobby!
UNDOCUMENTED CROSSER: Yes!
BORDER PATROL: Oh! Really good, boss. Go ahead, go ahead.

Jesús explained that his employer was friends with one of the main Border Patrol agents. As a result, the grower received advance notice when Border Patrol was planning to conduct raids in farms along the border. The grower used this information to warn his workers to hide in the fields or to come late to work. However, even when undocumented workers were caught and deported through the San Ysidro port of entry, they quickly returned. They were able to do so through the then-remote region of Mesa de Otay, where at the time, the only thing that separated Mexico from the United States was thin barbed wire.

While San Diego County growers supported clandestine crossings, they also encouraged some workers to think about obtaining legal status so they could cross through the port of entry on a daily basis and offered to help them fill out the paperwork. Many of the ex-braceros I interviewed accepted their employer's help to become legal permanent residents. Jesús recalled that his employer helped workers transition their status from guest workers or daily undocumented crossers to legal permanent residents.

He [the owner of Edwards and Smith Co.] helped legalize many of us. During the time, the foreman, who they called "Shorty," was told by the boss, "Shorty, I want you to sign up twenty-five men. They are no longer going to be braceros and I want you to help them legalize their papers." [The foremen replied], "Okay, that is fine." The employer helped me directly. He had already told me that he was going to legalize my papers. . . . He made a list of twenty-five. . . . Yes, many became legal residents. They became legal residents, but then they forgot who gave them the hand, that he [the employer] had immigrated us. So what they wanted was to get their residence and go to a place where they made more money. I did stay. I stayed there. I worked thirty-one years and left in 1985. . . . Then, the farm closed.

Jesús raised two important points in this narrative. First, the employer played a central role in regularizing workers' status. Second, some workers felt obligated to their employers after they provided them with access to legal status, though others did not. Jesús worked thirty-one years for his employer even though—or rather, because—his employer helped him obtain a Green Card during that time. Jesús believed that any worker who received legal status through his employers had a moral obligation to work for them for their entire careers. In contrast, Agustín, the migrant who left the fruits of his labor in the cornfield of rural Zacatecas, did not believe that it was necessary to give one's labor to his employer in exchange for a Green Card. He left his employer shortly after receiving his Green Card because he did not feel he was compensated well enough, and sought other employment opportunities in South San Diego County. He used his grower connections as a means to an end. He moved from being a hired hand to a driver for a strawberry farmer and then finally obtained a job at a nursery, where he continued to work until he retired. He explained:

AGUSTÍN: Well, before finishing the bracero contract, I began to apply for my legal residence. Henry was my boss. . . . I got my Green Card on the 5th of November in 1959.
SERGIO: Why did your boss help you?
AGUSTÍN: He helped me perhaps because I was a good worker. I am not sure.
SERGIO: You never asked him?
AGUSTÍN: Never asked him. But he not only helped me, he helped many people, many workers. He even helped out entire families! If I was not the first, I was the second who he helped. And my friends, when I came to Tijuana, did not believe me. They could not believe that I would come to visit. From then on, I worked for that boss for about six months as a legal resident. At that time, I got married in Tijuana. And I settled in Tijuana. I have always lived on the border and never lived over there [points toward the US side of the border].

Agustín departed Zacatecas on November 6, 1956, and almost exactly three years later, he became a legal resident, joining the thousands of Tijuanenses who crossed the port of entry each morning to labor in neighboring San Diego County. This cross-border labor force was beneficial to growers, workers, and the US and Mexican governments. Growers benefited because they had a permanent transnational labor force. Workers obtained full-time jobs with wages in American dollars, but spent nearly their entire paychecks in Mexico, which in turn benefited the Mexican economy. The US government benefited because they did not have to provide health care or education to immigrants and their children because they resided in Mexico. Sociologist Michael Burawoy argues that the maintenance (day-to-day activities) and renewal (biological reproduction) of migrant labor often take place in different nation-states.[31] In the case of border commuters, their lives were both maintained and renewed in one geographic location (Mexico) and they worked in another (the United States). Even though they were legal residents, their incorporation into the United States was limited to farm life. This was one of the opportunities that the border offered—namely, the opportunity to live in Mexico and only cross the border to work.

Employers played an intricate role in the development of a cross-border commuter labor force. In particular, south San Diego County employers helped create a cross-border commuter labor force comprising primarily male migrants. However, after the termination of the Bracero Program, the US agricultural labor force began to integrate entire families. In this process, the torch of labor recruitment was passed from employer to employee. For example, a letter shared by Lázaro, the ex-bracero border commuter, illustrates one Oregon employer's strategy of replenishing the agricultural labor force:

> We want to take this opportunity to thank you for having helped us during the season. We greatly appreciate the good work that you have done for us this year and we hope that you will return to work for us the following year. If you have friends or relatives that are interested in working for us, we will be here to receive them. . . . Don't forget to keep in communication with us.

This letter illustrates the shift in worker recruiting mechanisms after 1964. Employers who once relied on the US government for worker recruitment now depended on employee networks. After men were integrated into the cross-border labor force, they began to incorporate their relatives into the farm labor force as well.

Jesús was hired by Edwards and Smith Co. to lead an all-female crew of farm workers planting and harvesting tomatoes. Jesús parked his truck at the San Ysidro port of entry every morning and waited to transport the women to their worksite. These women entered the labor force to contribute to the household income, especially after their children entered Mexican schools. Luz María, for example, began working for Edwards and Smith in 1971. She had never before worked for wages, instead doing housework or working alongside her parents in agriculture to supplement their income. She began to work for Edwards and Smith during a time when male workers were striking for higher wages. Although she was first hired as a strikebreaker, Luz asserted that she outworked many of her "lazy" male counterparts. She was eventually hired full-time and remained with the company for sixteen years.

Luz María not only provided sixteen years of her own service; she also recruited female friends and relatives to form a tightly knit female work crew that lived in Tijuana and crossed the border to work. For female cross-border commuters, living in Tijuana and crossing the border to work in San Diego provided benefits. It allowed them to earn US wages and to live in Tijuana, where they had access to family members, friends, and neighbors who helped them with childcare services while they worked. In south San Diego County, being part of an occupational network with ties to farmers defined one's life chances and determined one's incorporation into the regional agricultural labor market.

Once ex-braceros were integrated into San Diego's agricultural labor force, they obtained other work opportunities by virtue of employer networks. Growers played an intricate role in the development of a commuter population. They controlled all aspects of the labor process, including hiring. In interviews with ex-braceros, I found that growers recommended their workers to other growers when they did not have work available. Thus, once ex-braceros and their family members were embedded in the agricultural labor force, employers directly assisted their future labor opportunities. Agustín explains how he found work once his Japanese employer passed away.

> One time I was going to ask for work with a Japanese [farmer]. He asked me my name.
> "Agustín Méndez."
> He says, "Let's see." And he took out his book. There I was! There was my name! And he says, "Yes, man, you know how to drive a tractor?"
> I said, "A little bit."
> "You'll stay here" [the Japanese farmer responded]. He did give me work but the rest of the workers there did not like it.

Employers in the borderlands created logs in which they kept the names of individuals they considered good or bad workers. Agustín explained that he was put on the list because he had a reputation as a hard worker who never caused any problems. These books also often contained details about workers' skills; in Agustín's case, the log stated that he knew how to drive a tractor and that he was not a worker who would cause problems for his employer. Similarly, Jesús explains how he found work when Edwards and Smith, his employer of almost thirty years, closed operations.

> JESÚS: In 1985, he closed and nothing more. We left!
> Sergio: And when the farm closed what did you do next for work?
> JESÚS: Oh well, I came to Puerta Blanca [border entrance] with an Anglo. There, I got work with him [as a crew supervisor for farm labor]. . . . And from there, a woman from Sinaloa who had a ranch there . . . gave me the chance to have a crew because she knew that I was a worker for "Bobby" and that I was a crew leader there.

When farmers could no longer provide work, they often referred their ex-employees to other growers within the agricultural labor-force network. Several braceros I interviewed mentioned that when they were unemployed and searching for work, all they had to do was say they had worked for "Bobby." That was enough to help them land other agricultural jobs. Agustín Méndez reiterated this very point in describing how he found a job. He explained:

> AGUSTÍN: He left [a letter to other growers]. For if someone wanted to look for work.
> SERGIO: Why did he do it?
> AGUSTÍN: Because he liked us. That boss was really nice with all people. And he would make sure that we would not struggle to find work. So that they would give us work. And me, yes, they identified me as a worker of his.

For ex-braceros who became cross-border farmworkers, their affiliation with US-based growers ultimately defined their occupational careers in the years following the Bracero Program. These men settled in the borderlands because they were allowed to live in Mexico but cross the border on a daily basis. Their affiliation with growers in San Diego County eventually provided them with the legal status to cross freely for their remainder of their careers. As a result, rather than return to their places of origin or settle in the United States, these ex-braceros settled in the borderlands and became part of a cross-border labor force.

Occupational Mobility in a Low-Wage Labor Market

Rural sociologists use the concept of the "agricultural ladder" to describe farmerworkers' movement from unpaid family laborer to wage worker to landowner.[32] In the US-Mexico borderlands, growers constructed an alternative to the "agricultural ladder"—the "occupational mobility ladder." Farmworkers aspirations were based not on the ultimate goal of landownership but rather on climbing to higher-status jobs within agricultural firms, which constitute what sociologists call an "internal labor market." Ex-braceros continued to cross the border because they gained legal status and because farm work in south San Diego County provided some occupational mobility. In farms at the US-Mexico border, a commuter could start as a farmhand and move up to positions with more prestige and higher wages, such as tractor driver, foreman, shed worker, or irrigator.

Table 2.1 illustrates the different wage rates paid to Mexican farm workers by south San Diego County growers. The lowest-paid workers were "general field and harvest" workers, or farmhands, who received $4.35 per hour. These workers generally performed unskilled work such as planting and harvesting crops. They were also required to report on the progress of crops to farm operators. Irrigators set up and monitored irrigation equipment and maintained irrigation ditches. Irrigators earned 10 cents an hour more than farmhands. The two highest-paid occupations were tractor driver and mechanic, which paid $4.90 and $5.70 per hour, respectively. Although all farmworkers' wages were low when compared to other US workers, they were still higher than average wages in Tijuana—though in some cases, not higher than the wages of their ex-bracero peers who

TABLE 2.1 Hourly wage rates for agricultural workers in the borderlands (1981)

OCCUPATIONAL CATEGORY	HOURLY WAGE RATE
Mechanic	$5.70
Tractor driver	$4.60–$4.90
Irrigator	$4.45
Field loader	$4.45
General field and harvest	$4.35

SOURCE: "Collective Agreement between Named Company and the United Farm Workers Association of America (1980)."[36]

worked in Tijuana. US farm labor jobs also provided workers with some employment security.

Andrés, a career farmworker, was one commuter who experienced mobility in US agriculture. Andrés commented that working for the right grower mattered because there were "good" and "bad" employers in the borderlands. Bad employers offered mostly sporadic employment with no job security, poor wages, and no opportunity for social mobility. Andrés worked for Edwards and Smith Co. He considered the company a "good" employer because it offered year-round employment to some workers and provided some room for mobility, even within a low-wage occupation. Andrés was able to move up the agricultural ladder within months of obtaining a job as a laborer. A *mayordomo* (crew supervisor) who was a relative helped him get a job as an irrigator.

Not only did the job pay better than being a farmhand, but it also guaranteed full employment year round. Andrés had a job even in bad weather conditions: when it rained, his employer would find work for him at one of the local sheds performing maintenance on farm equipment. The work kept Andrés happy and busy, further tying him to his company. Andrés worked for twenty-five years as an irrigator until Edwards and Smith Co. closed its operations in the mid-1980s.

When Trinidad, a former farmworker turned security guard, first immigrated from Jalisco to California, he began at the bottom rungs of the agricultural labor force. However, after a few months of working in the United States, Trinidad's employer gave him the opportunity to become a tractor driver. Trinidad learned how to operate a tractor within a few days and was immediately promoted. Trinidad recalls how becoming a tractor driver gave him more opportunities to work for other employers. With more responsibilities also came higher wages:

> It helped me a lot [to have learned how to drive a tractor] because I earned more money. . . . [Compared to picking produce], they paid me better. The rancher then recommended me to other rancher friends of his. They used to recommend me to other ranchers when there was no work [with my employer]. . . . At the time, they used to pay me two dollars and then I got a raise and it was $3.50 an hour and the other workers earned only 75 cents an hour and that is why I liked what my boss did for me.

Agustín Méndez was first hired as a farmhand to work for growers in the US-Mexico borderlands. After becoming familiar with how the labor market operated, Agustín became a cross-border *raitero* (driver who transported workers to and from Tijuana) for US growers. Studies on border commuters note that this formalized system of transportation was "crucial to mobility across the border for employment" because it helped workers get from their neighborhoods to their US workplaces.[33] Research on *raiteros* in other regions of California found that the drivers often served as brokers who matched employers to workers.[34] In Tijuana, they were transnational workers who recruited other residents with the goal of replenishing the agricultural labor force for San Diego County farmers.

In the 1970s, Agustín purchased a Ford station wagon that seated eight people, which he used to transport workers between their homes in Tijuana and the fields of South San Diego County. Agustín and other *raiteros* either were compensated by employers or charged a direct fee to workers for transporting them to their worksites. San Diego County growers also turned to *raiteros* to serve as brokers to recruit seasonal agricultural workers from Tijuana's working-class neighborhoods. *Raiteros* would provide transportation to workers who did not have driver's licenses. Agustín considered his job as a *raitero* to be high status and well paying. Once he reached the worksites, he was expected to perform light duties, such as inspecting the quality of picked fruit and vegetables or supervising workers. Moreover, Agustín's employer gave him the important task of recruiting workers when they were needed or when an employee did not show up for work. Agustín estimates that he recruited hundreds of farm laborers from Tijuana and transported them to the fields of south San Diego County, helping to expand the cross-border labor force. Here, Agustín echoes what urban ex-braceros experienced through their work in the borderlands. Their labor contributed to something larger than themselves—in this case, the making of a cross-border commuter labor force.

Ex-braceros who became lifelong commuters entered agricultural labor at an opportune historical moment that provided them with income security and job benefits. In 1976, the United Farm Workers of America (UFW), under the leadership of Cesar Chávez, organized farmworkers to negotiate against growers throughout California and in south San Diego County for better working conditions. The ex-braceros and their family members commented that once the UFW reorganized work relations, they received work-related benefits that made it desirable to prolong their careers as migrant farmworkers. It is important to note that although the UFW fought to end the Bracero Program and unauthorized immigration because they compromised the working conditions of legal immigrant workers in the United States, by the time the union arrived in the borderlands, most braceros had transitioned from unauthorized crossers to

Green Card commuters. As such, they joined the ranks of the UFW precisely because they were legal workers whom employers could no longer threaten to deport.

The UFW institutionalized better working conditions by regulating labor practices. The men and women I interviewed remembered that in the years before the UFW, they often worked overtime without pay. Once the UFW came to represent workers, employers were required to pay 1.5 times normal wages for overtime work or for any work conducted on weekends. Moreover, employers were required to pay employees a minimum of four hours just for reporting to work, regardless of the work availability for that day. Workers also received both paid and unpaid vacation time to travel to visit family members in Mexico or to care for sick relatives. Additionally, the UFW instituted the Robert Kennedy Farm Workers Plan, which gave migrant workers and their families US-based health insurance. Finally, the UFW established a pension fund to help migrant workers.

Twenty years after ex-braceros stopped working for growers, they continued to receive pension payments from the UFW. In addition to higher benefits, commuters and their family members also commented that the UFW instituted better working conditions. Some south San Diego County employers did not provide workers with safe drinking water or bathrooms until they were pressured by the UFW. Employers were also required to provide ten-minute paid breaks for every four hours of work performed. In the borderlands, the UFW formalized economic relations between employers, workers, and the union. The UFW required employers to deduct income taxes and union dues from employees' paychecks. By requiring workers to pay taxes, the UFW helped formalize the work status of cross-border workers.

The ex-braceros who continued to cross the border for farmwork spent a significant part of their work lives in the low-wage agricultural sector. These ex-braceros chose employment in the United States over Mexico because of the benefits that accrued from growers. Employers helped them obtain legal status and job tenure, and they also provided workers with some limited opportunities to achieve occupational mobility within a low-wage labor market. In the years following the Bracero Program, this group of workers identified themselves as "campesinos fronterizos" for Edwards and Smith Co. Some were field hands but others became irrigators, tractor drivers, and foremen. Regardless of their location on the occupational ladder, they spent their entire working lives as commuter farmworkers. During that tenure, they were also members of a workers union that that provided them with pension payments that supported them well into retirement when I met them in the mid-2000s.

Misfortune at the Border

The post-bracero occupational narratives presented to this point showcase men who knew how to navigate structural constraints and turned the border into a place of opportunity. These men developed occupational careers according to their needs and desires, and took the necessary steps to become either urban workers or border commuters. However, not all braceros were able to turn the border into an opportunity for social mobility. Instead, some braceros experienced misfortune, either after arriving in Tijuana or in the latter part of their lives. This shows that the livelihoods of this group of migrants were not durable given their economically vulnerable position.

Some ex-braceros experienced misfortune because they entered the informal economy, where they sold goods to tourists in the streets of downtown Tijuana. For example, José Robledo was an ex-bracero who worked two contracts in the 1950s. When I met him, he was selling belts and key chains. José purchased cheap and generic belts for $1.00 each from a distributor and sold them for $5.00, making a $4.00 profit. On a good day, he could make as much as $100, though most days he worked from 8:00 a.m. to 5:00 p.m. and sold only enough to eat; sometimes he did not sell even a single belt. Additionally, when José Robledo relocated to Tijuana, he cut ties with his family for reasons he would not tell me. He never learned to cook and today lives on street and restaurant food. Each day, he spends anywhere from $4 to $15 dollars on food. Since the Bracero Program ended, he has worked mostly informal jobs in agriculture and construction in Tijuana. The informal labor market provided some ex-braceros that I met with an immediate source of daily income, but in the long run, informal employment produced economic insecurity. By relocating to the border, José had severed ties with his family in rural Mexico, and thus had no familial emotional or economic support. Today, he yearns for social and economic support. José was not the only bracero who was in this situation, as others who relocated to the border had over the years had severed ties with their family members. These ex-braceros live on their own, relying on the sale of goods in the streets of Tijuana to afford basic food and housing.

Even those ex-braceros who found economic opportunities in the borderlands eventually experienced economic difficulties. Agustín Méndez, for example, spent his career working for US growers in south San Diego County and experienced occupational upward mobility. However, for most of his career, he earned just above minimum wage because he labored as a farmworker, a job that is poorly remunerated. He was able to get by because, even though he earned just above minimum wage, his income was still higher than that of most of his neighbors in Tijuana. By living in Tijuana, Agustín was able to stretch the purchasing power of his dollar. However, when I interviewed him, he had a very limited savings account and was at the whim of financial fate.

Florentino also originally turned the border into an opportunity, earning a good income throughout the course of his work history as a taxi driver. Yet due to spending mismanagement and excessive drinking, Florentino was unable to save money to support himself in retirement. As a result, at the time that I interviewed him he had a home, a personal vehicle, and a taxi that he rented out, but he was also struggling to pay for his food, medicine, and other basic necessities.

Throughout this chapter, I have described individual agency in ex-bracero's decisions to navigate the social, economic, and political structures of the borderlands throughout their work histories. Their stories illustrate how historical changes shape individuals' ability to act as they move from place to place and across time. Many of the stories evidenced ex-bracero's ability to adapt to the border and establish their livelihoods on one side or the other. However, it is important to recognize that most of these workers held a low position in the broader social and economic structure of the borderlands; as such, they did not have the resources to reinvent themselves over and over again. Given these ex-braceros' limited education and formal training, it is not surprising that the advantages they were able to find at the border were not durable.

Conclusion

After the termination of the Bracero Program, many ex-braceros settled in the United States or returned to their places of birth, as documented in previous literature on Mexican migrants. Yet a large group of ex-braceros also relocated to borderland cities like Tijuana to take advantage of the economic opportunities the border provided. Building on previous border research from scholars like Laura Velasco Ortiz and Oscar F. Contreras, this chapter shows that opportunity and social mobility were not restricted to one side of the border or the other.[35] One group of ex-braceros found their niche in the expanding urban border labor market of Tijuana. Another group continued to cross as agricultural workers in neighboring San Diego County. During the open-border period, ex-braceros were able to live in Tijuana and find jobs that provided economic and noneconomic benefits that supported their decision to labor either in the United States as cross-border farmworkers or in Mexico as reskilled urban workers.

Taken together, the experiences of these two groups illustrate how in the borderlands, workers' labor trajectories and social mobility respond to both Mexican and US labor markets. Ex-braceros formed their labor market strategies in relation to the economic conditions and government policies on both sides of the border. On the whole, the ex-braceros I met gravitated toward jobs that offered security, social mobility, and an enduring occupational identity. As he decided where to work and in what occupation, each ex-bracero attempted to capitalize on the borderland economy by making choices that suited his unique lifestyle, aspirations, and needs.

Even though ex-braceros were relegated to low-wage jobs, they were able to establish upward mobility in terms of both occupation and lifestyle using the border as a resource to obtain employment, upgrade their skills, develop new contacts, obtain border-crossing documents, or obtain jobs with opportunity for advancement that were lacking in their communities of origin. The ex-braceros I interviewed found success in Tijuana and never returned to their rural homes. While this chapter focuses specifically on the experiences of ex-braceros, it is important to note that the stories about ex-braceros are also stories about migrants. Their life histories illustrate how migrants adapt to new urban social systems. While this chapter highlights the role of the Bracero Program in the making of a cross-border labor force, in the following chapter I turn to the experiences of modern-day crossers with the goal of understanding how the commuter labor force has reproduced itself across time.

CHAPTER 3 | Becoming a Border Commuter

ONE UNIQUE ASPECT OF living in the borderlands is that people's livelihoods are shaped by cross-border social and economic exchanges. To live in the borderlands means that residents—with access to legal documents—enter the United States and participate in markets, whether as consumers or as workers. However, US border and immigration policies have in recent years restricted who can cross the border to take advantage of markets in both countries. This chapter examines how people obtain legal documents to engage in migration and border commuting practices that allow them to construct binational labor market strategies and become part of a border commuter labor force. As such, this chapter addresses the following questions: What strategies do current-day border residents employ in an attempt to turn the border into a source of opportunity? How do they obtain legal documents to work in the United States? How do they use these documents to build livelihoods that straddle the border? I highlight not only how people build livelihoods that straddle the border but also describe how changes to immigration laws and border enforcement have altered the strategies that they employ to become participants in the transborder economy.

To answer these questions, this chapter investigates the strategies employed by border residents to obtain legal documents, such as a BCC, Tourist Card, or Green Card, which they then use to engage in border commuting and/or long-distance migration to diversify their economic lives. In particular, I focus on the different types of resources available to migrants and border residents in the early 1980s, just before the period of the Immigration Reform and Control Act (IRCA; 1987–1993) and the years following its enactment. Then I focus on the years following Operation

Gatekeeper (1994). I argue that as the political and economic structure of the borderlands changed and restricted mobility, border residents exercised agency by navigating the constraints of immigration and border policies to obtain the necessary documents at each moment to pursue livelihoods that straddled the border. Before the dawn of IRCA, border residents migrated to the United States by obtaining the necessary resources and contacts to cross the border clandestinely or with the use of BCCs. This group eventually obtained Green Cards through IRCA, allowing them to return to Tijuana, where they became commuters. For crossers in the era following Operation Gatekeeper, entry into the labor market became more tenuous, as this group largely relied on BCCs to cross the border to work without authorization. This chapter details the strategies that both of these groups used to become part of a cross-border labor force and how they participate in the borderlands economy. The crossing strategies employed by these groups of crossers help to construct a transborder economy comprising people whose livelihoods extend beyond the confines of the nation-state.

Previous scholarship has found that border commuters engage in this form of work-life as a strategy to minimize the economic costs associated with the reproduction of daily family life. Migrant workers minimize costs by residing in a country of origin with lower costs of living and crossing the border to earn wages that are higher than those of where they reside.[1] These studies highlight the influence of IRCA on the cross-border labor force and the transnational nature of social and economic linkages between Mexico and the United States.[2] I build on these studies by discussing how migrants and local residents became border commuters in Tijuana by developing the necessary contacts, occupational experience, and knowledge to capitalize on the resources and opportunities that the borderlands offers, including legal documents to cross. The narratives presented in this chapter illustrate the wide diversity in strategies and labor market practices migrants used to join the cross-border labor force. BCCs allowed migrants either to commute back and forth across the border or to migrate to the United States. For commuters, crossing cards provided access to a wide variety of livelihood strategies.

Transfrontier Livelihoods

For geographer Lawrence Herzog, Tijuana and San Diego form part of a transfrontier metropolis as an urban region comprising settlements on either side of an international border.[3] Though a border divides these settlements, residents who cross for work, entertainment, and education transform the space into a single metropolitan region. The San Ysidro–Puerta México port of entry is the busiest port in the western hemisphere—62,792 vehicles and pedestrians cross daily. On an annual basis, this amounts to forty-two million people and fifteen million passenger vehicles entering through the pedestrian lines or the twenty-four automobile gates.[4] Together, the San Ysidro and Otay Mesa port of entry accounted for 17.2 percent of all border crossings into the United States in 2002 just before I started my fieldwork.[5] These Baja California crossers spent $1.6 billion in goods and services in the United States, while US visitors spent $812 million on entertainment and medicine in Mexico in 2002.[6]

While these crossing practices may suggest an integrated urban social system, Tito Alegría argues that structural differences between countries prevent true integration.[7] First, there are no restrictions on US residents wishing to visit Mexico, but there are restrictions on Mexican residents who want to visit the United States, Second, there are major inequalities between the two countries especially with regard to wages. In 1998, the average hourly wage of a worker in San Diego was $10.40 more than that of a worker in Tijuana. In manufacturing in particular, the average hourly rate was $12.20 in San Diego but only $1.90 in Tijuana.[8] In 2014, the average minimum wage for a California worker was $8.00 per hour while the minimum wage for a Baja California worker just over $5.00 *per day*.[9] Higher US wages are attractive to residents on the Tijuana side of the border, but very few are ever able to obtain those wages. Thus, as a result of the structural differences between Tijuana and San Diego, Tito Alegría concludes that there is no such thing as a transborder integrated market. Yet even as the unequal and segregated labor markets of Tijuana and San Diego fail to constitute a single, transborder market, the transfrontier metropolis is nevertheless home to a small but significant binational workforce of BCC and Green Card commuters. They may not be integrated, but they are connected, even if it only for a small percentage of the Tijuana population. In fact, Tito Alegría himself finds that as wage disparities between the United States and Mexico have increased, so too has the population of border commuters.[10]

But how exactly are Mexican residents able to live in Mexico and cross the border on an everyday basis? IRCA provided Tijuana residents with access to Green Cards. These allowed many migrants to remain in the United States, but others chose instead to live in Mexico and cross the border daily.[11] Since the early part of the twentieth century, border commuters have been an integral part of the US-Mexico borderlands and have entered the United States using legal documents such as Green Cards that allow them to live and work permanently in the United States.[12] BCCs have also long granted Mexicans passage into the United States for shopping and visiting friends and family in the United States, and some utilize these cards to work without authorization. In her historical study of consumption in Tijuana, Magalí Muriá shows that since 1929, people from the interior of Mexico have had to obtain visas to enter the United States. In Tijuana and other US-Mexico border cities, by contrast, residents were allowed to use BCCs to enter.[13] However, for much of the history of the Tijuana–San Diego border, Muriá found that US laws were in fact loosely enforced such that people could falsely declare US citizenship to cross the border. Many of the respondents that I interviewed recalled that during the 1970s and 1980s, obtaining a BCC was a relatively hassle-free process, in which an applicant simply had to prove residence in Tijuana for a year or more.

Few records document changes in the BCC application process, but it is clear that national-level immigration enforcement policies such as IRCA of 1986, Operation Gatekeeper of 1994, and the Illegal Immigration Reform and Immigrant Responsibility Act (IIRIRA) of 1996 complicated the process and increased surveillance at the border. These policies increased the number of Border Patrol agents and US Customs and Immigration officials at the port of entry and expanded border fences.[14] In recent decades, the US government began to imprint biometric information (such as fingerprints and a photograph) on BCCs to track the movements of the border population. The US Department of Homeland Security also began to use the IDENT system shortly after 1994, which allows the Border Patrol to track and apprehend migrants by taking their fingerprints and photographs when they are caught crossing clandestinely.

In an era of increasing border enforcement, many border residents obtain BCCs or tourist visas as an extralegal method to access US employment. Tijuana is one of only nine Mexican cities with a consulate office that grants BCCs and Tourists Cards. Figure 3.1 shows the US consulates in Mexico that gave out the highest number of nonimmigrant visas in 2005 and 2013. What is important to note is that, of border cities, only Ciudad Juárez gave out more nonimmigrant visas than Tijuana. The rest of the consulates are located far from the US-Mexico border. These consulate offices provide border residents with BCCs that allow the cardholder to enter the United States to shop or visit relatives but not to work. It becomes a resource for internal migrants who arrive in Tijuana.

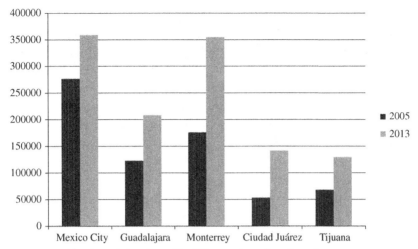

FIGURE 3.1 Number of visas issued by US consulates for selected years.
Source: "Nonimmigrant Visas Issued by Issuing Office (Including Border Crossing Cards), Fiscal Years 2004–2013."[36] Based on the report, http://travel.state.gov/content/dam/visas/Statistics/AnnualReports/FY2013AnnualReport/FY13AnnualReport-TableXIX.pdf.

To become eligible for a BCC, fronterizos must first establish long-term residency through home ownership and permanent employment. The current application process consists of a Mexican passport, online application, and an application fee of $160. Once obtained, the BCC allows the card-bearer to enter the United States within a twenty-five mile radius north of the international boundary for as long as thirty days. The cards have an expiration date of ten years, though they can be renewed more than once. The key factor that US immigration officials take into consideration when deciding to approve a BCC is whether the applicant has permanent "ties to Mexico" that will discourage the cardholder from overstaying their visit.

Sociologist Frank Bean and his associates conducted interviews with US immigration officials who issued BCCs to residents of Ciudad Juárez, Chihuahua, and found that "the law grants INS officers almost total discretion in determining a BCC applicant's eligibility for entry to the United States."[15] The immigration officers also assessed applicants favorably if they had a permanent job of more than one year and savings in the bank.[16] However, even for applicants who presented all of the necessary documents, had a stable job, and had savings in the bank, many were still denied the BCC. Echoing Bean's findings about the discretionary nature of BCC applications, the Tijuanenses I interviewed perceived little consistency in the granting of cards. Despite the level of arbitrariness involved in the process, however, BCCs and tourist visas, like the passport in John Torpey's study, represent an attempt by the state to monopolize the legitimate means of movement by creating procedures and policies, "establishing which types of persons may move within or cross their borders."[17] Given the subjective nature of obtaining the cards, as we shall see, contemporary commuters who cross to work using BCCs attempt to locate full-time jobs that give the appearance that they are rooted to the Mexican economy.

IRCA and the Creation of Green Card Commuters

BCCs, Green Cards, and tourist visas are attractive resources for Tijuanenses because they provide the opportunity to expand their livelihood options across the border.[18] Accessing these resources is a long, slow, and highly contingent process that unfolds through a series of life events. One set of border residents gained the ability to cross legally only after first crossing the border as unauthorized migrants during the later years of the open-border period (1965–85). These border residents migrated to the United States either clandestinely or by overstaying a BCC or visa prior to the enactment of IRCA, which extended legal permanent residence to many unauthorized migrants currently in the country. These migrants later moved to Tijuana, eventually becoming part of a cross-border labor force.

Fifty-two-year-old Fidel Ramos was an avid weekend soccer player and a typical border commuter who gained his Green Card status through IRCA. By the time Fidel was thirteen years old, he had already migrated twice with friends and considered himself a seasoned migrant. On his first trip, he set out on his own without a single peso in his pocket. His father had passed away, so he left to search for work to help support his mother and his siblings. He recounted that his first trip was "horrible," involving twenty-one days of hitchhiking from a small town just outside of Guadalajara to Tijuana. Rather than migrate to the United States, Fidel stayed in Tijuana on this first trip because he had siblings who lived there. Within a few days, he found work in the informal sector, first shining shoes, then washing cars, and then selling gum and newspapers.

After returning to visit his family in Guadalajara, Fidel migrated to Tijuana for a second time. This time, he worked and saved his earnings, which he then used to pay a smuggler to bring him to Los Angeles. He went on to spend the next two decades moving back and forth across the border. At one point, while living in Los Angeles, Fidel learned about the *amnistía* (IRCA), which would grant him legal permanent residence if he could prove that he had lived continuously in the United States between 1982 and 1986. To do so, he would have to present paystubs, utility bills, or letters from employers proving that he had lived in the United States during that time. Fortunately, Fidel had kept a suitcase under the bed of his one-bedroom apartment in Los Angeles containing all of his utility bills and paystubs. With those documents in hand, he was able to make a case to immigration officials for a Green Card.

After Fidel obtained his Green Card through IRCA, he returned to Tijuana so that he could live a *vida fronteriza* (binational life). He wanted to have the same lifestyle as many of the customers he had previously interacted with as a shoe shiner and car detailer. These customers lived in Mexico but freely crossed the border into the United States. Thus, rather than integrate socially and economically into the United States, like millions of other Mexican immigrants, Fidel chose to become a border commuter. In Tijuana, Fidel felt that he was able to progress "more here in ten years than I would have in twenty years over there [the United States]." He "progressed" in Tijuana by stretching the value of the dollars that he earned as a US construction worker while paying Mexican prices for living expenses. By residing in Tijuana, his rent was one-fifth what he had paid in the United States. Moreover, he also lowered his utility bills, and on weekends, it was cheaper to take his family out for dinner and a movie. Fidel said that even a haircut was much cheaper in Tijuana than in the United States. Life was good in Tijuana.

Fidel's multistage migration strategies resemble what scholars refer to as "stepwise" migration.[19] These scholars find that people engage in a series of migration steps with the goal of reaching a final international destination where they are able to obtain better employment opportunities. Stepwise migrants take a series of internal and/or international migration steps with the goal of obtaining information, resources, and money that can facilitate their reaching a final destination where they will be able to obtain better wages. In contrast to the typical stepwise migrant, however, Fidel's goal was not migration to another country but a return to Mexico. He was a "stepwise return migrant" who migrated in a series of steps before finally becoming a border commuter. First, he migrated from his origin community to Tijuana, where he gained access to income and social support before embarking on a trip to Los Angeles. In Los Angeles, he turned to his brother to help him find employment, and with the help of his US employer, Fidel qualified for a Green Card. With his Green Card and US work history, Fidel returned to Tijuana to settle as a border commuter.

At the time of our interview, Fidel daily crossed the border to work construction in the United States. During other periods, his brother, who was a construction contractor, invited Fidel to the United States for an extended period to live and work with him. Unlike stepwise migrants who move in a linear fashion from points A to B to C, stepwise return migrants like Fidel eventually return to point B for personal and economic reasons. A key aspect of stepwise return migration is that people must draw on a variety of resources and social networks during each stage of the migration process. For example, a border resident may turn to one set of contacts to help them obtain a BCC, then turn to another set of contacts to find work in the United States. This means that border residents must cultivate a broad base of helpers in order to build resources and to circumvent immigration policies that seek to restrict their livelihood choices.

Turning BCCs into Green Cards

Fifty-four-year-old Ramón García, one of Fidel's best friends, was also a stepwise return migrant. Ramón originally moved from Jocotepec, Jalisco, to Tijuana in 1968, then to Los Angeles, and finally back to Tijuana. Unlike Fidel, who migrated to the United States clandestinely before obtaining a Green Card, Ramón's migration to the United States was facilitated by a BCC. After his father became ill, Ramón migrated to Tijuana from Jalisco to live with his aunt during his late teenage years. She helped him locate work in the city. For the next twelve years, Ramón had a steady job in Mexico working for a radio station. His Mexican employer paid him in dollars and provided him with an apartment. He was well established and had no desire to migrate to the United States because he had a high-status job in Tijuana. In the mornings, he dressed in a suit and drove a Ford Torino around the city collecting dues from businesses that wanted to advertise at his radio station. However, two major events would shape his future trajectory. In 1982, Ramón broke his leg while playing soccer at a time that coincided with the peso devaluation that displaced Mexicans economically. He could no longer perform his job and found himself unemployed. Because he had a long record of living and working in Tijuana, he was able to apply for a BCC that he used to visit family in Los Angeles and to shop in San Diego County. Whenever he visited Los Angeles, his compadre (godfather) encouraged him to stay and find work.

In 1980, Ramón took up his compadre's offer and moved to Los Angeles. He spent the next fifteen years living in LA and returning to Mexico on the weekends to visit his wife and four children. He was able to do so because his compadre helped him find a job in a vegetable warehouse and then helped him apply for amnesty. Ramón considered himself lucky to have arrived in Los Angeles at the right historical moment and with the support of his family. Moreover, Ramón's exposure to US work life before IRCA was established came in handy when it came to applying for legal status, just as it did for other border migrants. He applied to become a legal permanent resident as a *rodino*, which meant that he was required to demonstrate continuous employment in agriculture for ninety days between May 1, 1985, and May 1, 1986. Ramón was never employed as a farmworker but applied for legal permanent residency this way because many friends told him that it was much easier to apply in this manner. During the application process, government officials attempted to trick unauthorized immigrants to see if they had truly worked in the United States. Immigration officials asked questions like, "How tall are the trees on which strawberries grow?" Because Ramón had labored in many different types of jobs in Los Angeles County and because he passed through strawberry fields in northern San Diego County en route to Los Angeles, he had enough knowledge of how people worked in the fields and responded in a confident manner, saying, "Strawberries do not grow on trees, but lemons do."

For Ramón, becoming a border commuter was a long process that involved myriad resources on both sides of the border. Ramón's Mexican employer provided him with stable employment that helped him qualify for a BCC, and his US-based relatives helped integrate him into US society by recommending him to an employer and encouraging him to become a legal permanent resident. Yet the final step in his migration occurred when his wife, Chelo, and their four children eventually persuaded Ramón to return to Tijuana. In fact, at one point Ramón received a letter in the mail asking him if he wanted to petition any family members to become Green Card holders like himself. Ángel, one of his sons, recalled, "We were small and we all began to cry . . . my dad used to talk to my mom and my mom would tell him no one wanted to stay in [Los Angeles]. We only liked to go on vacation like it was a trip." As a result, Ramón did not pursue the Green Cards for his family, even though it was instrumental to his and his family's livelihood, because he figured that the opportunity would always be there. Moreover, he was tired of living in the United States and did not want to have to relocate to Los Angeles or anywhere else in the United States. Ramón's return to Tijuana allowed him to live with his wife and children in Mexico only twenty minutes from the port of entry where he crossed to work in the United States.

Like that of Ramón and Fidel, twenty-nine-year-old María Robles's relocation from Chihuahua to Tijuana provided her with newfound opportunities that eventually landed her a Green Card. María came to Tijuana after her father was transferred for work over twenty years earlier. María obtained her first job at sixteen in a video rental store in Tijuana and eventually became an assistant in a pharmacy, where she developed customer service skills. Through this work, María was developing an occupational history that eventually qualified her for a BCC. Using the BCC to cross, she migrated for six months to Los Angeles, where she met her now ex-husband, a US citizen, who helped her obtain a Green Card.

Sociologist Katharine Donato points out that the Bracero Program and the amnesty provisions of the IRCA largely favored men but that women were also able to obtain legal permanent residence through sponsorship from male relatives.[20] By accumulating resources in Tijuana and engaging in "stepwise migration," María met and married her husband in the United States and he helped her access legal permanent residence. Whereas previously, María used a BCC to cross the border to shop and even to migrate, at the time of our interview, she crossed the border with a Green Card to work in a hardware store in the United States, a job she found through an online ad on a US site. She was also in the process of regularizing the status of her son, who was born in Tijuana.

Although she held a Green Card, María did not settle in the United States for financial reasons. She viewed the United States as a calmer and safer place to live than Tijuana, but she could not afford California's high cost of living on a retail salary. Her time in the United States was spent in cramped living conditions, and especially after her divorce, María realized that she would need to return to Tijuana to make ends meet. María did not like the culture of the United States, preferring that of Mexico. For her, the United States was all about work and less about family and leisure. People were always in a rush to get to and from work and seldom set aside time to spend with neighbors, friends, and family. Moreover, people in the United States were more individualistic in comparison to Mexico. But despite her love of fronterizo culture, María ironically also did not like the fast-paced nature of life of Tijuana, where people were always rushing to get to their jobs in the United States. For her, Tijuana resembled the United States too much largely because much of its population depended on its economy for their livelihoods, and thus adopted particular lifestyle choices that were just too similar to the United States. So, for both Ramón and María, family events—reunification for Ramón and divorce for María—were primary motivating factors for their return to Tijuana. But their decision to live in

Tijuana and work in the United States would not have been possible without access to legal documents—in their cases, Green Cards that provided the ability to both cross and work legally.

Sociologist Anju Mary Paul studied Filipino domestic workers who moved from less desirable countries to preferred destinations in a stepwise fashion.[21] At each step, migrants upgraded their skills and obtained money and social contacts that facilitated their trek across a hierarchy of destinations from the Middle East to Southeast Asia (Singapore and Malaysia) to East Asia (Hong Kong and Taiwan), with a preference for the West (United States, Spain, Italy, and the United Kingdom), where higher wage rates, better working conditions, and the possibility of permanent residency were factors that shaped their desires for further migration. For some migrants, Anju Mary Paul found that the move to a final destination could take as long as a decade to complete.[22] Like these Filipino migrants, the Mexican border residents in this study engaged in "stepwise" migration to obtain skills, money, and social contacts. In Tijuana, these resources helped pay their border-crossing fees and find work in the United States. Distinct from the Filipino migrants, however, Mexican border residents did not see the United States as their ultimate migrant destination. Instead, Tijuana served as a jumping point to the US labor market and then became point of return once legal documents—and therefore ongoing access to employment across the border—had been secured. There were two types of migration practices that border residents employed. Some border commuters engaged in "stepwise" return migration. Others migrated directly from their hometowns to the United States and settled in Tijuana only after acquiring legal residency. For both of these groups, Tijuana became the final resting point and location where they could access the best of both worlds: higher wages in the United States and the lower costs and cultural comforts of living in Mexico.

Fidel, Ramón, and María all exemplify cases of people who spent significant time living in Tijuana and the United States before becoming border commuters. However, Fidel and Ramón entered the US labor market at a unique historical moment—what sociologists Alejandro Portes and Rubén G. Rumbaut would term "a favorable context of reception" from the US government.[23] IRCA provided Fidel and Ramón with access to Green Cards that allowed them to become legal crossers. Decades later, María obtained a BCC that allowed her to live in Los Angeles, where she met her US citizen husband who would eventually provide her with legal residence. While these commuters obtained Green Cards to join the cross-border labor force, the newer generation of border crossers introduced in the next section primarily employed an extralegal strategy to join the cross-border labor force by acquiring BCCs, which entitled cardholders to visit the United States and to shop there, but not to work. BCCs were the primary mechanism for young border commuters to access the US labor market.

BCCs in a Post-IRCA, Post-Gatekeeper Period

The generation of border commuters who obtained their BCCs prior to 1986 included many stepwise return migrants who were able to eventually acquire Green Cards through IRCA, giving them the opportunity to live in Mexico and work in the United States with legal authorization. Fronterizos who decided to pursue the goal of commuting after 1986 were unable to apply for amnesty like Ramón and Fidel, and few were able to meet other requirements for the Green Card like María.[24] For later generations of commuters, BCCs were one of the only viable pathways to cross the border for livelihood opportunities in the United States. As such, these individuals employed a variety of strategies to access BCCs. They made a concerted effort to gather contacts, occupational experience, knowledge, and information about how to obtain BCCs. This was especially true in the period after Operation Gatekeeper (from 1994), when increased state surveillance at the US-Mexico border forced Tijuanenses to enter the US labor market through formal channels. In the absence of an amnesty or Bracero Program, the most recent generation of crossers had to obtain legal documents to cross the border to work—in particular, BCCs.

Armando Nava's story illustrates the long and complex process of obtaining a BCC. Almost immediately upon arrival in Tijuana, he began strategizing to obtain a BCC. Armando (age twenty-five) was the son of Aurelio Nava, the ex-bracero discussed in chapter 2, who relocated to Tijuana and became an independent entrepreneur before finally becoming a taxi owner. Armando followed his father to Tijuana from Mexico City. Armando's first job in Tijuana was as a driver, delivering frozen chicken to Chinese restaurants. I met Armando as he awaited the decision on his third application attempt for a BCC; he had made his first attempt four years earlier. I ran into Armando at his father's ice cream shop on the day he received the news about his third application. He was rejected yet again and told not to file another application for two years. He asked me if I would drive him to the local market to buy heavy cream and berries for his father, who was going to make strawberry ice cream. During our drive to Mercado Hidalgo, a large open-air market, Armando vented his frustration with the BCC process. He complained that despite holding a steady job and earning twice the "miserable wages" of his friends who worked in maquiladoras and obtained BCCs, he was denied.

Armando was desperate to obtain a BCC because he wanted to cross the border to buy new rims for his truck, and he also wanted to use the card either to migrate to Los Angeles, where he had family, or to join the thousands of people who crossed the border on a daily basis to work in the United States. While he still was uncertain as to whether he would migrate or commute, it was clear that he wanted to use the BCC to work without authorization in the United States to earn higher wages than in Mexico. Even if he did not cross to work in the United States, a BCC would allow him to cross the border to buy automobiles that he could resell in Tijuana. Armando coveted the BCC because it would increase his earnings by providing access to a labor market and/or to consumer goods that he did not have in Tijuana but others around him did. After his third rejection, he was mad as hell at the process of disbursing BCCs, which he believed was arbitrary and subjective.

Armando was what Anthony Giddens would call a "knowledgeable agent."[25] He knew he wanted to work in the United States and he knew what strategies to take to reach that goal. He took all of the necessary steps to obtain a BCC. He began by establishing a savings account. For several months, he syphoned gas out of the company's delivery van to use in his personal vehicle. This allowed him to save on daily transportation costs. Occasionally, he sold extra fuel to taxi drivers for cash, which he deposited in the bank. Within a year, his bank account showed a balance of $10,000. To establish records and save even more money, he gave up the house he had rented, because his landlord did not furnish him with a renter's receipt, and purchased an inexpensive home in a low-income area. Even after being rejected twice, Armando decided to try a third time for a BCC because he believed he had a strong case to bring before the immigration official. Before the third attempt, he also paid $200 to a person who claimed to have connections with US government officials who would erase his two previous attempts to obtain a BCC and any notes on his file. Unfortunately, when Armando appeared at the US consulate, he discovered that this person failed to make good on their agreement. The immigration official told him that the computer showed two prior attempts to obtain a BCC and ultimately rejected Armando for a third time.

Five years after this third rejection, I revisited Armando and his family. By this time, the rejections had gotten to him and had given up applying for a BCC. On each attempt, Armando had lost his application fee (which reached $140 by the last attempt) and hours spent away from work to stand in line at the US consulate. His father, Aurelio, advised Armando in no uncertain terms to stop wasting his time and money; one Sunday afternoon at a family gathering, Aurelio yelled at Armando, "Stop throwing away your fucking money, it is only being used to build a bigger wall!" After the Nava family had witnessed so many family, friends, and neighbors lose their applications for a BCC, Aurelio came to believe that the promise of a BCC was in fact a ploy by the US government to take money from Mexicans to fortify the wall between Tijuana and San Diego.

On this last visit, Armando no longer had the energy to continue applying for a BCC, but his priorities had also changed in the intervening years. He was no longer preoccupied with crossing the border because he was immersed in personal issues in Tijuana. His girlfriend had recently broken up with him, causing him to spiral into a deep depression. To heal from the breakup, he began to lift weights and compete in local bodybuilding contests. After multiple failed applications for a BCC, Armando began to divert his attention to other ways of making money. He invested in a purchase of two taxis. Though he still wanted a BCC, it was no longer one of his main priorities.

Armando's story illustrates the difficult process faced by border residents attempting to get a BCC, as well as the power of the state in regulating who can cross the border. Although Armando was content living in Tijuana, he felt constrained. The border, the physical boundary that separated both countries, placed limitations on his life goals. After taking all the necessary steps to obtain a BCC, the process appeared to him and so many other Tijuana residents as entirely arbitrary.

The process of allocating BCCs is an example of what John Torpey refers to as the state's role in monopolizing the legitimate means of movement by reserving the right to cross for a select number of beneficiaries.[26] While some border residents would spend their entire lives in the borderlands without qualifying for a BCC, others with weaker qualifications might obtain a BCC on their first try. Yet even as they lacked any guarantee of success, residents employed three strategies to increase their chances of obtaining a BCC: developing an occupational history, proving a history of ties to educational institutions, and mobilizing kinship ties.

Developing an Occupational History in Mexico

Border commuters sought a BCC with three goals in mind: (1) to use the card to cross the border daily to work in neighboring San Diego County; (2) to cross to work in the interior of the United States, in some cases permanently and in other cases temporarily, as seasonal migrants; (3) to cross the border to purchase used goods or automobiles to resell in Mexico at a profit. Yet to obtain a BCC, applicants had to hide these desires and prove to US officials their strong ties to Tijuana, as well as their ability to contribute to the US economy as consumers shopping across the border. To do so, applicants worked to establish an occupational history in Tijuana that consisted of stable, full-time jobs in the formal economy that provided paystubs and reported earnings to the Mexican social security office. Given Tijuana's dynamic labor market, there were many sectors in which people could develop an occupational history. Employment in factories was one common source of such employment.[27] Sociologist Christina Mendoza studied domestic workers in the border region of Laredo–Nuevo Laredo and found that about a third of the twenty-six women that she interviewed had obtained their BCCs as a result of working in maquiladoras.[28] Similarly, sociologist Kathy Kopinak interviewed migrants in San Diego County who had previously lived in Tijuana and found that in many cases, by working in maquiladoras, people received letters of recommendation and, in some cases, help navigating the US immigration bureaucracy as well.[29] While living in Tijuana, I interviewed some border commuters who at one time had worked for SONY, JVC, and Panasonic, employment that they believed helped them obtain a BCC.

Before becoming the manager of a US-owned factory, Emilio Flores, born and raised in Tijuana, worked as a factory laborer. At the time of our interview, Emilio was a US citizen living an American lifestyle in Tijuana. His home, located in a Mexican middle-class neighborhood, looked like a US tract home, with three bedrooms and a garage. During our interview, his wife Consuelo and two sons arrived after having bought groceries from Costco in San Diego. While Emilio considered himself lucky, given his history as a factory laborer, he had taken a long and difficult journey to achieve this comfortable lifestyle. When he was only sixteen years old, Emilio started to spend his summers working part-time as a welder at an electronics assembly plant within walking distance of his house. After Emilio had worked in the factory for six years, his employer recognized his leadership skills and promoted him to a supervisory position. With the promotion came many benefits: a higher salary and a higher-status job (he no longer had to perform the same monotonous and repetitive tasks) supervising forty to fifty workers on a daily basis. Shortly after his promotion, Emilio applied for and was granted a BCC. Although he did not originally plan to use the BCC to work in the United States, Emilio explained that the temptation was too great. After a friend who owned a taco shop in the United States invited him to work at a fast-food restaurant earning minimum wage, Emilio quit his job and spent the next year and a half crossing the US-Mexico border, because he earned as much working in a taco shop two days a week as he did in a full week as a factory supervisor.

While working in the United States, Emilio developed an extensive work history and friendships. These experiences allowed him to find a job working in a factory on the US side of the border that paid much higher wages than the minimum wage he earned at the taco shop. After spending several years working for the factory, Emilio was promoted to supervisor, and the US-based company asked him to relocate to their factory in Tijuana. At the time of our interview, Emilio worked for the same US-based company producing spa covers that were shipped to the United States. Although he lived in Mexico, he was paid in dollars.

As a teenager, Emilio obtained a factory job in Tijuana that provided him with the stable employment and letters of recommendation he needed for a BCC. In addition, his years of hard work in a factory allowed him to climb to a supervisory position. This position offered higher wages and showed his strong ties to the labor market in Mexico. After this position helped Emilio successfully obtain a BCC, he became a border commuter for some time, only to eventually return to working in a new factory in Tijuana at higher wages, thanks to his US work experience.

But not all interviewees agreed with Emilio that factory work was the best option to obtain a BCC. Many respondents believed that "maquiladoras pay miserable wages." Indeed, entry-level factory workers earned as little as 700 pesos (about $65) per week, just enough to pay for transportation and food expenses at the time of my field research. In response to the low wages available in manufacturing jobs, several respondents chose to work in the service sector. These respondents often moved from job to job within the service sector with the goal of securing a salary that would help them qualify for a BCC. One respondent recalled that when she presented her paystubs to the immigration official, he laughed and commented, "With these miserable wages, what can you do in the US?" To receive permission to cross the border and enter a country where the cost of goods and services was higher, applicants were well aware that they needed to secure a strong salary to prove their ability to afford to spend in the United States.

Manuel Sánchez was a confident twenty-seven-year-old who dressed in Calvin Klein jeans and pristine white Adidas sneakers. Although he worked in a pork-processing plant in the Midwest, he displayed no signs that he was a member of the proletarian labor force. Manuel originally migrated from rural Oaxaca to Tijuana after his oldest sister and a friend informed him about the vast employment opportunities available in the region. Before migrating to Tijuana, Manuel had limited labor market experience. He moved to Tijuana to find better employment opportunities and to establish his work history in well-paying occupations before applying for a BCC. He explained to me that in rural Oaxaca, the only employment opportunity he had had as a high school graduate was working on his father's small dairy farm. Instead, he chose to move to Tijuana, where the urban labor market offered many more opportunities.

After arriving in Tijuana, Manuel slowly worked his way up the occupational ladder. He started off working at a bus terminal and then transitioned into working as an operator at a long-distance telephone business. These jobs paid only subsistence wages, which he knew would not be enough to qualify for a BCC. He continued to search for other work, eventually replying to an advertisement for an optometrist's assistant at Plaza Rio, the local mall, where he was trained to fit eyeglasses. When he started the job, Manuel earned about $75 a week, but after he became skilled at selling eyeglasses, in a good week he earned as much as $175 in commission alone. He remained in this job for three years and was able to qualify for the BCC.

Manuel had several siblings living in the United States without legal authorization—a sister in Los Angeles and brothers in Lafayette, Indiana. When he first arrived in Tijuana, Manuel's brother encouraged him to migrate clandestinely to Indiana or Los Angeles. Manuel was not interested in clandestine migration, however. He explained:

One year after arriving in Tijuana, my brothers told me to migrate to the Midwest. So, I already had the idea of going [to the Midwest]. But I always said that I was not going to cross as a "wetback." I wanted to do it right and pass through the port of entry, you know what I mean. Eventually, I had the opportunity because I was well established [with residency in Tijuana] and had a good job.

Although Manuel worked without authorization in the United States, he did not consider himself a "wetback," a derogatory term used to describe immigrants who cross the Rio Grande. Rather than evade US authorities,

Manuel entered the country legally. If caught working without authorization, Manuel would lose his BCC and be deported to Mexico for violating the terms of the tourist visa. But this did not worry Manuel because it was rare for immigration officials to conduct worksite raids; most of the money allocated to enforce immigration law in the United States was spent on the border and not at worksites.

In addition to crossing the border legally, the BCC allowed Manuel to use his Mexican driver's license to drive in the United States and to fly to Indiana. This was one of the primary reasons why Manuel chose to enter the United States via inspection. To stay in Indiana or Los Angeles on his BCC, Manuel simply had to obtain an I-94 form (or record of admission) for a small fee. This form allowed him to travel to the interior of the United States as long as he returned the form to immigration officials on or before the mandated date. The I-94 form was another resource in Manuel's livelihood strategy, which involved working without authorization in Indiana. He did this for ten years of the allotted BCC time he was given by the US government.

On a return visit to Tijuana from Indiana, Manuel met me for an interview after a gathering with former coworkers and neighborhood friends. Manuel told them that there was plenty of work in the meat-processing industry in the northeastern United States, including the factory where he worked. When I asked if he had helped anyone obtain work in the United States, Manuel stated that he just "oriented them." In particular, he gave advice on how to obtain a BCC. He advised his friends: "Get your papers first before you decide to migrate to the US." He then explained to them the process of getting a BCC and how to use the BCC as a strategy to work in the interior of the United States.

Manuel's sister, Carmen Sánchez (age twenty-two), also migrated to Tijuana and moved up the occupational ladder until she obtained a BCC, which she used to migrate to the United States. Like Manuel, Carmen was encouraged by her Tijuana-based siblings to move to the border, where she found abundant opportunities for work. While her siblings encouraged her to move to Tijuana, her eventual transition to the US labor market was shaped by her coworkers. When she first arrived in Tijuana, Carmen started at an entry-level position. Her first job was as a cashier in a local department store that paid $45 per week. Though this job paid low wages, she developed many important work skills, including how to charge customers in both pesos and dollars. She then moved on to a clothing store that recognized this ability and paid her $62 per week plus a commission on sales. While working at the clothing store, Carmen met a friend who provided guidance on how to cross the international border and secure US employment. Carmen recalled that her friend "was the first to obtain it [a BCC] and then she told me to go apply. She helped me with the paperwork and we asked for letters of recommendation and all of that to be able to get it." After Carmen was approved for the BCC, her friend found them jobs in a food-processing plant in Los Angeles. The two friends became inseparable over the next year, traveling together to Los Angeles and returning every few weeks to Tijuana to visit relatives and friends and renew the I-94 form. One year after I met Carmen, she had purchased her own car and moved in with a boyfriend she had met at work in Los Angeles.

Stories like Carmen's and Manuel's illustrate how family, coworkers, and employers were a resource in the process of applying for a BCC. Whereas family and coworkers provided advice and connection to jobs in the United States, Mexican employers provided border residents with letters of recommendation and paystubs they could use to make their case to immigration officers. A well-paying full-time job helped border residents ease immigration officials' worries about potential BCC abusers.

Tijuana's dynamic economy allowed people to develop work and residential histories to support their BCC applications—but Mexican employers also provided benefits that were not immediately apparent to would-be border crossers. One afternoon, I visited Manuel's and Carmen's sister Susana Robledo, a twenty-eight-year-old divorcee and mother of an infant. She worked at a pharmacy located within walking distance of the US-Mexico border where many Americans shopped for medicine. Like all of her siblings, Susana wanted to obtain a BCC, either to migrate to the United States or to cross the border on a daily basis to work in San Diego County—she had not yet decided. Her immediate goal was simply to get the BCC before figuring out what to do next.

Despite having only a high school diploma, Susana was confident in her job at the pharmacy, interacting cheerfully and courteously in broken English with her US-based customers. She always greeted them with a "good morning" or "good afternoon," and made them feel comfortable by asking them how their day was and where they were visiting from. To explain her professionalism, Susana told me that she had received training from Mexican psychologists, who taught the pharmacy workers that "the client comes first because they maintain our pharmacy [through sales]." The psychologists also instructed the workers, "Sick people come in stressed, so we have to understand that they are sick. You have to make them feel better, even if they yell at you, so you need to be attentive to them. If you welcome them, they will forget about their sickness, so attend them well."

In the process of applying for the BCC, Susana took a number of important steps to strengthen her case. She rented an apartment under her name and she obtained a sales position where she earned about $160 dollars a week before commission. In addition, and perhaps unbeknownst to her, Susana was also developing *intangible* assets that would bolster her case when she appeared before the immigration officer. Through her work at the pharmacy counter, Susana developed her English skills and her interpersonal skills—areas of strength exhibited by many BCC holders. Thanks to her training from the psychologists, she also knew how to deal with frustrated and angry customers. This experience would help her contend with suspicious immigration officers during the BCC application process and beyond, when—as a border commuter—she wished to convince them that she planned only to shop in the United States and not to work. She would also know how to withstand the harassment and intimidation commonly reported from immigration officials.[30] Many migration scholars who have studied BCCs recognize the importance of full-time employment in the application process; however, obtaining a job provides more than just tangible assets like paystubs.[31] The ability to interact with customers translated into a valuable skill for many BCC applicants as an intangible asset that helped them navigate a difficult and sometimes arbitrary process.

Emilio and Martín were former factory workers who obtained a BCC that they eventually used to become part of a cross-border labor force. In contrast, Manuel, Carmen, and Susana were former rural-based migrants who moved to Tijuana and worked their way up the occupational ladder until they obtained a job that paid well and helped them qualify for a BCC. All of these respondents also followed in their siblings' footsteps. Siblings relayed information not only about "good jobs" in Tijuana but also about the process of obtaining a BCC. These internal migrants had siblings living in Los Angeles, Phoenix, Indiana, and also Tijuana. The narratives of Manuel, Carmen, and Susana illustrate one particular path taken by migrants to Tijuana. Each of these migrants moved to Tijuana with the intention of eventually migrating to the United States, but the process unfolded slowly over time. They were socialized into a border society where they had many job opportunities that could pave the way to US employment.

Each case also illustrates the importance of connections to employers and job market information in the migration process. Employers were not primary actors but rather an integral part of the migration process in that they provided the opportunity to develop a residential work history that border residents used to make a case for their ties to Mexico. The narratives I presented here illustrate the importance of developing a work history in the formal labor market. Although I mention these two sectors, many respondents had also worked in government agencies and museums, cable and telephone companies, and in schools and universities. Some border residents had even been business owners. Mexican employment helped all of these workers ultimately obtain a BCC.

Educational Affiliation

While the Mexican labor market was perhaps the most important avenue for gaining access to BCCs, schools in Tijuana also played an important role for a subset of the respondents that I spoke to: educated young men and women. Some border residents obtained their BCCs by virtue of their affiliation with an educational institution. Some obtained their BCC as children in elementary schools and others did so as adults in college. Regardless of the age at which they obtained the BCC, their affiliation to an educational institution helped to demonstrate that they were not at risk for working in the United States. Border residents believed that presenting their children's school documents in combination with their paystubs increased their chances of obtaining a BCC.

Alejandra Guzmán (age twenty-five) applied for a BCC as an elementary school student in Tijuana. Alejandra recalled that her mother taught her about the importance of self-presentation and grooming when they presented their case to the immigration official. Alejandra's mom instructed her to "wear [my] school uniform so that they [immigration officials] don't think we want to go live over there [United States] and work." Alejandra and her mother knew many friends, family, and neighbors who had been rejected by immigration officials at the US consulate when they applied for a BCC. As a result, her mother wanted to present a convincing case to the US government that they were not at risk for overstaying. When they first applied for the BCC, they did not have plans to work in the United States until a family emergency forced them to work in the US for higher wages.

Socorro Ramírez (age twenty-four) used her ties to a local university to apply for a BCC. Socorro came from a family of international migrants. Her brother and sisters had all migrated clandestinely from Colima, Mexico, to Stockton, California. Her two youngest sisters had migrated to the border—Juanita to Ciudad Juárez, where she obtained her BCC, and

Lupita to Tijuana, where she earned money to pay a coyote. As a result, Socorro was well aware of the negative ramifications of being undocumented. In Stockton, her siblings were all employed in fast-food restaurants, earning only slightly more than minimum wage. Thus, when I first met Socorro, she had one goal in mind—completing her master's degree in environmental studies. She wanted to obtain the BCC for two reasons: to visit her boyfriend, who resided in Los Angeles, on a more regular basis and to eventually have the opportunity to work in the United States.

Unfortunately, Socorro's applications for a BCC had been rejected twice because she labored mostly in the informal economy in Mexico. One Thursday afternoon, however, Socorro contacted me via text message, informing me: "I can now cross the border!" On her third attempt, Socorro had received her BCC. When I asked her why she thought she had finally been approved, she replied that it had everything to do with her affiliation to her local university. She explained, "institutions [in Mexico like her college] are used as a bridge to obtain documents to cross into the US." She explained that she had originally enrolled at her particular college because she had heard that many of its students were successful in obtaining their BCC. She also stated that though the documentation of her enrollment "did not guarantee that I would obtain the visa, it was a good document to present when I was interviewed by the immigration official." In addition, by the time she qualified for the BCC, Socorro had lived in Tijuana for over a year and had saved some of her scholarship earnings in a bank account.

In her rural community of Colima, Mexico, Soccoro did not know many people with the experience of applying for a BCC. However, after moving to Tijuana, she was surrounded by peers, friends, and neighbors who knew about the process. Her peers provided her with information that she would not have received back home on how to increase her chances of acquiring a BCC. She was a keen observer and once told me that she "was always attentive to the comments everyone gave me throughout the process. Their experiences and even advice on how to dress mattered. They used to say to be friendly, to not get nervous, to go well dressed, and that your bank account mattered." On her third visit to the US consulate, Socorro finally obtained her BCC and subsequently began to cross the border frequently to visit her boyfriend and stayed for extended periods of time. Unable to find employment with the master's degree that she had obtained in Tijuana, she eventually moved in with her boyfriend, and a few months later, they married. Socorro went on to work in a low-income health clinic, where she learned English and developed US-based skills. When I last spoke to her, she was in the process of retraining as a nurse. By this point, she already had her legal permanent residence as a result of marriage to a US citizen and was also contemplating applying for US citizenship. For some border residents like Alejandra and Socorro, educational institutions took the place of occupational connections as a method for border residents to make their case to obtain a BCC and eventually enter the US labor market.

Drawing on and Expanding Kinship Ties

Obtaining a BCC is a cumbersome process that can take years for some applicants. Parents play an important role in helping their children obtain a BCC and in socializing them to navigate the process. When Jorge (age forty-five) was a young adolescent, his father initiated the application process for the BCC and applied as a family. His father, who owned a small print shop with two employees, hoped to obtain BCCs so that the family could cross the border to shop for grocery items that were not available in Mexico and wash their clothes in a San Diego laundromat, where the soft water was less damaging to clothes. The family never planned to use the BCC for work; it was only when they experienced a crisis that they decided to take advantage of the higher wages in the United States. Thus, during the peso crisis of the mid-1980s, Jorge used his BCC to work in the United States for one year while his father's business was struggling.

Viviana Perez (age thirty) was one person who received extensive coaching from her mother to navigate the BCC application process. She remembered the day her mother, who worked in a local pharmacy, gathered all of her paystubs and electricity bills and prepared to take a taxi to the US consulate. In the days leading up to the scheduled interview, Viviana's mother coached her on how to dress and present herself to the official. Her mother also instructed her to get her school identification and a letter from the school along with a paystub from a job that she used to pay for her education. As a pharmacy salesperson, Viviana's mother earned enough income that she was able to include Viviana in her application as a dependent. Viviana's mother illustrates the role of parents in coaching their children on the bureaucratic process of obtaining a BCC. Viviana's mother had likely gained this information from others, and she passed it along to her young daughter.

After relocating to the border, people expanded their networks through marriage to people who were not from their hometowns. In some cases, their marriage partners provided access to US citizenship or Green Cards. For example, Emilio, mentioned earlier, married Elizabeth, a US citizen, who helped him obtain legal permanent residence in the United States. Armando, meanwhile, became interested in obtaining a BCC after observing both his sister-in-law and brother-in-law obtain a BCC. Without these contacts at the US-Mexico border, Armando would have known little about the BCC process and the ways that it could be used to generate income. Both of his in-laws, for example, used the BCCs to work in the United States, a behavior that he wanted to mimic. The sociologist Rubén Hernández-León argues that kinship and paisano ties, which may not necessarily be mutually exclusive due to marriage, are the two most important social networks rural migrants draw on for social support to migrate internationally.[32] Through marriage, border residents expand their networks, which provide access to new resources such as Green Cards or knowledge of how to navigate the BCC process, as well as a whole new array of social ties in Mexico and the United States. As illustrated in Table 1.1 in chapter 1, almost a fifth of the commuter population was born in the United States. These border commuters identified more with Mexico than the United States and preferred Spanish over English, Mexican over US food, and living in Mexico over living in the United States. Some even preferred dating Mexicans in Tijuana to Mexicans or Chicanas/Chicanos/ Mexican Americans in the United States. In the borderlands, unlike interior communities in the Mexico, border residents had the ability to form relationships with US citizens who could then aid in crossing the border. Potential spouses could provide access to legal documents or information about jobs in the United States.

Kinship ties were an important part of the BCC application process because they gave younger family members access to a BCC that they could later use to work in the United States. Sociologist David Spener examined which types of border residents were more likely to obtain BCCs.[33] He found that immigration officials generally favored border residents who worked in the formal economy and could provide a "paper trail" of records proving their ties to Mexico. He also found that some households included residents with access to BCCs while others did not. As a result, kinship ties were important to the BCC application process. Many respondents explained that their family members loaned them money to help pay the application fee. Some individuals moved in with extended family, who tended to charge them less for room and board than an unknown landlord. This helped BCC applicants to establish savings accounts. It should not be surprising that kinship ties helped facilitate the BCC application process because family members assist in the migration process in many societies.[34] The case of border commuters, however, illustrates the specific importance of ties to kinship networks with respect to accessing legal documents, knowledge about the application process, and economic resources that increase the odds of obtaining a BCC.

BCCs as Livelihood Strategies

For successful applicants, BCCs open up a wide variety of potential livelihood strategies. BCCs can be used to cross the border to work in the regional labor market of San Diego as a border commuter. They can also be used to access interior labor markets beyond the borderlands in places as close as Los Angeles and San Diego or as far away as Indiana, as we saw in the case of Manuel, who used Tijuana as a stepping stone for international migration. The BCC can also be used to earn extra income by purchasing goods in the United States and reselling them for higher prices in Tijuana.

Extended Stays in the US Labor Market

Crossing the border daily to work in the United States is a risky behavior. Cardholders who work without authorization in the United States subject themselves to inspection every time they cross through the port of entry. Rather than risk losing their BCC, some border residents elected to migrate to the United States on a temporary basis. One example of this was Román Padilla (age thirty-eight), a local artist who spent his free time drawing caricatures that he sold from his home. Though he was originally from the Mexican state of Morelos, Román had lived in Tijuana for seventeen years and considered himself a fronterizo. One Sunday afternoon, I arrived at Román's one-bedroom house at 4:00 p.m. He had just arrived with his wife from a trip to Food-4-Less in Chula Vista, California, where he had purchased corn at a price of ten for a dollar. He planned to steam some of the corn for our dinner and to resell the rest to neighbors for a dollar apiece. After explaining the purpose of my research, we talked about his experiences living in the borderlands. He told me that he had spent the past seventeen years shuttling between Tijuana, San Diego, and Los Angeles, with and without papers. In recent years, he had crossed the border legally after obtaining a BCC as a result of having worked as a *taxista*. Román explained that he used the BCC to work periodically in the United States by shuttling migrants to and from work. When he ran out of money or when sales of his caricatures were low, he also crossed the border to work in San Diego, washing dishes at a local Mexican restaurant. When he worked in the United States, Román spent Monday through

Friday living in a crowded one-bedroom apartment with several friends and then returned to Tijuana on the weekends. Explaining the value of the BCC to his economic livelihood, Román said:

> It gives me the opportunity to work in the US. That is why I like to protect my BCC. It is a resource that I have for when the moment arises and I can't find work here in Mexico. I will use it to go work to get food for my family. There are many people here who go to the US to work but they will never say they work with BCCs.

The BCC was a "resource" that allowed Román to live as a binational worker and to diversify his income-generating activities. Though Román preferred to work in Mexico, his BCC gave him the flexibility to work in the United States when he needed to supplement his income. Román used his BCC in the same way as his seasonal migrant counterparts, who migrated to the United States during the peak of the job season in such occupations as agriculture and construction before returning to Mexico for the remainder of the year.

One group of borderland residents I interviewed used the BCC as a resource to migrate to the United States. Some, like Manuel and Carmen, migrated with no plan to ever return to Tijuana. Others used the BCC to migrate, but eventually returned to Tijuana after spending some time living and working in the United States. This is one of the key features that distinguishes Tijuana from most other Mexican migrant-sending communities: border residents have access to the BCC, which they can use to migrate seasonally or on a permanent basis to the United States.

Daily Commuting

Border commuters engaged in various job-market strategies to earn extra income. One group of workers I studied crossed the border once or twice a week to work in irregular or part-time jobs, where they could earn income under the table. This job strategy was an effective way to earn income in the United States without calling attention to frequent border crossings. When she was only eighteen years old, Alejandra Guzmán began to cross the border on Saturdays and Sundays to earn extra income to pay for her school supplies. Each weekend morning, she told the immigration official that she was crossing to shop at the local swap meet—a half-truth. In reality, she worked at the swap meet. On Saturdays, she was informally employed as a sales assistant by a vendor selling hats, shirts, and Levi jeans. On Sundays she sold beer, sodas, tacos, donuts, and snow cones for a second vendor. Even though she was paid only $50–$80 for the entire weekend, she chose this labor arrangement because she ran a smaller risk of losing her BCC by crossing the border only twice a week. Through each border crossing experience, Alejandra's social networks and job experiences grew, and she began to branch out to other job opportunities. Eventually, she left her job at the swap meet and became a babysitter and then a housecleaner and finally a party organizer. Alejandra's story of transitory and informal work is representative of the experiences of border commuters who obtain jobs in the United States but cross to work only one or two days a week.

Unlike Alejandra, many other border commuters crossed the border daily to work in formal jobs in construction as framers, in the service sector as fast-food workers, and in personal services like gardening. As border card holders, they worked in the same low-skill and low-paying jobs as many other immigrants in the United States. Within this group, some participated in "job splitting" to lower the risk of losing their BCC. Job splitting consists of splitting a weekly schedule between two workers to lower the number of border crossings. For example, Viviana Torres (age twenty-three) was offered a job as a waitress at a Mexican restaurant in San Diego that would have required her to cross the border six days per week. Because Viviana felt the job required too many crossings and would interfere with her schooling, she and her boyfriend, also a BCC holder, applied for the job together. They each took three days per week.

By obtaining BCCs, people were able to capitalize on one of the key advantages of living in the borderlands. They were able to cross the border to earn higher wages and purchase cheaper household items, but at the end of the day, they returned home to Mexico, where their families awaited them and where rent was much cheaper than in the United States. This shielded commuters from severe poverty.

Reselling Commodities

Unlike commuters who irregularly or regularly crossed to work unauthorized in the United States, some border residents were able to generate income transnationally without violating the terms of their BCC. These commuters crossed to purchase goods—sometimes new but more often used—to resell in Tijuana. These goods ranged from small household items to used cars, purchased cheaply in the United States.

Physical-education instructor Jorge considered himself rare because he was born and raised in Tijuana but had not lived in the United States for more than a month. He was invited by a friend to work in San Diego at a zoo and by uncles in Denver, Colorado, and San Jose, California, to work in construction, but each time he turned them down. He loved Tijuana too much to leave. Jorge was a fronterizo with in-depth knowledge of how to cross the port of entry quickly. He was by far one of the most knowledgeable border residents I met while living in Tijuana, a product of having spent his entire life in the borderlands. During one of our many conversations, Jorge explained to me that he began crossing the border as a young child. He and his family crossed on Saturdays to wash their clothes at a laundromat in San Ysidro. While in the United States, they also filled up their gas tank because, according to Jorge, gas from the United States lasted much longer. Over the years, Jorge and his family members continued to navigate a binational life through work and consumption. On a typical weekend, he would purchase goods like corn flakes and laundry detergent in the United States before stopping by a store in Tijuana to pick up fruits and vegetables.

This long history of border crossing led Jorge to become a transnational vendor before Mexican customs inspectors began to closely scrutinize entry into Tijuana. Every Saturday morning, he departed his home at 5:00 a.m. and headed to the port of entry in his Volkswagen Jetta, alongside hundreds of men with cargo vans, who were similarly crossing the US-Mexico border to purchase used equipment that they would resell in Tijuana. I accompanied Jorge on numerous occasions to buy used goods in San Diego and worked alongside him selling the goods from his driveway. After crossing the border and eating breakfast, Jorge arrived at his first garage sale at around 7:00 a.m. to get the best deals. He spent the next ten hours sorting through used items at garage sales in San Diego and returned to Tijuana with goods of all types that he would ultimately sell from his own home.

Jorge began his business by crossing to work at a thrift store and then selling used sporting goods to college students in Tijuana. Jorge later learned to visit garage sales in rich white neighborhoods to find more profitable items. At the time of our interviews, Jorge earned $100–$200 a week selling DVDs, CD, shoes, sports equipment, toys, designer jeans, and stereos. This was a substantial contribution to the household income, considering that as a part-time instructor, he made only $33 per week, a low salary to support a wife and two children. Fortunately, Jorge lived in a home that his father had given him, so he did not have to pay rent. By selling goods obtained across the border, he was able to make ends meet.

The BCC helped Jorge capitalize on the economies of both sides of the border. Jorge's trips across the border also provided resources to people living in Tijuana who could not cross the border to work in the United States. One afternoon, a young Mexican man in his early twenties came to talk to Jorge. The man was well dressed in a white t-shirt and pressed pants. He explained that he was looking for a CD, which he named in perfect English. I was amazed by his impeccable English and asked where he had learned it. He explained that he had lived his entire life in the United States but was recently deported back to Tijuana. As a result, he was dependent on border crossers like Jorge to provide him with the US goods he grew up with.

Doña Maria had a similar experience to the young man who spoke perfect English. Doña Maria was once a legal border crosser, but for reasons she never explained, she lost her Green Card. As a storeowner, she was dependent on others who could cross to buy US goods at a discount store, which she then resold. When I interviewed her, she explained that neighbors brought her "toothbrushes, toilet paper, paper towels and six packs of soda." To end the interview, Doña Maria echoed what many other residents told me on numerous occasions—she wanted the card to be able to "shop for myself." Like other residents, she viewed the BCC as a valuable resource to access regional or interior labor markets as border commuters, to migrate internationally, or to shop. Unfortunately, Doña Maria could not obtain a BCC because she did not have a formal job and because she lived on an irregular land plot and stole her electricity from nearby poles. She had no way to prove her existence in the borderlands and would never be a good candidate for the BCC.

Conclusion

This chapter has discussed the various strategies border residents utilize to become part of a binational labor force that lives in Mexico but crosses to work in the United States. In particular, I highlighted the different strategies that people employed just before the enactment of the IRCA and during the period after Operation Gatekeeper. What we find is that the earlier group of border crossers migrated in a series of steps that gave them access to resources and contacts, which helped them to eventually obtain Green Cards. This group of legal border crossers eventually became border commuters in today's service-sector economy. In contrast, contemporary crossers rely exclusively on BCCs to enter the United States. For this newer generation of crossers, the process of entering the United States has become more burdensome, especially with immigration and border restriction. For this group, obtaining a BCC was difficult and arbitrary process, but applicants devised careful strategies to increase their chances of success. Once obtained, a BCC provided the opportunity to migrate internationally as a stepwise migrant, join a cross-border commuter labor force through regular or irregular employment, and resell commodities as part of their individual livelihood strategies. Thus a close examination of these two groups of border commuters reveals how they enacted agency at different historical periods and how they navigated a constantly changing political economy at the border.

Previous scholarship shows that after IRCA legalized the status of formerly undocumented immigrants, many transitioned from *sojourners* to *settlers*.[35] That is, as formerly unauthorized immigrants obtained legal status, they began to settle permanently in the United States, bringing their families with them. However, this pattern of settlement was not universal. Many immigrants instead chose to use their immigrant status to return to Tijuana, where they joined a transborder labor force of Green Card commuters. Border residents like Ramón originally migrated domestically to Tijuana to use the city as a "stepping stone" for international migration, where they develop the necessary contacts, labor market experience, and knowledge to cross the border. But after obtaining legal permanent residency through IRCA, these migrants participated in stepwise return migration that brought them back to Tijuana, where they could enjoy their US wages with a Mexican cost of living and lifestyle. Their migration trajectories entailed a domestic, international, and return migration that I defined as "stepwise return migration."

Yet stepwise return migration was only one of a variety of strategies migrants used at the border to meet their economic, personal, and familial needs. Based on their particular life circumstances, each border commuter I interviewed succeeded in turning the border into a source of opportunity. To secure a BCC, border residents carefully strategized to establish the qualifications that would convince an immigration official, seeking higher-paying jobs, establishing back accounts, and establishing their affiliations to schools. Once individuals received their BCCs, they had the option to join the cross-border labor force as commuters or to migrate to interior labor markets in US locations such as Los Angeles or the state of Indiana as international migrants. Tijuana was thus a rich site for the development of the social and economic resources to mine the border for opportunities. Once people mobilized these resources, relocation to the border offered a variety of pathways to the US labor market that did not entail a move abroad on a permanent basis.

CHAPTER 4 | Strategies for Crossing the Border
through (Non)inspection

FOR DAILY COMMUTERS, THE process of crossing the border is fraught with obstacles that they must overcome. The border is dynamic in terms of both structure and enforcement, and changes in the border necessarily alter commuters' crossing practices and strategies. This chapter details histori-cal changes in the crossing experiences of migrants and commuters who live in Tijuana and work in the United States. In particular, I focus on the experiences of unauthorized crossers who circulated on a seasonal and daily basis during the open-border period and of authorized crossers who entered frequently through inspection during the post-IRCA and post–Operation Gatekeeper periods. I focus on the two groups in their respec-tive historical periods because they were the dominant mode of gaining access to unauthorized employment at that moment in time.

The border-crossing narratives presented in this chapter illustrate that the border is more than a physical structure that separates one nation from another; it is also a set of social relations. From this standpoint, I see the border as interactional and constantly under construction, as evidenced through face-to-face encounters between border crossers and US Customs and Border Protection (CBP) agents. Recently, scholars have highlighted the vulnerability of legal Mexican crossers who are subjected to intensive scrutiny by US state agents.[1] Héctor Padilla Delgado argues that at the point of crossing, Mexicans are subjected to discrimination and inequality from CBP agents, who dictate when and if they will be allowed to cross, even when they have documents.[2] He also demonstrates extensively the harassment that border crossers must endure at the hands of CBP agents even though they have legal documents. At the San Ysidro port of entry, the border crossers I interviewed confronted this scrutiny with creative strategies that matched the enforcement strategies of the period. A focus on the encounters between these two sets of actors—CBP agents and commuters—thus illuminates the generative agency of crossers as they confront structural constraints to their mobility.

As the border is remade by both law enforcers and border crossers, border-crossing practices change over time.[3] As such, this chapter chronicles the transition of the border at Tijuana–San Diego from a time when "there was no line," according to respondents, to a time of increased surveillance and an expanding physical boundary separating the two nation-states. In particular, I focus on two periods: before and after the introduction of Operation Gatekeeper in 1994. Operation Gatekeeper marks a critical time in which "la frontera se cerró [the border closed]," according to narratives from respondents, curtailing most unauthorized migration in the Tijuana–San Diego corridor. Prior to Gatekeeper, unauthorized crossers circumvented inspection at the port of entry through a variety of informal modes and used occupational ties to US agricultural employers to increase their chances of entry. In contrast, after Gatekeeper, people who were authorized only to cross engaged almost exclusively in Goffmanian strategies of "the art of impression management" and "face work" when crossing through the port of entry to conceal their unauthorized US occupational affiliation.[4] Neither type of crosser took for granted their ability to cross; both groups required knowledge, experiences, and resources to navigate across a border that has been continually remade throughout its history. A focus on these two historical periods illustrates the tense relationship that exists between national politics and law making that seek to control labor flows but do not take into account the local realities of economies in the borderlands.

Border History

Over the years, the border agencies have slowly restricted unauthorized crossings in the Tijuana–San Diego corridor. Following the termination of the Bracero Program in 1964, the decades between 1965 and 1985 are known both as the open-border period and as the era of unauthorized migration, because US agricultural employers began to rely on their workers to recruit friends and family to farms throughout the southwest. As a result, the number of unauthorized immigrants residing in the United States and circulating back and forth between the United States and Mexico grew considerably in these years.[5] The Immigration Reform and Control Act (IRCA) of 1986 marked a major shift in the way the US government handled unauthorized migration. First, it legalized the status of almost three million formerly unauthorized immigrants. Second, it created sanctions for firms that hired unauthorized workers. Finally, IRCA expanded Border Patrol staff. Although this legislation was intended to stop unauthorized migration, IRCA's success was limited because the US government policed primarily the border and largely neglected the workplace. Therefore, if an unauthorized migrant could cross the border into the United States, his likelihood of being caught and returned to Mexico was small. As a result, IRCA *generated* waves of unauthorized migration as return migrants told their friends and relatives about US jobs.[6] Even with added border enforcement, it was relatively easy for migrants to cross the border if they had the knowledge to cross or could buy assistance from smugglers.

In the late 1980s, anthropologist Leo Chavez observed many unauthorized migrants as they attempted to cross the Tijuana–San Diego border at Cañon Zapata, also known as the Soccer Field.[7] Located inland from the Pacific Ocean, the Cañon Zapata area was the unofficial port of entry for clandestine crossings. The following passage speaks to the arbitrary nature of immigration law and territorial boundaries prior to restricting unauthorized crossings at the Tijuana–San Diego corridor:

> The Soccer Field (like other places along the border) is a place of geographic liminality. Although legally inside the United States, it is an ambiguous place betwixt and between the United States and Mexico. It is in the United States but migrants use it as a staging area, a place to gather and wait for the right moment to try to migrate north. Even though they stand on sovereign US territory, the people at the soccer field are not treated as if they have officially entered the United States. The Border Patrol watches what goes on in the soccer field, but makes little attempt to assert control over it. . . . The Soccer Field, metaphorically speaking, stands between the domestic and the foreign from the perspective of people on both sides of the border.[8]

In *Shadowed Lives*, Leo Chavez describes the social interactions between Border Patrol officers and unauthorized border crossers as they observed one another. His ethnography documents an instance when an officer told an unauthorized migrant waiting to cross through Cañon Zapata en route to the United States, "Good luck. I'll be seeing you," reminding the crosser that the next time they met, the officer might be in pursuit of the migrant.[9]

However, many migrants continued to cross through Tijuana because border enforcement at the time was "a game of cat and mouse." When migrants were captured, they were deported to Mexico. This allowed them to retry crossing the border until they were successful, creating a never-ending cycle of catch and release for unauthorized migrants and ensuring that people would cross the border if they attempted enough times.[10]

To gain control of the border, the US government instituted Operation Gatekeeper in 1994. Within four years of Gatekeeper's implementation, the number of patrol agents had soared from 980 to 2,264, the miles of fencing expanded from nineteen to forty-five, and the number of underground sensors grew from 448 to 1,214. The 1996 Illegal Immigration Reform and Immigrant Responsibility Act (IIRIRA) led to further increases in surveillance. Whereas one Border Patrol officer was responsible for guarding 1.1 miles of the US-Mexico border in 1975, there was one guard for every 1,000 feet by 2004, at the time that I started conducting this study.[11] Moreover, IIRIRA also sought to control clandestine crossings by fingerprinting offenders before deporting them back to Mexico and making repeated entry a felony.[12] Peter Andreas states that border enforcement made Tijuana crossings "less visible and more dispersed" and created an "*image* of a more secure and orderly border" (emphasis mine).[13] In other words, the image of Tijuana as representing a controlled border was a false one because migrants began to cross through more isolated areas like the Arizona desert and the South Texas landscape, where populations were more dispersed and there was less media presence. Unauthorized migrants declined considerably in Tijuana but expanded in other areas of the US-Mexico border.

Gatekeeper was successful in curbing unauthorized migration to a large degree. Before Gatekeeper, 50 percent of all unauthorized Mexican migrants bound for the United States crossed through Tijuana. In particular, 98 percent of all California-bound migrants used Tijuana as a crossing point.[14] The masses of unauthorized migrants who congregated in Tijuana and their encounters with Border Patrol agents were a common spectacle. Following Gatekeeper, however, the once-easy trek across the international border became impossible to undertake without help. Despite heightened surveillance at the US-Mexico border, unauthorized migration persisted, though border-crossing behaviors changed. The geographical shift from traditional urban crossing points to remote locations led to a decline in the number of apprehensions in fortified sectors by 64 percent between 1993 and 2004.[15] Migrants also began to turn to smugglers, who had the knowledge to help them cross through uncharted territory.[16] As demand for smuggling services increased, the average fees charged by smugglers grew from $143 prior to Gatekeeper to $2,000 by the mid-2000s.[17] As injuries and even death grew more common during border crossings, smugglers became essential to helping migrants navigate dangerous terrain.[18] These obstacles changed the nature of international migration. Unauthorized Mexican migrants no longer circulated across the border but instead chose to remain in the United States for longer periods of time.[19]

Not all border crossers enter through noninspection, however. Some border crossers enter the United States through inspection, using BCCs issued by the Department of Homeland Security and the State Department to allow Mexican nationals to shop and visit relatives but not work in the United States. Some of these border crossers enter through the San Ysidro port of entry with legal documents. They enter either through a pedestrian line, on a bus, or in a car through one of twenty-four gates where they are greeted by a CBP agent. The agent asks, "Purpose of visit?" and their cards—equipped with biometric information such as fingerprints—are scanned to ensure the authenticity of the crosser. But a card does not guarantee entry; crossing depends on the discretion of CBP agents.[20]

Strategies for Entering without Inspection before Gatekeeper

Before Gatekeeper, there were two groups of people who crossed without inspection through Tijuana and became unauthorized workers in either interior cities like Los Angeles for extended periods of time or in San Diego County on a short-term basis: *transient unauthorized crossers* and *daily unauthorized crossers*. Transient unauthorized crossers circumvented port inspection by drawing on the support of family and friends or local smugglers to cross the international border, before moving on to interior labor markets within days of arriving in Tijuana. After developing experience crossing the border, these workers often crossed without the assistance of friends and family. These transient unauthorized crossers came from areas all over Mexico such as Guanajuato or Jalisco and they selected Tijuana as the place where they would cross the border. In contrast, daily unauthorized crossers or agricultural commuters relied on the support of family and friends and especially US growers to enter San Diego County's regional agricultural labor market. For daily crossers, declaring their occupational status as agricultural workers and asserting their ties to San Diego farmers often gave them a free pass to circulate across the border. Daily unauthorized workers were residents of Tijuana who circulated on a daily basis. Despite their different migration journeys, the groups had one thing in common: they both circumvented inspection at the port of entry through their largely informal mode of entry.

Friends and Family as a Border-Crossing Resource

Crossing the US-Mexico border can be a traumatic experience for migrants with limited knowledge and experience. Migrants confront bandits, harassment from corrupt Mexican police officers, unscrupulous coyotes who take their money without providing services, and Border Patrol agents who block their entry and physically or verbally assault them. To mitigate these risks, the older generation of migrants who crossed through Tijuana relied on the assistance of family members and friends. Family members and friends played a direct and indirect role in helping would-be migrants cross the border. They shared information about the best crossing routes and recommended crossing times. They also recommended transient migrants to trusted smugglers who would ensure a safe border-crossing experience. Friends and family members who had settled in the United States drove to San Ysidro to wait at a local restaurant for migrants who had crossed to drive them to destinations such as Los Angeles or Sacramento.

In the late 1970s, Richard Mines found that migrants from the Mexican state of Zacatecas had created a migratory station in Tijuana for transient migrants bound for interior labor markets in California. One particular family had established a boarding house that served as a temporary refuge where US-bound migrants could rest, sleep, and eat before they made their trek across the border. He argued that the social support that these migrants received from their border counterparts gave them an added advantage in crossing the border compared to those without ties in the border region.[21] Many of the respondents actually had family members or friends in Tijuana who taught them the ins and outs of everything, from getting a job to crossing the border, giving them an advantage just as those in Mines's study.

Self-Smuggling "a la Brava"

When migrants return from the United States, they return not only with US dollars but also with information. With each migration experience, migrants develop knowledge about advantageous strategies and tactics.[22]

One strategy that transient unauthorized migrants adopt when crossing clandestinely is to travel with experienced migrants familiar with crossing routes. Rafael Torrez, for example, crossed the border through both South Texas and California by the time he was twenty-nine years old. By his third and final migration trip in the 1970s, Rafael knew the borderlands so well that he felt he was a veteran crosser. He did not hire smugglers during any of his crossing attempts. During the 1970s, clandestine cross-ers like Rafael seldom used smugglers; only 13.5 percent of unauthorized migrants apprehended by the US government in the southwest corridor during the 1970s had employed smugglers.[23]

When I interviewed Rafael about the last time he crossed clandestinely through Tijuana into the United States, he told me that he had left his hometown in the state of Michoacán with his brother and several friends. They arrived at the Tijuana bus terminal and, from there, took a taxi to the isolated Cañon Zapata. When night came, Rafael and his friends ran through the canyons and ravines until they reached San Ysidro. He remem-bered, "The first time I came to Tijuana in 1974 it was really easy. I was the type of person who did not need anyone [smugglers] to help me cross. I crossed with other people and we were told to simply cross the line and wait in San Ysidro, California, for someone to pick us up." Rafael crossed the border with ease because the border patrol was almost nonexistent at the time of his last crossing. Moreover, his friends provided him with bus ticket money and guided him across the international border. Once in the United States, they were picked up by another group of friends who drove them to Washington State, where they picked apples. Since that last cross-ing, Rafael had not returned to the United States to work.

All of the unauthorized crossers originally left Mexico because they had a difficult time finding steady jobs. Migrants who crossed through Tijuana during the era of limited restriction were generally rural migrants who earned subsistence wages and/or surplus goods from the harvest in Mexico. Because unauthorized crossers did not have money to pay smug-glers, they depended on experienced migrants to guide them across the border. I met Chuy on the streets of Tijuana, and later interviewed him when I gave him a ride to Los Angeles. As we crossed the port of entry and drove along Interstate 5, Chuy recounted the time he had crossed through Tijuana in 1980. Chuy explained how he and his friend had trav-eled through Cañon Zapata without a smuggler during his first crossing. They had crossed alone because they had little money and because they wanted to prove it was possible to cross with limited knowledge and with-out a smuggler. Chuy and his friend had continued to cross without the assistance of a smuggler for years, picking up pieces of useful information from family and friends and from their own repeated trips.

As we drove, Chuy recalled one border-crossing experience in which he and his friend walked the entire 130 miles to Los Angeles. When the two of us were stopped at the San Clemente checkpoint, Chuy pointed out the railroad tracks that had guided them to Los Angeles. They had mapped and memorized safe walking routes during their previous treks and developed detours to safely bypass the secondary inspection checkpoint on Interstate 5. The poorly guarded border at the time meant that the odds of successfully crossing were high, especially if migrants relied on experienced friends and family members who knew entry routes.

Like some other transient migrants, Chuy and his friend claimed they came to the United States for "adventure" and wanted to cross the border "*a la brava* [without permission or authorization]." Their main strategy consisted of repeated entries until they reached the US point of destination. During their trips, they were able to eat food that had been discarded by restaurants, going through garbage cans to find it. While Chuy and his companion crossed without a smuggler or even money, some migrants were not as daring. When unauthorized crossers did not know the route, they hired local smugglers to guide them safely to the United States. They hired either local *pateros* (guides), who walked them across the border, or coyotes or *polleros* (smugglers), who not only guided them across the international boundary but also drove them to their US destination.

Buying Crossing Knowledge before Gatekeeper

In 2004, while fishing in Playas de Tijuana, I met Fidel Ramos (age sixty-two), a retired automobile mechanic from Los Angeles. Fidel had many stories about growing up in Tijuana, but none stood out more than his days as a smuggler. He revealed that he had been a *patero* at one point in his life. Fidel helped guide people across the border during his teenage years. Sometimes he charged people $10. Other times, he let migrants name their own price in return for instructions on how to jump the international fence and in which direction they should run once on US soil. Guides like Fidel were able to sell their services to unauthorized migrants because they knew where the Border Patrol hid. They used their knowledge of agents' monitoring habits to move clandestine crossers during times when the odds of capture were lower. For a small fee, Fidel and his fellow guides were able to share their knowledge of borderland geography to help unauthorized crossers enter successfully even when the Border Patrol was present. However, these guides did not actually accompany migrants across the border. They simply told migrants which direction to run and when. Their role was not one of helping would-be migrants to cross the border, but rather of encouraging clandestine crossers and selling information for a fee.

When the services of local guides were not enough, transient migrants hired more experienced smugglers with more resources at their disposal. The ex-smuggler El Guerro at one time worked for a sophisticated smuggling ring after his cousin had introduced him to the job. When we first met, however, he largely worked in the informal economy, selling machetes and necklaces, or taking photographs of tourists posed with the famous Zonkey, a white burro painted with black stripes. In 1979, when El Guerro was only twenty-five, he began working at the bottom of the smuggling occupational ladder as a guide. His job was simple—all he had to do was walk people across the border near El Soler, a neighborhood close to the US-Mexico boundary, and hand them over to waiting relatives. El Guerro earned $100 for each trip. He was eventually promoted to pilot, a job that consisted of transporting people from San Ysidro, California, to destinations in San Diego, Los Angeles, and Fresno. El Guerro worked hard to gain his clients' trust by providing them with the best information and ensuring their safe passage.

El Guerro decided to extend his services to his hometown in Zacatecas after realizing how easy it was to cross the border in the era when there was little enforcement. He bought business cards and distributed them in communities throughout rural Zacatecas. When El Guerro handed his cards to aspiring migrants, he told them that they did not need any money as long as they had a family member in the United States who would agree to pay their fare upon delivery. He would also provide free room and board, the day before migrants attempted to cross the border, at one of the local participating hotels and restaurants that served as part of the smuggling network. Finally, El Guerro would explain how easy it was to cross the border and the abundant employment opportunities that awaited them in places like Los Angeles. Many transient migrants requested his services during this period because he allowed their family members in the United States to pay the fare upon their delivery.

Local smugglers developed many tactics for crossing the border. After he made several unsuccessful attempts to cross the border through the remote hills of Tijuana on his own, Hugo hired a local smuggler to help him. At the time, Hugo was an inexperienced migrant in his mid-twenties. When he was younger, however, he recalled crossing through Playas de Tijuana (a public beach located along the Pacific Ocean) in the 1980s: "I crossed by the beach, running—it was really easy. My brother and I crossed pretending to be surfers." While some local smugglers' strategies consisted of evading Border Patrol agents, Hugo's smuggler gave him instructions on adopting the identity of a surfer. His smuggler disguised him to blend into the local surfer culture of Imperial Beach, California, through his clothing. Other local guides dressed their clients in athletic clothes (running pants and shoes) and had them jog right past Border Patrol agents. When they ran past the immigration officials, they quickly glanced over at them and waved with confidence. In these instances, the unauthorized crossers were successful because of their local guides. The guides they hired had carefully studied the international border's weaknesses and, in particular, the agents who patrolled it. They packaged this knowledge and, for a fee, passed it on to those who wanted to go to the United States. They instructed crossers on which types of identities and behaviors would not be subject to scrutiny from immigration officials. Then, the border crossers were instructed on how to perform these identities when crossing the border. In Goffmanian terms, these unauthorized crossers utilized theatrical tools by performing roles and using disguises to present an altered self that was allowed to move freely in the borderlands during this historical period.[24] These tools worked with Border Patrol because at this time, taking a jog or walk across the border was customary.

Transient migrants did not always attempt to evade inspection. In some instances, they crossed directly through the port of entry. Friends and relatives sometimes encouraged their unauthorized loved ones who were well educated or light skinned to attempt to cross the border by claiming they were US citizens or Green Card holders who had lost their identification while visiting Tijuana. These border residents remembered a time when immigration was not strictly enforced by border officials. If a crosser could maintain a false persona without being nervous, they were likely to be allowed to enter the United States as long as they were not perceived as a threat. One border resident who worked for a pharmacy near the port of entry recalled how he was allowed to enter the United States without any documents. When he crossed the border, he would simply ask the Border Patrol agent if he could cross the border to purchase hamburgers for his coworkers. Each time, he wore his pharmacist's white coat to signify his occupation and to show that he had ties to the Mexican labor market. Because of this, immigration officials were unlikely to perceive the pharmacist as at-risk to stay in the United States. He was allowed to enter the United States but was reminded to return after purchasing his hamburgers.

In other cases, transient migrants borrowed documents from friends or relatives who were physically similar. This practice was more common before Operation Gatekeeper because the use of fake or borrowed documents was not a felony at the time.

During this early historical period, there were many ways to cross the border both clandestinely or through the port of entry, but crossing still required knowledge and strategy. Sociologist John Price conducted an ethnography of the Tijuana–San Ysidro port of entry in 1969 and 1970 and found that "border officials use a loose working definition of national customs and immigration laws that emphasizes the spirit of the law more than the letter of the law."[25] Therefore, crossers had to learn how to navigate the whim of the officials in order to circumvent the law that was subjectively applied to Mexican nationals circulating back and forth between both nation-states.

Declaring Ties to Growers

While transient unauthorized crossers depended on the assistance of family, friends, and local guides, another group of unauthorized crossers circulated through the borderlands on a daily basis through other means. These unauthorized migrants drew on their ties to US growers in San Diego County. The vast majority of these border residents were men and women who had settled with their families in Tijuana to be close to US farm jobs. Some of these daily unauthorized commuters had participated in the Bracero Program but had not regularized their legal status. After the program ended in 1964, these men became part of the reserve army of labor that lived in Tijuana but crossed to work in the United States. They continued to cross the border on a daily basis and recruited their friends and family to work in the fields of south San Diego County as well.

Daily unauthorized crossers formed part of an occupational network whose unlawful entry was facilitated by intermediaries, the US-based growers who hired them, and labor contractors who sometimes guided them across the border. If Border Patrol agents stopped these migrants at the international boundary, the migrants simply declared the name of the grower who hired them. Border Patrol agents then allowed them to enter the United States. Seventy-one-year-old Jesús, who spent six years as a farmworker before his promotion to foreman, told me that before the 1980s, if migrants stated the name of their employer, Border Patrol agents allowed them to enter but reminded them to return to Mexico at the end of the workday. An informal work arrangement existed between the Border Patrol and US growers. The Border Patrol tolerated clandestine crossing because Tijuana residents provided labor to farms located along the US-Mexico border. The main feature distinguishing clandestine crossers and daily unauthorized commuters was the verbal recognition of their occupational ties to a particular grower in the borderlands.

Cresencio "El Primo," an eighty-two-year-old migrant, had once helped recruit workers for US growers in the bars and restaurants of Zona Norte and Colonia Libertad. In the 1970s, however, he earned his money by recruiting people to work in San Diego. To ensure that his recruits were not mistaken for transient unauthorized crossers bound for internal labor markets, Cresencio taught his workers how to respond to authorities if they were stopped en route to the farm. He instructed the men to give the name of their employer, to describe the type of produce that they were recruited to pick, and to explain how it was tended or harvested.

Sociologist Timothy Dunn argues that the Border Patrol and growers in the American southwest have long had "a de facto relationship" defined by the supply of and demand for labor.[26] This seemed to be the case in the Tijuana–San Diego agricultural labor market, as the Border Patrol often assisted growers by facilitating the entry of workers. Jesús, the ex-bracero and labor foreman mentioned previously, remembered, "Back in those times, the Border Patrol would pick you up. . . . He would take me to work in Nestor, California. He would give me a ride and leave me there [at the farm]." Once the Border Patrol came to know Jesús as a daily crosser with permanent ties to Tijuana and as an employee of Edwards and Smith Co., he was allowed to enter the country. To confirm Jesús's claims, I interviewed one of his former employees who stated that one of his employers threw frequent parties to thank Border Patrol agents for allowing his Mexican workers to enter the United States freely. He explained:

My boss, he used to throw a party every fifteen days for the Border Patrol. . . So when we crossed, they asked us, "Who do you work with?" and we replied, "Martínez," and they would say "Okay, come on in!"

By "Martínez," Raul referred to the labor contractor who managed the farm where he was employed. Some Border Patrol agents not only knew the names of major employers in south San Diego County, but also the names of the contractors who ran the farms or recruited labor from Tijuana. In an effort to keep cordial relations between the Border Patrol and unauthorized workers, US growers frequently hosted parties for the agents.

The older generations of unauthorized crossers I interviewed in Tijuana remembered a border with limited restriction through which migrants circulated freely on a seasonal or daily basis. Though both groups entered without inspection, transient workers and daily commuters employed distinct strategies to cross the border successfully. Their narratives revealed that before Operation Gatekeeper, crossing patterns were informal, due to the lack of institutional regulations controlling labor flows and the close ties between employers and Border Patrol agents.

However, unauthorized crossings declined significantly after Operation Gatekeeper was introduced in 1994 in the Tijuana–San Ysidro border. Gatekeeper was effective in curtailing the flow of clandestine crossers in the region. Peter Andreas argues that while Gatekeeper allowed border enforcement to enact "successful image management," unauthorized migration continued through the discovery of new modes of entry.[27] After 1994, the primary means of entry to the United States shifted from clandestine crossings, the assumption of false personas, and claiming US employment to the presentation of legal documents to immigration agents. This does not mean that people did not use BCCs to work without authorization in the United States before Gatekeeper. Rather, after Gatekeeper, BCCs became the only safe way to work in the United States without authorization while also maintaining residence in Tijuana.

Entering via Inspection after Gatekeeper

Unlike unauthorized crossers who circumvented inspection, contemporary authorized crossers did not evade state authorities. Instead, they obtained and strategically used BCCs to cross into the United States through the official port of entry in an era of increased surveillance that channeled unauthorized crossers to the port. When I arrived in 2004, ten years of Gatekeeper had effectively stopped unauthorized crossings in Tijuana and diverted human flows to the Arizona desert. Nonetheless, people continued to cross from Tijuana to the United States, but this migration stream comprised people using BCCs intended for tourism and visitation to access unauthorized employment. After the transition to an increasingly fortified border, respondents engaged in Goffmanian strategies when crossing from Mexico to the United States to outwit CBP agents.

Some Tijuana residents viewed the BCC as a labor market resource. They could use the BCC to enter the regional labor market in San Diego as daily commuters or to migrate on a more permanent basis to the interior of the United States.[28] They could also use it to supplement their Mexican income with part-time or full-time US employment. As border enforcement under Operation Gatekeeper made unauthorized crossings through contemporary Tijuana all but impossible, the BCC became the most secure way for Tijuanenses to enter the US labor market. Thus, authorized crossers' first strategy to enter the United States was securing a BCC. They did so by obtaining a job and establishing residency in Tijuana (see chapter 3). However, simply obtaining a BCC did not guarantee entry because authorized crossers still had to convince immigration officials that they were not BCC violators to cross securely on a regular basis and protect their cards from confiscation. Furthermore, entry into the United States was left to the discretion of CBP agents who questioned crossers to ensure that they were not crossing to engage in unlawful acts, such as working without legal documents.[29]

The Subjective Nature of Enforcement

Whereas unauthorized crossers tried to evade inspection by crossing through unofficial entry points, authorized crossers had to cross through the official port of entry. Every day, authorized crossers came into contact with CBP agents whose job was to stop the flow of contraband, such as drugs, and prohibit the entry of unauthorized crossers. Though it was difficult for immigration officers to detect drug smuggling or the use of fraudulent documents, it was also difficult to identify people who crossed the border legally to obtain unauthorized employment, due to the lack of concrete evidence. The only clear way for immigration officials to identify these individuals was to find hard evidence of a violation, such as a US paycheck, or to get a crosser to admit that they were crossing to work. According to the border crossers I interviewed, immigration officials relied on subjective assessments of the border crosser's honesty to determine who might be in violation of US immigration laws.

Ángel, the son of Ramón, whose story opens the book, was a bilingual and bicultural native of Tijuana who had been crossing the border since he was a child and who had learned these lessons the hard way. He crossed the border for almost two years to work in US construction jobs, but was stopped one day on the suspicion that he was using his BCC to work. Though the CBP agent never proved that he was working in the United States, Ángel's BCC was revoked. He recalled the day in detail:

> The immigration officer asked me, "Hey, so why are you going so early [in the morning]?" I told him that I was going to pick up my father. He told me, "No, you are going to work." He kept telling me and telling me that I was coming to work, and each time, I would say "no." He tried to force me to tell him that "yes," I was going to work in the US. But I never admitted that. He told me that "a [BCC] is a privilege . . . that we give to Mexicans, and we take away the privilege when we want to and today, your BCC is cancelled." But I asked him, "Why? For what reason? What rule did I break?" The official said, "No, we are just going to cancel it right now!"

According to Ángel, his border-crossing experience illustrates the subjectivity with which CBP agents could label a crosser a violator, even without evidence. This example illustrates the state's power in granting entry to Mexican nationals. Unfortunately, the experience of losing BCCs was common in the García household. As described in chapter 1, Ángel's father Ramón had his card confiscated when he questioned an immigration official who forcibly grabbed a woman who stood in the wrong line. His brother Richard also lost his BCC one weekday afternoon when it fell from the worn-out back pocket of his Levi jeans after returning from a twelve-hour workday.

Rodrigo, a BCC holder who crossed to work construction as a framer, shared a similar story of a capricious CBP agent:

> One time they were about to take my passport away. . . . [The agent was] from Iraq or Iran, they were like Arab. He was really sure that I worked [in the United States]. I told him, "no, no." He made me turn off the car and was really mad. I then told him [clears throat and begin to cry as he recalls story], "I ask that for the sake of my children, don't take away my passport, I really need it!" Then, he began to think and then said, "Okay, here is your passport. The next time I see you, I will take it away." He gave me the passport and off I went. I went to work and was really nervous [thinking about the incident]. Two days later, I got him again [as an inspector at the port of entry]. I said to myself [over and over], "He is going take it away, he is going take it away." When he saw me, he only laughed and gave it back to me.

Rodrigo's narrative illustrates how some CBP agents attempted to instill fear in BCC violators. Suspecting Rodrigo of being a BCC violator, the immigration official attempted to intimidate him into admitting that he worked in the United States. Although his entry was eventually successful, Rodrigo worried that he would lose his card in the future. Yet facing the very same agent two days later, Rodrigo was waved through without incident, to his surprise.

Mexican border crossers also believed that they were treated unfairly in comparison to non-Mexican crossers. This was because CBP agents assumed they were in violation of the BCC agreement. In examining essays written by college students who crossed the border to attend the University of Texas at El Paso, one of Héctor Padilla Delgado's primary findings was that agents presumed all Mexican crossers were suspect for some type of illicit behavior until they proved otherwise.[30] Border commuters believed that CBP agents scrutinized the papers of Mexicans more carefully than those of white Americans. For example, twenty-one-year-old Carmen crossed the port of entry dozens of times and concluded from her observations that selective enforcement was clearly based on race and ethnicity. From her home in Colonia Pancho Villa, Carmen recounted how Mexicans were more likely to be subjected to surveillance and inspection of personal property:

> I have seen that if a white American passes, sometimes they will not even ask them for an ID. Or sometimes they check it really quickly. But if a Latino passes, they will ask you where you are going. "How long will you be over there [in the United States]?" They will ask many questions. They will also ask what you have in your purse. Sometimes I carry my small bag and they will ask, "What do you have in the bag?"
>
> I say, "Clothes."
>
> They will then ask, "Where are you going?"

In his historical study of the US-Mexico border, Joseph Nevins points out that the creation of political and ideological differences between "Americans" and "Mexicans" and "citizens" and "aliens" is an important part of institutionalizing the border.[31] The complex living arrangements in the borderlands intensified these distinctions and the ensuing encounters between authorities and border commuters. According to the US Citizenship and Immigration Services, a Green Card holder must "live permanently in the United States provided you do not commit any actions that would make you removable under immigration law. Work in the United States at any legal work of your qualification and choosing."[32] Yet many Green Card holders chose instead to live in Tijuana. Likewise, many BCC holders who had authorization to shop or visit family also chose to work in the United States. Commuters' ability to cross or even to reside in the United States was in tension with laws preventing them from working there as residents of Tijuana. This tension manifested in fraught encounters with CBP agents over commuters' status as "suspects" and "violators."

Queuing Immigration Officials

Every day, CBP agents sort through thousands of driver's licenses, passports, tourist cards, and BCCs. Immigration officials know that many residents in Mexican border cities have access to BCCs, and it is their job to question BCC carriers to ensure that carriers do not violate the terms of the cards. CBP agents ask border crossers routine questions such as, "What is your purpose for visiting the United States?" "How long were you in Mexico?" "Where are you going?" "How long will you stay?"

To avoid detection as border commuters who worked in the United States, BCC holders diversified their mode of entry or the timing of their entry to avoid standing out to CBP agents as a crosser with a regular schedule. Some crossers chose to cross infrequently, choosing jobs such as house cleaning or catering, where they had more control over their schedules, or relying on family members living in San Diego County or Los Angeles County to host them during their workweek. Viviana Ramos was a twenty-three-year-old infrequent commuter who crossed the border on Sundays and worked in a Los Angeles restaurant Monday through Thursday. A friend with US citizenship transported her suitcase each week so that immigration officials would not question why she planned to stay. She recalled:

> On Sunday, I remember that we would get in line [at the international port of entry] and we were all heading to work, and well yes, I would get nervous because I would cross with everyone who was going to work and they are going to find out that I do not have any papers. But I had a friend who was a really good friend of mine and she was a US citizen. She used to always cross my suitcase for me because I could not cross my suitcase and I would then get in a different line so that they would not think that I did not have any papers.

Commuters who could not cross frequently developed other strategies to avoid detection. People who crossed by car changed vehicles to prevent immigration officials from tracking their license plates. These BCC holders borrowed vehicles from friends and family members to confuse authorities. Those with more than one vehicle rotated among their cars. Regular drivers also biked or walked across the US-Mexico border on certain days. Whenever possible, BCC holders also carpooled with legal permanent residents or US citizens because immigration officials often regarded the documents of the driver with more scrutiny than those of the passengers.

For commuters who crossed the port of entry by foot, evading detection was more challenging. These BCC holders developed strategies to cross successfully based on the belief that certain US immigration officials were more likely to grant entry than others. One strategy was to look for the fastest-moving inspection line. A fast-moving line indicated that a CBP agent might not scrutinize passports or probe for border-crossing reasons. Perhaps the CBP agent with a fast-moving line was in a good mood on that particular day. Commuters usually moved to faster-moving lines regardless of the CBP agent's ethnicity. However, when commuters could not identify the fastest-moving line, they tried to study the CBP agent. They chose their lines based on the CBP's demeanor, such as whether they greeted border crossers or smiled at them. They also paid attention to the immigration official's time on the job, age, and gender. And border crossers also chose their lines based on race and ethnicity, taking care to avoid immigration officials of Mexican descent because they were known as the greatest boundary enforcers.

At the US-Mexico border, white immigration officials were considered the most welcoming and least stringent. In contrast, border crossers believed that "their own people" made entry difficult—an observation that has been documented by scholars as well.[33] Cecilia, a twenty-three-year-old who sold clothing at a San Diego swap meet and cleaned homes for upper-middle-class Americans without authorization, explained, "We have always said that Asians and Mexican Americans were the ones who used to check your passports more." Along these same lines, Alejandra, a twenty-five-year-old who crossed the border every Saturday and Sunday for seven years to clean homes in San Diego, nicely summarized border crossers' criteria for queuing immigration officials at the port of entry, "One's dream is to get a rookie immigration official, a young or old white official, an Asian, a Mexican, and lastly a woman. ... Because they are the ones who are most insistent." For Alejandra, a white male rookie was the ideal immigration official because they were friendly and enthusiastic, and not yet burned out by the routinization of the job. In contrast, Alejandra and other border residents perceived older, female Mexican American CBP agents as the most willing to dig into BCC holders' motives for crossing the border.

Through the act of crossing the border, immigration officials and border commuters reinforce and challenge boundaries based on nation, race, and ethnicity. In Weberian terms, political and ethnic boundaries are constructs that immigration officials use to enforce social closure.[34] By scrutinizing Mexican crossers, Mexican American CBP agents established their own position as "American" insiders. Jacinto, a commuter of almost two decades and also a US citizen, explained how this sociopolitical boundary strained his relationship with a former high school friend when he saw her years later working at the port of entry:

> When I was in high school, I had a friend. . . . The next time I saw her, there she was working at the border as a customs agent. One day I passed, and I said "hi." I like to say "hi" with respect so that they respect me in return. I told her, "Good morning madam."
>
> She turned around and only said, "Good morning" [sternly].
>
> Then I said to her, "Hey Adriana, how are you?"
>
> "Do I know you?" [she responded].
>
> I told her, "Oh, excuse me Adriana. You don't remember me?" She kept looking at me. I said, "Look, here is my ID. Jacinto. You don't remember me?"
>
> [But she kept insisting] "Do I know you?"
>
> I then got mad, "Okay, you don't know me? You don't remember me when we went to school? You know what? Fuck you! Bye!" She was with me in school for four years. We were really good friends! When we were in high school, we used to ditch and come over to Tijuana. All those years of friendship for nothing.

When I asked Jacinto why his former high school friend would not acknowledge him, his explanation was that she was now a US government agent. Her role as a state agent and her job enforcing boundaries required her to define herself as an "insider" and Jacinto as an "outsider," despite the fact that he was a US citizen. However, he was a US citizen who did not neatly fit into identifiable categories. Jacinto was born in the United States to unauthorized parents. Although he was a US citizen, he lived in Mexico and only crossed the border to work in the United States. Though Jacinto understood that he and his high school friend now had a different relationship, he could not understand why she was so hostile toward him. Instances like this reinforced the idea that Mexican border crossers, even those who were born in the United States like Jacinto, were "outsiders" who must convince immigration officials that they were worthy of crossing.

Anthropologist Josiah Heyman studied interactions between Mexican border crossers and US immigration officials of Mexican descent to examine whether these officials felt empathy toward Mexican immigrants who frequently crossed the US-Mexico border.[35] Not surprisingly, his research shows that US immigration officials of Mexican descent distance themselves from noncitizen Mexican border crossers to protect their own class interests. The border crossers I interviewed agreed with this assessment. For their part, crossers were not interested in developing ethnic solidarity with US immigration officials. They just wanted to avoid the extended delays and unnecessary questioning that could potentially arise when they fictitiously declared that their visit was for the purposes of consumption.

Having Confidence

When border commuters picked the wrong CBP agent, one of two things would happen. In the best-case scenario, they were denied entry for the day. In the worst-case scenario, CBP agents permanently revoked their border-crossing privileges for the remainder of the period on the card or even for the holder's lifetime. As a result, some commuters prayed to God or to a revered saint when crossing the border. Choosing the correct line and immigration official could also make the difference between being waved through and losing one's BCC. But even crossers who chose the correct line had to be careful to avoid arousing suspicion and to withstand intense and humiliating questioning.

Some BCC holders believed that some US immigration officials were trained in psychological tactics. These BCC holders believed that if they controlled their emotions and maintained poise while they were in the point of entry, immigration officials were less likely to try these tactics. BCC holders learned valuable lessons about maintaining poise through personal experiences, observations, and folk stories, and by observing border arrests. Waiting in line, they often witnessed immigration officials extensively questioning young women and men who were of prime age to work in the United States. The situation often became tense when immigration officials stuck their hands into crossers' pockets, wallets, and purses or compared crossers' fingerprints to the ones on their cards. Border crossers caught using borrowed documents were ushered into a back room for secondary inspection.

Cesar Villa, a thirty-three-year-old who was three when he first obtained his BCC, was sent to secondary inspection during a few of his crossings. In secondary inspection, he was subjected to intense questioning about his travels and his documents were then checked in computer databases. Officials extensively questioned his border-crossing behavior and even inspected his vehicle to make sure he was not smuggling contraband into the United States. He explained, "They ask you many questions and they send you to secondary inspection and then they begin to check your car." Jacinto was also sent to secondary inspection on one occasion. Immigration officials ordered him to disrobe because they did not understand why he had a birth certificate but could not speak English. When I interviewed him in his Tijuana home, he explained his strategy to avoid secondary inspections. Jacinto made sure to appear confident and to look immigration officials straight in their eyes. His motto was to never show fear to CBP agents.

Watching from the line at the port of entry as others were arrested or pulled into secondary inspection was an unnerving experience for many border commuters, but these instances also provided valuable lessons about how to avoid detection. BCC holders observed that individuals who looked nervous, out of place, or who avoided looking immigration officials in the eyes when handing over their documents were more likely to be scrutinized. Of the many arrests I personally observed, one that stood out was that of a young Mexican migrant in his early twenties who wore a San Diego Padres baseball cap but otherwise seemed out of place. He kept looking around the port of entry, which was unusual because people in line generally looked straight ahead or engaged in conversation with others. When he got to the counter, he took out his identification card, laid it on the counter, and looked away, placing both hands in his pocket. He never looked the immigration official in the eye and he did not say a word. The immigration official asked the crosser to show him his fingerprints. After comparing the fingerprints to those on the card, in one smooth move, the official placed his arm around the young man's neck, took his right arm and placed it behind the back, handcuffed him, and escorted him into a back room as border crossers and US tourists watched. He handed the young man to another immigration official and returned to his computer within about two minutes, smiling at the next two border crossers as if nothing had happened. No matter how shaken up they may have felt, these crossers had to be careful to look the officer in the eye and talk with him amiably as they passed.

One woman explained to me that the ability to cross depended both on luck and on "the face that they see on you," indicating that presentation of self based on confidence and poise mattered at the border. Her comment reflects Erving Goffman's "impression management," in which individuals consciously work to influence others' perceptions of them. One way in which people perform "impression management" in social interactions is through the use of "face work." Goffman explains how people use "face work" on a daily basis to control social interaction processes:

> When a person senses that he is in face, he typically responds with feelings of confidence and assurance. Firm in the line he is taking, he feels that he can hold his head up and openly present himself to others. He feels some security and some relief—as he also can when the others feel he is in wrong face but successfully hide these feelings from him.[36]

In interview after interview, respondents named "tener confianza," or having confidence, as the single most important behavior to master when crossing the border. It was only when border crossers had confidence and were not intimidated by CBP agents that they were able to withstand intense questioning about their activities in the United States. For example, Daniel, a manager at a fast-food restaurant in the United States, once had a CBP agent accuse him without proof of working in the United States. Daniel stood his ground with the CBP agent, and the two had a bitter exchange of words. On two other occasions, the same CBP agent accused Daniel of being a drug dealer and of using his card to work without authorization. Daniel insisted the official was falsely accusing him and that he was only crossing to purchase groceries. According to Daniel, "My mouth became dry. And I had only been working in the United States for three weeks, but that immigration official had me scoped out."

Instead of becoming bitter and fearful after these incidents, Daniel learned a valuable lesson. He learned to keep his composure, stare directly into border agents' eyes, and remain confident and consistent about his reasons for crossing. Likewise, Jorge, a garage-sale commuter, recalled an instance when a CBP agent threw his passport in his face. "I did not say anything to him. I only looked at him. But inside myself, I told him to fuck off. I knew that if I said something, he would take my passport away or rip it up." Border crossers like Jorge and Daniel used a strategy that Erving Goffman terms "character maintenance," or "standing correct and steady in the face of sudden pressure."[37] By developing their ability to maintain character in the face of hostility, they were able to cross the border successfully for years. Rather than enter into a verbal altercation with a CBP agent and risk losing their cards, most border crossers remained poised, suppressed their feelings of marginalization, maintained a confident demeanor, and developed a thick skin. Their reward for doing so was access to the US labor market and higher wages than those they earned in Mexico though it meant swallowing their pride.

Scripts and Artifacts

Anthropologist Josiah Heyman studied border enforcement at the El Paso–Ciudad Juárez checkpoint. He found that immigration officials look for certain characteristics when they profile Mexicans.[38] According to Heyman, BCC holders who look like upper- and middle-class Mexicans are less likely to be detained or questioned extensively. The symbols that immigration officials use to differentiate crossers by class include clothing, vehicles, and skin color. Border commuters in Tijuana shared his assessment. They were well aware that CBP agents used class, race, and ethnicity to profile border crossers and, as a result, they tried to avoid negative attention by dressing in the best possible clothes and driving cars that were insured and in good working order. In addition to these efforts to project a higher class status as they crossed, I found that border commuters spent considerable effort concealing their US occupational identity. They developed extensive scripts and strategies to avoid tipping CBP agents off to their US-based work.

Cesar, a BCC holder who worked in a shoe store in La Jolla, described his script for crossing:

> I used to carry a lot of documentation of my business [in Tijuana], and almost always, I say that I am going to see my girlfriend. That way, when they ask me, "Why do you cross so much?" Well, I tell them that I am going to see my girlfriend. And then they can't ask me any more questions.

Cesar convinced authorities of his employment ties to Mexico by carrying proof that he owned a business in Tijuana. In addition, by mentioning that he had a girlfriend in the United States, Cesar presented a script that provided a convincing reason for his frequent crossing. Cesar's eagerness to cross the border quickly and "meet his girlfriend" showed at the port of entry.

Other BCC crossers avoided carrying items that would indicate their work in the United States, such as lunch bags or paystubs. Omar, a twenty-seven-year-old internal migrant, successfully crossed the border for four years. He witnessed many friends lose their BCCs while attempting to smuggle their work uniform in a purse or backpack. Omar realized that he needed to conceal his US-based occupation after watching these "common-sense mistakes." He said:

> Oh, about our uniforms, we had to hide them over there [in the US restaurant] because you could not cross with a uniform, and it was really difficult because you had to leave them in a place and we had to tell someone who could cross [to help us]. . . . Someone who could cross and wash the uniforms because we could not cross with the uniforms.

As he crossed, Omar dressed as a skateboarder or wore basic jeans and a hoodie to avoid detection. Like Omar, Miguel developed various travel strategies through his years of crossing the border. His main goal at the port of entry was to conceal all of his US affiliations, including those with his employers or friends:

> First, I never carry anybody's telephone numbers in the United States. Not even my work number. Never. I never carry business cards from work. Everything can compromise you. You never want to show that you have a relationship to a restaurant or that you know people in the US. If you want to have the number of friends in the US, you should have the area code as 664 for [Tijuana] and not 619 [San Diego]. Because I have experiences of friends who this happened to and they took away their BCC.

Miguel's strategy of disguising phone numbers was shared by many other commuters. BCC holders' strategies were largely the result of others' mistakes or of knowledge gained from folk stories. BCC holders carefully studied others' slips and altered their border-crossing behaviors and fictions accordingly. One border commuter who was forced to carry the names of her clients across the border in her cell phone altered the names in case the authorities took her phone and called her clients, a strategy that she learned from others.

In a study based in California's Silicon Valley, anthropologist Roger Rouse found that unauthorized migrants adopted the identity of "good consumers" to mask their legal status.[39] Likewise, BCC holders often used a consumption script to hide their US occupational status from immigration officials. The script was effective because shopping was the card's intended use. In 2002, there were 56.6 million legal crossings through the Tijuana–San Diego border for social visits, work, and shopping in the United States.[40] Though most depictions of border crossings focus on clandestine crossings for the purpose of immigration, millions of people regularly crossed between Mexico and the United States with documents in the closed-border era. One study found that when Tijuanenses crossed the border with documents, they did so for shopping and tourism 68.7 percent of the time and for work only 16.5 percent of the time.[41] Many people crossed the border to attend sporting events, purchase electronic goods, eat in restaurants, and even do laundry. In fact, during the time that I lived in and studied Tijuana, one out of every ten shoppers in South San Diego malls was a resident of Baja California, Mexico.[42] Thus, at this historical moment, Mexican border residents were embraced as consumers but discouraged as workers when crossing through the port of entry.

Though cross-border shopping was a common practice in the borderlands, participants quickly learned that simply mentioning a shopping trip was not enough to convince immigration officials of their honesty. To present a more convincing script about their shopping, BCC violators memorized the names of restaurants and stores and their hours of operation and location. Workers even studied bus routes in case immigration officials asked which bus they would ride. These detailed narratives provided convincing evidence of fictitious visits to relatives or shopping centers in San Diego County.

Diego, a twenty-three-year-old internal migrant from Jalisco, told me about his friends who lost their border-crossing privileges because they were not prepared to answer immigration officials' probing questions. Diego explained that to trick the border guards, crossers must pay attention to even the smallest details of their stories. He explained that one strategy "is to always carry money—approximately $100 dollars—because it would be ridiculous to say you are going shopping but you have no money." As a result, Diego carried the same $100 dollar bill each time he crossed the border. Carrying this bill was just as important to Diego as carrying his BCC. Similarly, another interviewee was advised by a friend to carry dollars or even a cancelled credit card whenever he crossed the border to give the appearance that he was a "good consumer." Some border crossers felt butterflies in their stomach when crossing the border at the end of the workweek because by then, they had spent most of their week's earnings.

BCC violators who frequently crossed the US-Mexico boundary strategically attempted to earn the trust of US immigration officials. One strategy was to conform to gendered consumption practices. For example, several women I interviewed described keeping old mall and outlet center receipts from the United States in their purses. Immigration officials who found the receipts would be more likely to believe their shopping narratives. Other respondents had individualized shopping scripts. One female respondent regularly crossed the US-Mexico border with a hamper of dirty clothes. When immigration officials asked why she was crossing, she explained that she planned to shop at US specialty grocery store Whole Foods after doing her laundry and stressed that Whole Foods carried products she could not find in Mexican stores. Other women explained their frequent crossings by saying that they were going to purchase food products that were cheaper in the United States than in Mexico. Yet another woman claimed to be picking up her son from an American private school, after which, she said, she would get her nails and hair done at an upscale US salon. These border crossers knew that gendered consumption practices provided a convincing border-crossing story. If these women could demonstrate they were crossing to consume a middle-class lifestyle, immigration officials would be even less likely to see them as BCC violators.

These scripts and artifacts were carefully orchestrated to convince CBP agents that border commuters intended to shop. However, successful border-crossing strategies were not always planned; sometimes unanticipated aspects of migrants' self-presentation had a positive effect on immigration officers. When twenty-two-year-old bodybuilder Rodolfo Rodríguez began crossing the port of entry, he won the officers' trust in the following way:

> I had a membership at the gym. . . . I used to cross by bicycle or by car and they used to ask me where I was going. I used to tell them that I was going to the gymnasium. And they would ask me which one and I would give them my membership card [to the gym]. Occasionally I used to run into the agents [immigration officials] at the gymnasium and we'd identify one another. . . . That was my strategy and I used to like to do exercise and go to the gymnasium.

Rodolfo did not join a gym to develop a border-crossing strategy. He just happened to enjoy weightlifting and football, and by participating in his hobbies across the border, he alleviated officials' suspicion of his unlawful employment. Every time he came across one particular immigration official at the port of entry, that official casually asked if he was heading to the gym. This interaction helped Rodolfo transform his gym membership into a strategy for safely crossing the border.

Some BCC holders were indeed able to tell immigration officials that they planned to cross the border to earn money. These commuters told the story of a "good consumer" who crossed to purchase used electronics, bicycles, and clothes from US garage sales, which they would later sell in Mexico. Even though this was a way of using the United States to make money, these individuals were considered "good crossers" because their money was spent in the United States and their profits were earned in Mexico. Thus, even when it was presented as a livelihood strategy, the script of the "good consumer" convinced CBP agents that commuters were fulfilling the intended purpose of the BCC.

Commuting across a "Closed Border"

Operation Gatekeeper emerged at the same time as the North American Free Trade Agreement, a contract that created an economic partnership between the United States, Canada, and Mexico. This strange coupling between immigration containment and economic openness manifested in interactions between border commuters and CBP agents in the closed-border period. The capriciousness with which CBP agents seemed to enforce boundaries seemed to indicate a tacit understanding that unauthorized employment would persist under Operation Gatekeeper. In my observations at the port of entry, I found that immigration officials did not always attempt to identify and catch BCC violators. In many cases, CBP agents quickly waved crossers through during work hours, sometimes barely examining their identification cards. I also observed instances in which US citizens who had either forgotten or lost their identification in Tijuana were allowed to enter the United States after passing a series of oral questions and claiming under oath that they were US citizens. This arbitrary and uneven border enforcement was explained by one female Tijuana resident who claimed, "The US knows that Tijuana is a working-class barrio for San Diego. They allow it because they get free labor and don't have to provide housing and medical services for transnational workers."

Likewise, Cesar, who crossed six times a week for a period of two years, told me "there are times when it is very evident that you are going to work, but some immigration officials let you cross." When I asked why the US government tolerated Mexican border residents working in the United States, he responded, "They know that we cross every day. We are the ones who maintain their nation. We are the ones who do the hard work." Other interviewees pointed out similar lapses in border enforcement based on a tacit understanding of the need for Mexican labor in the United States. For example, one sixty-four-year-old woman crossed the border for decades to care for the children of a CBP agent. She found it ironic that the same agent who regulated the entry of BCC violators employed one in his household. I also spoke to commuters who worked in fast-food restaurants within walking distance of the US-Mexico border. They often trembled as they took the orders of CBP agents who had questioned their reason for visiting the United States earlier in the day.

The crossers I interviewed considered officials hypocritical for allowing some BCC holders to cross into the United States to work but not others. These crossers did not believe that immigration officials should monitor the international boundary for illegal crossings, especially considering that Mexico provided such important labor to the US economy.

Conclusion

Thus far, I have contrasted border migrants' crossing strategies in the Tijuana–San Diego border region across two periods—the closed-border period and the open-border period. However, I want to reiterate that unauthorized and authorized border-crossing strategies were not mutually exclusive during the two historical periods I have discussed. I arrived as an ethnographer in Tijuana ten years after Gatekeeper was implemented. By this time, unauthorized crossings were greatly reduced as compared to the previous period. The open-border period was characterized by such a large number of unauthorized migrants congregating at the US-Mexico border that spectators could observe clandestine crossings and Border Patrol agents chasing unauthorized migrants. Additionally, there were also many daily crossers who used their ties to US growers to gain access to the US labor market. In contrast, during the post-Gatekeeper era, most crossers used BCCs at the port of entry to gain access to unauthorized employment by concealing their affiliation to the US labor market. The discussion in this chapter should not be taken to indicate that authorized crossings did not occur in the region before border enforcement or that unauthorized crossings did not happen afterwards. Rather, I suggest that the border enforcement policies of each historical period reshaped migrants' border-crossing strategies and behaviors. By describing the remaking of the border and border-crossing strategies across time, I have tried to answer Mustafa Emirbayer's and Ann Mische's call for the study of "historical changes in agentic orientations."[43]

Before Operation Gatekeeper was introduced, Tijuana was the preferred border-crossing location for US-bound unauthorized migrants. After Operation Gatekeeper, increased policing rerouted unauthorized migration patterns from Tijuana to the Arizona desert and other desolate crossing points, though authorized migrants continued to enter the United States to work through the port of entry.[44] In this chapter, I have described the experiences of people who crossed the border to work without authorization in the United States during these two historical periods, focusing especially on the experiences of unauthorized crossers who entered without inspection during the first period and border commuters who (mis)used BCCs to cross with authorization but work without it. Their narratives illustrate how changes in the US-Mexico border changed commuters' strategies to cross.

I found that in the open-border period, one group of unauthorized crossers either crossed alone or relied on smugglers to enter the US labor market. This finding is consistent with migration and border-enforcement studies that show the importance of social support in lowering border-crossing risks.[45] To gain access to the US labor market, border crossers who entered without inspection reported performing roles and utilizing disguises to be allowed to circulate in the regional labor market. I also identified another group of crossers who lived in Mexico but crossed to work in the farms adjacent to the US-Mexico border. For these crossers, declaring their occupational affiliation to growers provided them with entry into the United States. These findings support David Spener's assertion that border crossing is not a uniform process because each social actor (family, friends, smugglers, and employers) employs a variety of border-crossing strategies that lead to distinct outcomes.[46]

In contrast to unauthorized crossers in the open-border period, authorized crossers in the closed-border period depended less on the support of others and more on documents that allowed them to enter the United States to work. This group of crossers adopted strategies that operated within formal rules and regulations. To commute to work in the United States, crossers during this era ironically had to mask their affiliation with US employers to convince immigration officials that they were not BCC violators. Border crossers carefully planned their interactions with immigration officials to maintain poise under duress, employing Goffmanian strategies consisting of managing one's physical and emotional self. This impression management required a great deal of knowledge in order to cross an increasingly militarized border. This suggests that the border is not just a physical structure but also a set of social relations that are negotiated through face-to-face interaction.

The findings contained in this chapter contribute to the growing literature on border-enforcement and migration studies by illustrating how increased policing altered patterns and modes of entry at Tijuana–San Ysidro.[47] I identified unique border-crossing strategies employed by unauthorized and authorized border crossers, which demonstrates migrants' agency in the process of navigating the US-Mexico border. With the exception of Josiah Heyman's and Rubén Hernández-León's work, BCC holders have remained invisible and understudied in the migration and border-studies literature, yet there is so much to learn from their experiences.[48] I build on these scholars' work by showing how migrants with a legal method of entry but an unauthorized purpose for work negotiated their encounters with Border Patrol agents and adjusted their behaviors in response to the particular social situations they encountered.

Scholars who study the border-crossing behaviors of migrants have alluded to the importance of developing knowledge and skills, but this is the first study to outline the particular forms of skill and knowledge that pertain to different types of border enforcement. In this chapter, I have presented examples from what I saw when I crossed the port of entry on a regular basis and the experiences of my respondents to highlight the ways in which people accumulated border-crossing knowledge through personal encounters and careful observation of interactions between migrants and the state officials who attempted to keep them out. I also demonstrated that because the border is a social construct, it has been constantly remade. The strategies that border crossers employed to obtain unauthorized employment resulted in the state also employing strategies for controlling the movement of bodies across the border. As a result, the border provides an important place to study the ways in which structure and agency shape one another: the border and the rules which regulate border behavior provide a medium that encourages agentic behavior. The actions of border crossers illustrate that regardless of increased surveillance at the international boundary, people will continue to be creative and devise new strategies for crossing.

Finally, the study of border-crossing strategies reveals the contradictory nature of enforcement in an era of globalization. The border-crossing strategies of commuters reveal the fluid nature of the border and in particular that the line that separates these two nation-states is not so clear cut. Those who cross the border on a regular basis help unmask the contradictions that are inherent in border enforcement and immigration laws, which struggle to contain a population with social and economic ties that cannot be restricted to one nation. Here I have presented how border enforcement affects the daily life of people who cross regularly and how they adjust their behaviors to be able to cross the border even when immigration laws prohibit it.

CHAPTER 5 | Border Networks

WHEN RAMÓN MIGRATED to Tijuana in 1968, he left behind his parents, siblings, and friends in Jalisco and arrived in the city knowing only his aunt. Despite knowing almost no one when he arrived, Ramón would form ties throughout his life to find work in Tijuana, then to migrate to Los Angeles, and eventually to settle back in Tijuana. Ramón's network ties did not remain static but expanded and dissolved as he came in contact with hundreds of fronterizos. This chapter investigates the social life of border residents with a particular focus on how border migrants like Ramón craft networks to secure livelihoods in the borderlands. It investigates not just *what* network ties do for people but also *who* border residents interact with, *how* they interact with others, and *why* some ties are enabling and others constraining in an urban border context. In short, this chapter considers how people form network ties through face-to-face interaction in an urban context where the border exerts its constant influence on people's lives. The ethnographic findings presented here illustrate how social dynamics are shaped by the physical border and by immigration and border policies that disrupt the normal urban flow of social support.

Sociologists and demographers who study international migration have long noted the importance of network ties among low-wage immigrants living in the United States, particularly for those who originate from rural communities. According to Manuel Gamio, in the first decade of the twentieth century, Mexican migrants forged ties to find a job, to pay smuggler fees, and to pool resources during times of employment scarcity.[1] Since then, numerous studies have documented how rural migrants draw on and depend on the support of kin, friends, and paisanos from their hometowns to survive in a foreign environment.[2] While the US-Mexico migration scholarship may explain how migrants like Ramón form homeland ties to get to the United States and adapt to life there, we know little about how urban residents form ties in border cities. We also have limited information on how their network structures change in the borderlands as they are exposed to new livelihoods as well as new laws and policies that govern international mobility in the borderlands.

Border residents have access to current and former migrants as well as to border commuters who can and often do pass along information and/or become a resource for navigating social and economic life in the borderlands. Yet this dynamic context also means that border residents form and sustain relationships in ways that defy standard explanations of migrant networks based on kin or hometown ties. The borderlands present a unique context that shapes people's particular pathways to become a migrant, commuter, or nonmigrant through network ties that are created and recreated on a daily basis and across time.

This chapter describes how the border residents I followed in Tijuana sought information and assistance to decide whether to migrate or commute to the United States or to find work in Mexico. I not only interviewed people and asked them about their networks but also observed them as they crafted ties in their homes, neighborhoods, workplaces, and the port of entry over the course of my entire fieldwork and during revisits. As a result, I show how people reconfigured their ties to adapt to changing life circumstances, compensate for a lack of resources in their current networks, pursue new livelihood options, or replace lost network members. By studying the process of how people form relationships through everyday interactions, I show why some networks enable human action while others constrain it. In particular, I pay attention to the way in which larger structural forces (e.g., unemployment, border enforcement, immigration policies) influence individual life paths by shifting the everyday practices and interactions that foster network ties. By studying the intersection of these macro- and micro-level processes, I show how larger social forces shape relational ties and make some networks more useful than others.

Cecilia Menjivar asserts that scholars "have continued to treat the intermediate web of social relations through which individuals respond to structural forces as entities impervious to structural forces," and suggests that we should study how, as "broader forces are configured dissimilarly at different historical moments, so social networks may operate differently as configurations of time and place fluctuate."[3] Matthew Desmond studied the urban poor and found that evicted tenants formed *disposable ties* with acquaintances and strangers to obtain crucial resources like food and rent.[4] He found that the ties of the urban poor are not static but change as they deal with structural crises such as joblessness, rising housing costs, and incarceration. Similarly, structural factors particular to the borderlands, such as increased border enforcement and restrictive immigration policies, should be expected to influence the formation of ties among poor urban residents of Tijuana. How the border in its physical, legal, and symbolic manifestations shapes the formation of social ties is this chapter's central concern.

How Do People Form Ties?

Four decades ago, Mark Granovetter made two important theoretical observations about network ties. First, networks require extensive time, energy, and effort to form and sustain. Second, there are two types of social ties: strong ties and weak ties. For Granovetter, "the strength of a tie is a (probably linear) combination of the amount of time, the emotional intensity, the intimacy (mutual confiding), and the reciprocal services which characterize the tie."[5] Strong ties (e.g., siblings, best friends) share many of the characteristics just mentioned, while weak ties (e.g., workmates, friends of friends) exhibit fewer of these characteristics. Different ties serve different functions, providing network members with access to distinct resources. For example, a migrant is likely to turn to a strong tie with a close family member or a best friend for immediate needs like a loan to cross the border. Weak ties, on the other hand, serve as "bridges" that allow migrants to move beyond clustered ties, perhaps leading to new occupational opportunities.

The Mexico-US migration literature is filled with examples of how migrants draw on the social support of strong ties of close intimates from the place of origin and to a lesser extent on weak ties.[6] These studies show that migrants, with limited English skills and connections outside of their ethnic group, seek the help of close intimates to navigate unfamiliar places and workplace situations.[7] Meanwhile, border scholars have demonstrated that when migrant families relocate to the border, they accumulate ties beyond their hometown that allow them to start a new life in the United States or in Mexican border cities.[8] While these studies provide important insights into the ways networks are reconfigured at the border, they provide little information about how networks are formed in the borderlands through the course of daily interactions.

Mario Luis Small argues that the formation of ties depends on two key factors. First, people must have a place to interact and they must communicate on a frequent basis. Second, the formation of ties depends on whether interactions are competitive or cooperative in nature.[9] He argues that people who engage in cooperative tasks are more likely to produce friendships. In the United States, childcare centers, laundromats, coffee shops, restaurants, and barbershops are places that allow people to meet, interact face-to-face, and form ties. Similarly, the small-knit Mexican rural community has provided a place for migrants to form ties that can be used to migrate to the United States, based on a shared common history. But what about a border city known for its constantly changing population? In this chapter, I highlight how people form (and attempt to form) ties in a Mexican border city in common places where we would expect, such as the workplace and neighborhood, but also in unconventional places, like the port of entry. It is in these places that border residents form connections to migrants with previous international migration experience who can provide knowledge and resources for crossing the border or gaining access to US job opportunities.

How Newcomers Form Ties that Constrain

When internal migrants first move to Tijuana with the desire to continue their journey to the United States, they seek to develop contacts and accumulate resources for their eventual move to the United States. But who do the newly arrived turn to for help? Like international migrants, internal migrants rely on their strong ties to obtain information and assistance with the decision of whether to migrate to the United States or to stay put in Mexico. In particular, they draw on strong, kinship ties, but when they cannot obtain what they need, they turn to weaker ties with friends and acquaintances to obtain information and assistance for crossing the border.

The case of Rubén Nava illustrates that even when border residents have access to strong and weak ties to current and former migrants, these do not automatically translate into resources to access the US labor market as an international migrant or border commuter. Some network associates simply do not have the resources to help. Rubén, a twenty-five-year-old father of two boys, spent considerable time and energy forming ties when he arrived in Tijuana. At the age of seventeen, Rubén migrated to Tijuana from Mexico City with the intention of moving to the United States. When he arrived, the only people he knew in the city were his father and brother (his mother would arrive a few years later). Although Rubén's kinship ties were thin upon arrival, he formed a large friendship and acquaintance base that he would consult when he wanted to know what it was like to live in the United States or how to get a BCC. He had formed most of his ties at the ice cream shop where he worked. Because the shop was within a ten-minute walk of the San Ysidro port of entry, Rubén came in contact with all sorts of people with varying labor market experience in the United States. This included deportees, return migrants, border commuters, tourists, and US-based Americans of Mexican descent.

Although Rubén wanted to cross to the United States, the strategy that he planned to get to the other side varied day by day. Some days, he planned to obtain a BCC to relocate to the United States. Other days, he spoke about using the BCC to cross the border to purchase US goods to resell in Mexico. Sometimes he thought about jumping the fence and living as an unauthorized immigrant. To complicate matters further, he also wanted to start his own business in Tijuana. Regardless of whether he planned to become an international migrant, a border commuter, or neither, Rubén clearly had a strong desire to see what the United States had to offer. Therefore, he spent considerable time and energy developing his social connections to the United States by befriending customers at the ice cream parlor. He was quite good at it.

Through customer interactions, Rubén formed friendships with James and John (whom I never met personally). James was an African American man who lived in San Diego but crossed the border to visit Tijuana. Rubén and James initially bonded over their mutual interest in travel, and the relationship solidified when Rubén's father let James borrow their Mexico City home for a month. Rubén also befriended John, a Greyhound bus driver, who regularly visited the ice cream parlor when he came to Tijuana. Eventually, the relationship grew into a friendship, to the point where John encouraged Rubén to obtain a BCC so he could show Rubén America. John told Rubén that if he obtained his BCC, John would personally buy Rubén a bus ticket to travel throughout California.

Yet even though these friendships were strong, and James and John were both encouraging of Rubén, they did little to help Rubén cross the border. These friendships did not materialize into resources for Rubén's crossing because both of his associates were US citizens, with limited knowledge of what it would take to get a BCC. They also knew little about how to get a job in the construction industry where Rubén envisioned working. He originally befriended both James and John with the hope of gaining resources to cross the border to the United States, but Rubén slowly came to realize that his contacts did little for him.

Another source of information for Rubén came by way of his father, Aurelio, and many of Aurelio's friends who had diverse experiences in the United States. Aurelio worked in the United States as a bracero in the early 1960s, and then again as an undocumented immigrant in the mid-1980s. Aurelio believed that the United States offered abundant opportunities and regularly drew on his own life history to frame the narrative he told Rubén. Aurelio frequently talked about his time in Stockton, California, where he worked as many as eighteen hours picking tomatoes by day and canning them by night. Through this farmwork, Aurelio made more money than he could spend, which he eventually invested in several ice cream shops in Mexico. Even in his mid-sixties, Aurelio still liked to work long hours. He opened his business at 9:00 a.m. every morning and closed it at exactly 9:00 p.m. He also never took a day off. As such, Aurelio had little tolerance for people who did not work hard.

Aurelio's Protestant-ethic approach to work was a source of tension with Rubén. Father and son frequently bickered about Rubén's work habits and his dream of going to the United States.[10] During one argument, Rubén stormed out of the shop and did not return to work for a couple of days. The source of their bickering was Aurelio's belief that anyone who wanted to work in the United States had to be disciplined and willing to work long hours. Aurelio believed that Rubén did not have the work ethic of a migrant and referred to him as a "lazy ass," for staying up late playing video games. Because Aurelio saw Rubén as lazy, he did not advise his son to migrate to the United States. Instead, he advised Rubén to find his occupational niche in Tijuana.

Rubén received discouraging messages not only from his father but also from his close acquaintances who had worked in the United States. One acquaintance was El Guerro, an ex-smuggler and factory worker in Los Angeles. El Guerro now sold silver necklaces to tourists making their way from the port of entry to Avenida Revolución. El Guerro often stopped at the ice cream shop to order a cold strawberry drink and talk to Rubén and Aurelio. One hot summer afternoon, El Guerro chatted with Aurelio and Rubén about working life in the United States. Aurelio brought out his usual narrative of working from sunset to sundown and earning as much as $1,000 a week picking tomatoes back in 1964, an amount most of his friends had a difficult time believing. At one point, Aurelio told Rubén, "If they gave me the opportunity again [meaning the opportunity to get a work visa], I would earn that much money, if not more." El Guerro slowly sipped on his drink, stopped to think about what Aurelio had said, and in a low voice replied, "My friend, those days of making money in the US are long gone!" He explained that it was difficult to find a well-paying US job because labor markets such as those in Los Angeles were saturated with immigrants. He did not discourage Rubén from migrating to the United States but rather suggested that he should head for Indiana, where perhaps he could have better luck because there were fewer immigrants to compete with in the labor market. He also warned Rubén that if he ventured into the United States without legal documents, he would be subjected to exploitation and would have almost no rights as an unauthorized immigrant. During the discussion, Rubén sat back and listened to El Guerro's advice and asked him questions from time to time, without ever agreeing or disagreeing. He simply listened and stored the information that he received from El Guerro.

Although Rubén had an extensive network of friends with US experience, many of his friends were loners with limited social ties who struggled to make ends meet in the United States. These men hung out at the ice cream parlor because it provided them with a stable set of social relations in a city where people were constantly migrating. Chuy, who at one point walked from Tijuana to Los Angeles, was an intimidating figure at 5' 10" in baggy Dickies pants, shiny dress shoes, and a checkerboard flannel shirt. He did not have any family and lived alone. His only friends were Rubén and Aurelio. Before relocating to Tijuana, Chuy had lived in South Central Los Angeles, where he had become addicted to drugs and was homeless. When I met Chuy, he had been clean for almost two decades.

Chuy was a border commuter who crossed seven days a week. He worked in Chula Vista pushing an ice cream cart through a working-class neighborhood. During conversations, Chuy regularly told Rubén that many of his customers did not have money to purchase ice cream, so he carried a small notebook to jot down how much each customer owed him. Chuy also told Rubén that although he had worked in the United States for over two decades, he did not have any savings to show for it. Chuy labored in low-wage jobs and earned just enough to cover his living expenses. This was one reason why Chuy moved from Los Angeles to Tijuana, so he could get by on minimal wages. He lived in a roach-infested one-bedroom apartment with an outdoor bathroom but paid only $100 a month. Chuy and Rubén were close friends who not only exchanged information about life in the United States but also many other resources. Chuy frequently brought Rubén *Playboy* magazines, milk, and other food items. In exchange, Chuy received free coffee and also had someone to return to at the end of the day. Outside of the ice cream parlor, Chuy had few people that he interacted with and trusted.

Rubén's story illustrates how aspiring crossers form social ties on a consistent basis with experienced US migrants to obtain information about labor market opportunities in the United States. Rubén formed many of his social connections as a result of working at the ice cream parlor near the port of entry. However, Rubén's social circles did not provide him with the information or assistance that he needed. Much of the information that Rubén received did not paint a rosy picture of labor market opportunities in the United States. Eventually, he took the information to heart and decided to forgo the idea of crossing the border, at least for the time being. A few months after making this decision, Rubén stopped working at his father's business and bought a taxi, using a $5,000 loan from his brother. His wife Lupita had also encouraged him to become a taxi driver because she believed that it was the best way to obtain a BCC should he ever change his mind again about going to the United States.

The process of deciding to cross the border is an emotional one, filled with uncertainties for people with very limited information about what lies to the north and how to get there. As a result, migrants look to family and friends to provide some clarity about the process. However, as in Rubén's case, network connections can in fact constrain one's desire to migrate to the United States. The narratives that his network associates presented did not enable his aspirations to become a migrant or border commuter but rather created doubt. This doubt was enough to put a temporary hold on his dream of crossing the border. Yet even as Rubén's connections discouraged him from migrating to the United States, they were an important resource that he developed in the borderlands that provided him with the necessary information to decide that at this moment in his life course, he was better off staying put.

Family Members Providing Assistance

We know from previous studies on the labor market experiences of immigrants that they rely on their family and friends to obtain employment in the United States. But what happens when a border commuter loses his or her job in the United States and the ability to cross the border? We know relatively little about how nonmigrants provide assistance to migrants. This section investigates the role of nonmigrants and noncrossers in sustaining transnational social networks. In particular, I focus on how one family dealt with this crisis by drawing on household members who had access to different civil society ties in Tijuana. These family members provided yet another layer of network associates that can help when dealing with an economic crisis. Because these family members did not spend as much time crossing the border and working in the United States, they were able to form ties with neighbors, acquaintances, and friends throughout Tijuana in ways that regular crossers were unable to do. These family members had effectively created social ties in Tijuana that helped those with limited ties in Tijuana locate employment in Mexico.

One Sunday afternoon, Chelo (age sixty) knocked at my door. Chelo was an internal migrant who had relocated to Tijuana from Guanajuato. Shortly after arriving, Chelo met and married Ramón García. I had known her and Ramón for almost six months, and I was currently living with one of their extended relatives. When I opened the door, Chelo shook her head from side to side and said, "I have bad news. Richard lost his visa so now both Ángel and Richard [her sons] can no longer cross!" Since they were children, Ángel and Richard had crossed the border using their BCCs, but for the first time in their lives, they could no longer cross. Their employers encouraged them to cross the border without documents, but they were unable to find a way to make this work. As a result, they effectively lost their US jobs. They now had to find jobs in Mexico, which proved difficult. Even though they had lived in Tijuana since birth, Richard and Ángel worried that the ties that they had developed to find jobs in the United States could not provide them access to employment in Mexico.

Twenty-seven-year-old Ángel was the first to lose his crossing privileges when a border official confiscated his card. As a US worker, Ángel had achieved economic mobility. His employer promoted him to supervisor because he had learned how to remodel homes and was proficient in English, and his hourly wages had increased from $10 to $15. Losing his BCC was a major financial catastrophe for Ángel and his wife, who had recently given birth to their first child. His household income shrank overnight from $500 dollars a week to nothing because he could no longer cross the border. Ángel became desperate. For several days, he considered hiring a smuggler to get him to San Diego so he could return to his job. However, he knew that if he crossed the border, he would not be able to return each night to be with his wife and child as he had done for years. His family convinced him to wait and suggested that he try to obtain work in Tijuana.

For several days, Ángel searched for work but was unable to find it because he "no longer had an [employment] record here in Tijuana." Moreover, Ángel spoke Spanish with an American accent, which raised suspicion among Mexican employers that perhaps he had been deported for committing a crime in the United States. It was clear that Ángel's lack of Mexican-based ties was an obstacle to finding work in Mexico. Just like in the United States, jobs in Mexico depend on social contacts that could open doors to job opportunities. In the United States, Ángel relied on his father, Ramón, a crew leader, to help him find work in construction or to put him in contact with one of his labor contractor friends. However, Ramón had limited ties to the Mexican job market. Ramón primarily socialized with others who crossed the border to work in the United States. He spent much of his day at the port of entry and at work in the United States, which left him with very little time to form ties in Tijuana outside his family.

Unable to find employment in Mexico and with a newborn son, Ángel began to worry. Fortunately, Chelo stepped in to mobilize her social ties. Unlike Ramón, who had few friends in Mexico, Chelo had spent all of her life living and working in Mexico. She had once worked at a factory that produced televisions for Sears and had developed extensive contacts there. She also knew most of her neighbors, to whom she had sold used appliances at discounted prices. So when Ángel became unemployed, Chelo asked her former coworker, who was also a member of her extended family, for help. The relative then turned to a friend who ran a muffler shop to ask if he would consider hiring her nephew who had recently lost his job in the United States. The shop owner was looking for an assistant mechanic at the time and gave Ángel an interview. The interview went well, and Ángel began work at the shop.

A few months after Ángel lost his crossing privileges, his younger brother Richard (age twenty-four) also lost his BCC, creating further stress to the García household. Although Richard was young, people thought that he was in his mid-thirties because he always had a worried look on his face and was beginning to go bald. Chelo attributed his premature aging to the fact that "in *el Norte* [United States], it is a fucking struggle." Richard lost his card when it fell out of the back pocket of his tight wrangler jeans one afternoon as he crossed the turnstile gates at the San Ysidro port of entry. After losing his card, Richard fell into a deep depression. He could no longer bear to go outside for fear of running into friends who would ask him why he was not at work. He had been crossing the border for years; doing so was his normal way of life. Not once had he considered what it would mean to be unable to cross. This was the first time he had to confront the idea that the US-Mexico boundary was indeed a powerful barrier that limited his mobility. He had taken for granted the freedom of being able to cross the border.

Richard posted a sign at the entrance to Tijuana offering a $200 reward for the return of his card. No one ever responded. His parents speculated that perhaps someone had reached into his back pocket and stolen it. Shortly after Richard lost his card, I spoke to his wife, Maria. She told me that he struggled emotionally because he was no longer the family breadwinner. Because Richard had friends who worked in construction in Tijuana, he was able to find a job relatively quickly in Mexico. However, he was unsatisfied with this job because the work was infrequent and the wages were low in comparison to what he earned in the United States. Just a few weeks earlier, he had earned $500 a week. Now, he was earning $120 a week for the same work. He could no longer cover his $250-a-month rent plus household costs. Ramón helped him for the first few weeks by supplementing his son's income. He also received a final paycheck plus a bonus from his US employer. But without a better-paying job, Ramón could not maintain his household. One month later, Richard and Maria vacated their two-bedroom apartment and moved in with her parents.

To make ends meet, Richard and Maria began to find new ways to generate income. Ramón, who crossed the border every day to work for a demolition company, still provided ties to the United States that Richard was able to use to his advantage. Sometimes, the company that he worked for allowed him to keep discarded cabinets, tables, dishwashers, and ceiling fans for a small fee. Ramón began to bring discarded equipment to Richard to sell. One afternoon, Ramón returned from his US job with a car filled with ceiling fans that he had purchased from his employer for $8 apiece. Ramón gave the fans to Richard, who then sold and installed them for an additional fee. Because Richard had spent so much time crossing the border, he had not developed many ties in Tijuana, so Chelo helped him locate customers. Her frequent interaction with other neighborhood women and visits to the local clinic and community center became a valuable resource that allowed her son to locate customers.

While selling and installing household items helped Richard generate extra income, it was not enough to cover his family's expenses. As a result, Richard and Maria began to mobilize yet another layer of social ties in their neighborhood. This time, Maria decided that she would use her BCC to cross the border and clean homes with a local neighbor. Prior to this incident, Maria had not worked in the United States and had limited US-based contacts. Therefore, Maria turned to neighbors who cleaned the homes of middle-class families in San Diego to help her find work. After hearing what happened to Richard, Maria's neighbor "felt bad about [her] situation" and took her to work in the United States, where she was paid

$75 for cleaning two homes. Later, Maria received another job offer; this time she was paid $50. Unfortunately, at the time that I spoke to Maria, she had grown disenchanted with the process of crossing the border because she "had to get up at 5:00 a.m." She crossed the port of entry at 8:00 a.m. and then took the trolley from San Ysidro to San Diego and then transferred to a bus that took her to the neighborhood where she worked, a process that took five hours. She spent the next five or six hours cleaning the home before returning to Tijuana. "It was just too exhausting," explained Maria.

Maria's commute was not only time-consuming but also costly. It cost about $2 to get to the port of entry by taxi, where she then had to buy a $5 daily public transportation pass in the United States before spending another $2 to return from the port of entry. Thus, on transportation alone, she spent almost $10 of her daily $50 earnings. She also found that it was difficult to break into the house-cleaning niche because "those who have cleaning jobs hold onto them. They don't want to share information." As a result, Maria grew frustrated and decided to search for work in Mexico after only a month. She found subcontracting work blowing up balloons for a Mexican vendor who then resold them from anywhere from $2 to $5 dollars. The last time I spoke to Maria and Richard, they were still struggling to adjust to a life in which their primary income was no longer earned in the United States but in Mexico.

Even though Richard and Ángel were Mexican citizens who had lived all of their lives in Tijuana, the majority of their adulthood was spent crossing the border to work in the United States. As a result, when Richard and Ángel lost their jobs, they turned to female relatives and/or spouses who activated their Mexican-based ties for information and contacts. These examples illustrate the limitations of US-based networks and how people must mobilize a different set of social ties to deal with changing circumstances. It shows how networks adapt by integrating new members and mobilizing current members to gain access to resources not found within the immediate web of social relations. The case I presented here shows the importance of women in mobilizing different sets of relations to compensate for what men's networks could not accomplish; namely, to find ways to reintegrate into the Mexican economy when men could no longer cross the border.

Neighborhood Ties

Writing about urbanism in the 1930s, Louis Wirth characterized social relations in the city as "impersonal, superficial, transitory, and segmental."[11]

He—like Max Weber, Émile Durkheim, and Georg Simmel—argued that although urbanites "rub elbows" with many people on a daily basis due to population growth and despite the economic interdependence stemming from the high division of labor in cities, urbanites are less likely to form strong bonds to both kin and neighbors compared to rural migrants.[12] Rural inhabitants have stronger bonds because they interact regularly and because relations date back several generations. Elizabeth Fussell argues that the lack of strong ties among urban residents combined with diverse economic opportunities explains why Mexican cities such as Tijuana have lower levels of outmigration compared to rural communities.[13] That is, according to Fussell, potential migrants' strong ties to others with previous international migration experience in rural communities make them more likely to migrate.

Social relations in Tijuana are complicated by the fact that the city is used by some as a "trampoline," where people obtain money and contacts before moving to the United States. Migrants who use Tijuana as a trampoline may spend limited time and emotional energy establishing meaningful long-term ties to others. The type of migrant who moves to Tijuana is, to quote Georg Simmel, "the [person] who comes today and stays tomorrow—the *potential* wanderer . . . [who] has not quite got over the freedom of coming and going."[14] In Tijuana, however, I found that while there were certainly many people who moved there with the goal of moving on, there were also many people with very strong roots in this border city. Some urban residents developed strong bonds to peers through daily neighborhood interactions that dated back to their childhoods. These social relations remained intact even when respondents lived abroad for extended periods of time. Once established, these social ties became a resource for a select group of friends to draw upon to enter the US labor market, not as international migrants but as border commuters.

To investigate how people craft friendships in a neighborhood context and how these friendships supported access to US opportunities, I interviewed and observed a ten-member network in a neighborhood I call Colonia Frontera. The neighborhood is located within a ten-minute drive of the San Ysidro port of entry. At night, neighborhood residents can see the stadium lights lining the boundary stretching from Playas de Tijuana to the San Ysidro port of entry. Neighbors here have resided so long in their neighborhood that they remember the days when they played soccer in dirt streets and when few neighbors had running water or electricity. Today, however, the neighborhood has a family-owned print shop, an OXXO convenience store (similar to a 7-Eleven), restaurants, auto-mechanic shops, a

Catholic church, a bakery, and schools. Although most people in Colonia Frontera were long-term residents, few had lived their entire lives in Tijuana. Some residents had spent time in the United States as immigrant workers, particularly in Los Angeles and San Diego during the 1980s. As a result of living in the United States, many of these respondents received legal permanent residence through IRCA of 1986. Residents of Colonia Frontera with extensive US labor histories crossed to work in the United States as managers and supervisors in construction or small businesses. These positions enabled them to serve as important sources of potential information for Tijuanenses from this neighborhood searching for work in the United States.

Although the friendships I observed had formed over many years, ties between friends were tested and reassessed through daily interactions. Through these interactions, residents came to understand whom they could and could not rely on. One Sunday at around 3:00 p.m., the youngest member of the network, Cesar (age twenty-eight), stopped by Jorge's weekly garage sale. As we saw previously in the book, Jorge was a transnational vendor who bought goods in the United States and resold them in Tijuana. People frequently came to Jorge when they needed something: a bike, a pair of jeans, or a DVD. That afternoon, Cesar jumped out of his Jeep Cherokee and yelled at Jorge, "Hey, man! I need you to loan me your bicycle because I need to go mail this letter [to the United States]." The letter Cesar needed to mail was his application for US unemployment insurance. Normally, it took anywhere from forty-five minutes to two hours to cross the US-Mexico border by foot or car, but Cesar knew how to get around the delay. Cesar's plan was to drive to the port of entry with his drinking buddy Julio, park the car at the border turnstiles on the Mexican side, and jump on the bicycle. This strategy would cut the border crossing time to as little as ten minutes because, as a cyclist, he could line up at a special bike lane, cross within a few minutes, and drop the letter at a post office located just across the US-Mexico border.[15] Then he would jump back on his bike, cross the bridge over Interstate 5, and ride straight into Tijuana.

The only problem was that Jorge did not want to lend Cesar his bicycle even though they were close friends. He considered Cesar a "hooligan" and did not trust him with his expensive bike that he valued at $3,000 dollars. Jorge was planning to sell the bike so that he could buy a used car. Cesar felt betrayed by Jorge for not trusting him and grew infuriated as they argued over the bike; they were childhood friends after all. Meanwhile, Jorge grew frustrated with Cesar for not understanding the value of his bicycle as an investment. Cesar eventually borrowed someone else's bike to mail the letter.

Later that night, Cesar invited me and Julio to his home, where I got to know him better. Cesar stated that while he was a border commuter by day, at night he was also a successful business owner, and on the weekends, a well-known singer in Tijuana's club scene. Every day, Cesar crossed the border to work in the United States. Ironically, his job was putting up fences at construction sites to keep people out. At night, he helped manage a beauty salon. On another night, he invited a few men over for beer to showcase a new idea that he was working on, a bar inside of his home that contained a pool table, a big-screen television, a kitchen sink, a blender, and one large neon sign for Budweiser. All in all, he spent $40,000 constructing the bar, and he planned to charge visitors $20 to enter.

After listening to music and drinking beer for almost an hour that night, Julio Cárdenas, a thirty-five-year-old divorced father of two, made an announcement. People referred to Julio as "Sleepy" because he had been fired twice for oversleeping, once at home and another time while riding the San Diego trolley to work. Julio announced that he was going to start a new warehouse job. Cesar and Jorge mocked Julio, with Cesar telling him, "You will not last more than one week." "Shut the fuck up!" responded Julio in a high-pitched voice. He explained that the reason he had lost his previous job was because he was required to get up by 3:00 a.m. to be at work by 6:00 a.m. In his new job, he did not start work until 8:00 a.m. Julio also explained that his day job competed with his ability to generate additional income by placing bets at local sports bars. During the conversation, Cesar interrupted Julio and told him that the real reason he lost his last job was that he was lazy and did not know the culture of work. Julio was not a hard worker in comparison to other residents in the neighborhood. He still lived at home with his parents, did not have a car, and had been unable to keep a steady relationship. Moreover, he had also burned many bridges with friends from whom he had borrowed money which he had never repaid. But Julio sipped his beer, took a puff of his cigarette, and said that things had changed.

That night, when 10:00 p.m. hit, Julio turned in early. All night, he had been careful to drink only a few beers to avoid a hangover; he wanted to get a good night's sleep so that he would have plenty of energy the following day. As soon as Julio left, Jorge started talking about how tired he had grown of helping Julio. Most recently, Jorge had attempted to help Julio by bringing him along to garage sales. Eventually, Jorge stopped inviting Julio because, "Julio did not give me money for gas. He never bought lunch, and sometimes he would even outbid me for items." Jorge's complaints about Julio reflect what Alejandro Portes refers to as the "free-rider problem," where "less diligent members enforce on the more successful all kinds of demands backed by a shared normative structure."[16] But what normative structures allowed Julio to obtain resources as a free-rider even as his companions mocked his laziness or became frustrated with his behavior? Even though Julio had aggravated each of his friends on more than one occasion, they continued to help him because Jorge, Julio, and Cesar had all developed strong ties that dated back to their early childhood. They were first-generation Tijuanenses who had formed friendship ties over their life course as a result of having grown up and raised children in Colonia Frontera. On one occasion, Julio stated that he valued Jorge's friendship because, "I remember when I first had my son, it was Jorge who I told." Jorge made him feel at ease knowing that he was going to be a young father. Although Julio frequently disappointed Jorge, other neighborhood friends, and even his own brother with his selfish acts, Julio always seemed to have some friend he could rely on to borrow money, obtain beer and cigarettes, and find a job when he needed income. Julio was strategic in how he formed relationships with others, sometimes spending weeks with one friend then moving on to another when he had exhausted their resources, time, and energy. Despite his flaws, he was sought out for friendships because he was funny, confident, and a great storyteller, which mixed well with drinking.

Los Veteranos

The neighborhood serves as a central place where men interact on a daily basis and form friendships that date back to childhood experiences. Because many of Colonia Frontera's residents had a history of working in the United States as both migrants and border commuters, some of these friendship ties could eventually be used to obtain employment in the United States. In particular, veteran border commuters and migrants provided valuable information about employment opportunities, and in some cases even helped their neighbors by "putting in a good word" with employers. They were able to perform this function because veteran crossers had extensive labor histories in the United States and some were even foremen or managers of US companies. These connections gave veteran migrants respected status in the neighborhood.

One of these veteran crossers was Hugo Méndez (age forty-six), who was born and raised in Mazatlán, Sinaloa. Hugo lost his job in Sinaloa during the Mexican economic crisis of the 1980s, and migrated without authorization to San Francisco, California. There, he worked in various jobs, from washing dishes to working in a clothing department store. Eventually, he obtained legal permanent residency through IRCA in 1987, learned English, and was promoted to the position of foreman at a fencing company in San Diego County.[17] When we met, Hugo was one of the highest-earning employees at his company. Hugo's friends respected him as a responsible family man, a hard worker, and someone who had climbed the economic ladder and achieved the "American Dream, Mexican style," as he referred to his current lifestyle, enjoying the fruits of his US-based wage labor in Mexico. In Colonia Frontera, Hugo had a three-bedroom home with a garage, mini-bar, barbeque pit, and a computer room where his daughters did the homework assigned in their US schools. Despite achieving social mobility, however, Hugo did not forget about his friends. He maintained strong ties with other neighborhood residents and helped many to get jobs in the United States.

To better understand how this veteran migrant provided employment assistance to friends, I interviewed Hugo one Sunday afternoon as he sat drinking beers at a garage sale with Julio, Cesar, and Jorge. All of Hugo's friends considered him generous when it came to helping others. Hugo explained that he had helped countless others find work at the fencing company. When I probed him to name someone he had helped and to explain why, Hugo pointed to Cesar, the young man who had needed a bike to cross the border, and said, "*a ese güey*! [that fucker]." He explained:

HUGO: Look, I helped Cesar. And very many others. Many others.
SERGIO: How did you help them out?
HUGO: I have to talk to the boss and recommend them and tell them that they are good persons.
SERGIO: Why did you decide to help Cesar?
HUGO: Look, when that fucker was like five years old, he stepped onto the basketball court [at the local park]. . . . He told me, "I will play you." I did not want to play him because I was tired but I felt bad for the guy because no one else would play with him. So I played him and he played harder than any other five-year-old I had ever seen.

Even though the pick-up basketball game had taken place twenty-three years earlier, Hugo narrated the story as if it were yesterday. He explained to me that it was a moment that began a life-long friendship between him and Cesar. Once he decided to play the basketball game with Cesar,

Hugo said, "Okay, *mijo* [son]. Let's go." Hugo was impressed by young Cesar's determination and talent—Cesar had one of the best hook shots in the neighborhood. Late one Sunday night, I watched a two-on-two game between veterans Julio and Hugo and Jorge and Cesar, played in an illuminated courtyard located off a busy street. Down 13–1, Cesar turned to Jorge and said, "all me." Over the next twenty or thirty minutes, Cesar made shot after shot to win the game by a score of 19–17. This game illustrated Cesar's persistence and hard-work ethic that had won Hugo's respect twenty-three years earlier.

Throughout the younger man's life, Hugo helped Cesar on numerous occasions. He had introduced Cesar to his employer and taught short-tempered Cesar to use humility when dealing with the owner of the company. On one occasion, Hugo explained to Cesar, "You have to swallow your pride" to "get on the boss's good side." Cesar had a difficult time working in the United States because in Mexico he was very well respected. In Colonia Frontera, he was known as an entrepreneur, a gifted athlete, a respected street fighter, and a talented vocalist, who was invited annually to sing at the town square to commemorate Mexico's independence day. In the United States, he saw himself simply as a laborer who had very little control over the labor process.

Hugo helped Cesar find work at the fencing company, and in turn, Cesar helped other friends find work there as well. Cesar helped Julio get a job at the same company, though Julio eventually lost the job by oversleeping, because he liked to stay up late placing bets at a sports bar. Cesar had initially hoped that Julio would succeed at this job because he needed someone to help him drive to work each morning. Cesar had to get up at 3:00 a.m. to be at work in San Diego by 5:30 a.m., which he found "very stressful" and tiring. As a result, he recruited Julio to take turns driving across the port of entry. However, Cesar recounted, "he would drive [with me], but he always fell asleep." Cesar eventually recruited other friends from the neighborhood so that he would not have to drive every morning. Thus, one of the benefits of residing in the neighborhood was that residents could share the morning rush-hour commute at one of the busiest port of entry crossings in the world. Alone, the commute was tiring, burdensome, and unpredictable due to the nature of border inspections.

As a return migrant, Hugo served as an informal recruiter for the fencing company. By helping Cesar find employment in the United States, he set off a chain reaction of access to employment opportunities in his neighborhood. When Cesar built his bar with his US earnings, he hired day-laborer Rafael to help him with the construction. Cesar gave Rafael the job because he knew how to build and was unemployed. As a day laborer, Rafael was not tied to the US or Mexican economy but worked wherever jobs were available. In addition to building the bar, Cesar brought home used and discarded construction materials, such as doors, windows, and sinks from the United States. Too busy to sell them on his own, he bargained with friends to sell them on commission. For example, I watched as Cesar and Jorge haggled over a brand-new screen door. Cesar wanted $100 for the door, but Jorge told him that he knew his customers and he would not get that much. Eventually, they settled on $75. Jorge would not pay Cesar until he sold the door.

Even after residents moved out of Colonia Frontera, they returned on weekends to rekindle neighborhood friendships and recruit workers. Lemus García, who was born and raised in Colonia Frontera but had moved to the United States, would stop by the basketball court to play a pick-up game with old friends every time he visited the neighborhood. Lemus began working in an upholstery shop in Tijuana until he married a US citizen. In Tijuana, Lemus reupholstered cars and furniture for Mexican Americans and US tourists. After obtaining US citizenship, Lemus found work in an upholstery shop in San Diego, reupholstering the furniture of wealthy La Jolla residents. In Tijuana, he was a laborer, but in San Diego, he was the foreman who oversaw the hiring process. He told me, "I pick the people who I want to work with. I am almost like the owner. I have been there like twenty-seven or twenty-eight years, so the business operates because of me."

Although the company Lemus worked for was located in San Diego—a city with a large Mexican American and Mexican immigrant population— he hired workers from Tijuana. He explained, "For the most part, I take people from Tijuana because I know them. When I am over there [San Diego], I only dedicate myself to work so I know very few people." Over the years, Lemus helped many neighborhood friends from Colonia Frontera find employment in his shop. He also helped his brother, a former police officer, find work in the United States after obtaining legal permanent residency. Although there were hundreds of young men who would be interested in working at the US-based upholstery shop, Lemus was selective about whom to integrate into the network. Lemus chose workers who were legal residents so he did not have to worry about paying smugglers to help them enter the United States. And by recruiting workers from his old neighborhood, Lemus did not have to provide housing for workers who lived in Tijuana, only a short car-ride away from the upholstery shop.

Yet even as the trust and mutual obligation that existed between childhood friends in Colonia Frontera served as a resource for many network members to gain access to US employment, institutional constraints prevented other members from enjoying the full benefits of this resource. Lorenzo (age forty-two), Manuel (age forty), and Juan (age fifty-two), had all worked in the United States without documents at one point in their lives. All three of these men lived within walking distance of Hugo and other border crossers. Yet none of the three could cross. They did not have legal documents to cross, and Juan was prohibited from entering the United States after he was caught smuggling others across. These respondents turned to friends in Colonia Frontera for social activities and emotional comfort but they were outside the network when it came to obtaining work in the United States. Neighborhood friends who did not have legal documents were unable to capitalize on resources from return migrants because the border effectively separated them from opportunities in the United States. The friends could migrate clandestinely to the United States, but doing so would mean leaving their families and friends, a sacrifice they chose not to make because they had just enough work in Mexico to get by. The residents who were most able to benefit from the information and assistance provided by return migrants were those who had legal documents to cross.

Replanting Hometown Ties in Tijuana

Colonia Frontera was populated by families who had migrated from the interior of Mexico and settled in Tijuana. In particular, my ethnographic fieldwork in neighborhoods introduced me to a small network of "stepwise return migrant" border commuters from an origin community in Central Western Mexico who had relocated to Tijuana. Daniel Rojas Sr. was an internal migrant from the state of Michoacán, who relocated to Tijuana after he could no longer find employment in the avocado industry. In Tijuana, he started a pottery-making business that employed all of his family members. For years, as the patriarch of the family, Daniel Sr. ran a successful pottery-making business until many of his former employees started their own businesses and soon began to oversupply the market. Displaced from their previous livelihood activities in the early 1980s, many family members migrated to Los Angeles to diversify the household income. After living in the United States and obtaining legal permanent residency, the family returned to Tijuana where they became border commuters. With their US earnings and residence in Mexico, the family purchased a large hacienda that became the neighborhood's center of economic activity. From the hacienda, the younger generation of the

Rojas family established an occupational network in which several neighborhood residents crossed the border to work in the junkyard business in San Diego.

At only thirty years old, Daniel Rojas Jr. was an experienced return migrant. He had thirteen years of US labor market experience in the car-salvaging industry of northern San Diego County. Daniel got his job at the junkyard through his father-in-law. Once he got the job, he began to integrate his four brothers and then several other friends into the car-salvaging occupational network. Eventually, Daniel's brothers and friends comprised half of the workforce at the junkyard:

SERGIO: Did you help your brother Arti get a job?

DANIEL: Yes, Arti, and my other brothers, and many others. . . . Everyone knows me. Acquaintances always greet me. When friends come, they say, "I am looking for work." They have a passport or a Green Card. And yes, I have provided employment to many people. I have helped many people. And even if they do not know [how to do the work], I give them a chance with small tasks at a time. . . . Just as I was helped, I help them.

In addition to helping his brothers and friends find work in the United States, Daniel also helped train these men by assigning them tasks that allowed them to gradually build skills. For example, when they were first hired, Daniel would have them sweep the floors; then, as they gained experience, they began to take apart engines. He also transported friends to and from the junkyard. This was a valuable service, considering that some of his friends had BCCs that provided them with authorization to visit the United States but not to work. One afternoon, while Daniel worked under the hood of his Oldsmobile, I asked him why he had helped so many neighbors. He responded:

I do not know. I do it because with my brother, well, he is my brother. But with friends, well, I think it is because, well, we all have to help people when they need the help. . . . Because if you give a hand to others, others will also give you a hand. . . . Also because I don't like to see people suffer. Helping them is good for yourself that you can help someone.

Here, Daniel describes a common pattern observed by migration scholars among Mexican immigrants in the United States.[18] Like their international migrant counterparts, border residents form ties with neighborhood friends that provides a base of social support to migrate and to gain access to US employment. Border crossers like Daniel helped friends so that in turn, they would "give him a hand" if he ever needed help. Daniel helped his siblings out of familial obligation, but he helped his friends because of their common experience as transplants from rural Michoacán who were attempting to adapt to a border life. By relocating to the border, Daniel's network expanded to not only include his friends and family members from his origin community but also migrants from other regions of Mexico. He was someone who helped not only his paisanos from Michoacán, but also new friends that he developed in Tijuana that wanted to obtain work in the United States.

The Unintended Consequences of Waiting

Up to this point, I have described networks that border residents crafted through face-to-face interactions in workplaces, streets, and neighborhoods. The narratives illustrated borderland residents' conscious efforts to craft networks with people they know to exchange information, resources, and goods. However, not all network ties emerge among known associates, and not all network ties are deliberately formed. In *Unanticipated Gains*, Mario Small found that childcare centers provided mothers with "opportunities for strangers to meet, for acquaintances to become friends, and for friends and acquaintances to exchange favors."[19] Thus placed-based face-to-face interaction are key factors in the formation of useful network ties. In Tijuana, the port of entry served a similar purpose for commuters. As people waited in slow-moving lines for inspection, they interacted and formed ties with complete strangers.

One twenty-three-year-old woman who crossed the port of entry several times a week noted, "Oh yes, you develop friendships. I think it's because sometimes you spend so much time [crossing] that you make friends there." According to many respondents, the wait time had increased since September 11, 2001, due to closer passport inspection by the US government. During this long and unpredictable wait, border commuters exchanged information about US job opportunities. Though the border was intended to confine individuals to one country or another and limit social interaction, the wait at the port of entry had the unintended consequence of providing a space for people to strike up conversations about topics ranging from where to find the best sales to who was hiring in the United States. Though hearing word of a job opportunity does not always lead to an actual job outcome, my observations at the port of entry revealed that the exchange of labor market information at the point of crossing fostered ties among strangers as they were forced to wait.

Every morning, thousands of people left their neighborhoods by car, taxi, or bus to head toward La Linea (the port of entry). Once there, the time it took to cross the US-Mexico border by foot varied depending on the time of day. During my stay in Tijuana, my shortest border crossing experience was fifteen minutes, and my longest was two hours. As early as 4:00 a.m. (sometimes much earlier), the port of entry in San Ysidro was packed with foot and car traffic en route to the United States. While waiting in line, I documented in my notes the names of companies advertised on the door panels of vehicles, such as Martínez Landscaping Company or Diego's Construction Company. Men and women also wore their work uniforms from the US Postal Service, McDonald's restaurant, Hilton hotel, and mechanic shops that displayed their US occupational affiliation. These crossers were likely US or legal permanent residents and did not have any fear in claiming their US occupational affiliation. In addition, some US companies directly advertised in Tijuana about employment opportunities. For example, at the entrance to the port of entry in 2004, the Viejas Casino had a billboard with the tagline "Fabulous Employment for Fun People" accompanying a photo of a Latino-appearing man and a phone number for further information. During the morning rush hour, the labor power that Tijuana provided to neighboring San Diego County was highly visible.

While visual images conveyed information about American employers, most information about jobs was exchanged in encounters between crossers at the port of entry. I observed many instances in which border migrants exchanged information about wage rates, working conditions, and job openings in the United States. In fact, the questions I asked border commuters about their jobs in the United States were sometimes mistaken to mean that I was looking for a job. During one experience at the port of entry, I asked an airport employee how he had obtained his job. He began to give me "insider tips," including where to apply and how I should present myself at the airport. He also explained that jobs at the airport tended to pay higher wages than most entry-level low-skilled jobs. It was through these experiences that I became interested in learning more about how labor market information flowed through the port of entry.

During one of my border crossing experiences, I observed two women in their early forties as they crossed the port of entry at 5:50 a.m. One woman was taking her child to school in the United States while the other woman was headed to work at a five-star hotel. Though hundreds of people were dropped off by taxis and buses at the port of entry at that time, these two women who knew each other managed to end up in line together. The employed woman explained that she had recently taken her son with her during a "take your child to work" day. She intended to show him how difficult it was to labor in low-wage jobs, but "my son said that he wanted to leave school so he could work at the hotel!" The hotel employee went on to explain how she had moved up the job ladder from low-paying, privately owned hotels to a five-star hotel in La Jolla, California. According to the woman, she had worked at many "really bad and ugly" hotels where pay, benefits, and work conditions were poor. The mother then told the hotel employee that she was interested in working, but her husband did not want her to work. The hotel employee told her friend that if her husband ever let her work and she needed a reference, she should not hesitate to call. They continued to talk as they approached the customs officers, passed inspection, and boarded the San Diego trolley headed north.

Border crossers also shared labor market information as they traveled to their jobs on the San Diego trolley from Tijuana to their jobsites. I regularly observed people talking about their work experiences and exchanging job information. In one instance, I observed a Chicano in his mid-twenties, whose name, Joaquín, was printed on a white patch on his blue work uniform, as he spoke to another Chicano as they returned to Tijuana from their workday. Joaquín worked for a roofing company. He explained to the stranger that his boss was hiring entry-level workers for $9 per hour. After I joined the conversation, Joaquín explained that his company had recently hired two unauthorized workers from Tijuana. Those workers were too eager to impress and had unfortunately fallen while climbing a ladder with heavy roofing materials. As a result, the company needed replacement workers. Joaquín told us that roofing was a great job because the earnings compensated for the rigors of the work. Additionally, he explained that his employers paid for his training in the United States. This additional training enabled him to earn $30 an hour working an eight-hour shift. He pulled his paycheck from his back pocket to show us the $467 he had earned working only sixteen hours during the Fourth of July week. Before Joaquín got off the trolley, he gave us the name and phone number of the company in case we were interested in pursuing a roofing career.

I also observed border residents casually exchanging employment information in *taquerias* and bars en route to the port of entry or after returning from the United States. During these encounters, border commuters discussed the jobs they held, divulged how much they had earned, and complained about coworkers or the fact that their wages did not reflect their hard work. The exchange of information about employment opportunities was often a way to strike up a conversation with friends or to kill time, but sometimes these conversations had an economic incentive as well. In one instance, I boarded a collective taxi headed from the working-class neighborhood where I lived to the port of entry. One passenger told the driver that he sent $400 each month to his family in southern Mexico. The passenger was able to send that amount of money because his monthly rent in Tijuana was much cheaper than in California. He was able to make this money as an independent plumber. He told the taxi driver that he had recently completed an $800 plumbing job that only took him three days. To complete the job, he paid three of his friends from Tijuana $100 each and kept $500 for himself. As he recounted his quick earnings, another passenger in the taxi turned and asked, "How often do you need workers?" They then exchanged information as they got out of the cab.

During my time in Tijuana, I followed border commuters as they crossed the US-Mexico border and provided help to others. Pablo Torres (age forty-three) was a lawnmower mechanic who crossed the border every morning to drop off his son at a US high school by 7:00 a.m. He was not required to work until 10:30 a.m, so he had about two hours of free time each morning. Over the course of twenty years, Pablo developed extensive labor market experience. Throughout his time working in the United States, he learned various strategies to navigate US labor markets. He had obtained jobs through family and friendship contacts, newspaper advertisements, and employment agencies. He had also worked in both Los Angeles and San Diego County. When he first arrived in the United States, he worked as a dishwasher, factory worker, gardener, and finally as a small engine mechanic for landscaping equipment.

Because he knew the binational labor market well, Pablo often assisted others in finding work. On numerous occasions, I watched him counsel a group of Mexican day laborers from Tijuana at a restaurant just on the other side of the port of entry. Pablo taught these day laborers how to present themselves to employers, where to apply for jobs, and how to keep a job once they obtained it. He also introduced day laborers to new hiring sites away from the border and to home improvement stores near urban middle-class neighborhoods. Pablo explained to these laborers the advantages of working in white suburbs where residents and local police were more tolerant of men waiting for work on street corners. By working far away from the US-Mexico border, he advised, BCC holders were less likely to be targeted by immigration officials. He explained that suburban employers often paid higher wages than their counterparts in southern San Diego County because there was less Mexican labor competition. In fact, the average hourly wages reported by day laborers at the border were $7–$8 per hour, but in affluent areas, wages were as high as $12 per hour.

Although Pablo was generous in providing assistance and advice, he restricted his help to those who had successfully crossed the US-Mexico border. He reported seldom-provided job assistance to neighbors in Colonia Matamoros, despite the neighborhood's large internal migrant population who likely moved to Tijuana to become part of cross-border labor market. He did not provide extensive assistance because his ties were formed along occupational and border networks that were restricted to people with legal documents. One border commuter commented to me that Pablo was a good guy. Pablo had given his business card to this commuter in case he needed advice on finding gardening work. However, Pablo also saw sharing his card as a potential way to make money. In case the commuter or his contacts ever needed a lawnmower repaired, the commuter might remember Pablo's help and the business information on his card.

Stories like these illustrate that even as the border can serve as a barrier that limits social interaction, it also provides a place where interaction can lead to cooperation. This cooperation does not occur only among commuters but also between border commuters and immigration officials. On one occasion, I observed an interaction between a Latina immigration officer and a Mexican commuter who was obtaining a SENTRI permit at the US-Mexico border.[20] In the process of obtaining the permit, the Latina immigration officer asked the commuter about his occupation. The border commuter replied that he was building homes along the Baja California coast, just south of Tijuana. The Latina immigration officer responded that she was interested in buying a house near the coast, and the commuter told her about how much houses cost and where she might find good housing. This was an interesting exchange, in which a commuter provided a Latina immigration officer with information on how to find a place to live in Tijuana, not the United States. This was just one example of how daily interactions challenged firm boundaries at the US-Mexico border.

This is not to say that simply being at the port of entry necessarily translates into labor market opportunities. It does not. Yet cases of cooperation illustrate that the port of entry provides a space where border residents craft networks through interactions with strangers as they are forced to wait. At the same time, it is important not to underestimate the power of the state in shaping opportunities at the border. Only those who were able to line up and cross with either a Green Card or BCC were able to access this community of crossers and their information about employment opportunities in the United States.

Numerous ethnographies document how people form networks through sustained interaction in organizations and institutions. Mitchell Duneier's *Slim's Table* shows how African Americans at a Chicago restaurant formed collective solidarity through face-to-face interaction over a long period of time.[21] Javier Auyero's ethnography of poor Argentinians' welfare-office visits meanwhile illustrates how the forced wait led to "informal interactions [that] also serve to exchange information about existing soup kitchens, the availability and prices of housing in the city, required paperwork for a specific welfare plan."[22] Given the importance of place in network formation, Mario Small argues that sociologists should no longer think of diners, welfare offices, beauty salons, or churches only in terms of their intended purposes but also in terms of the unintended ways in which they foster interaction and human relationships.[23] The port of entry acted as a space for the development of an informal community of border crossers who had the common experience of having to wait, often for unknown and extended periods of time, at the border for CBP agents to let them enter the United States. This wait allowed for information exchanges about everything from getting a job to learning about the rules for crossing the border among strangers. Thus, for those with a certain level of access, the border fostered interaction that provided concrete resources and opportunities to border residents.

Conclusion

In this chapter, I have presented various snapshots of border residents' social ties to kin and friends that they formed in their workplaces, neighborhoods, and at the port of entry. These ties were important resources for border residents that provided information about and access to the US labor market. Scholars who write about Tijuana have historically depicted the city as a "trampoline" that migrants use as a jumping point to the United States. While many migrants may indeed use Tijuana in such a temporary manner, many border residents also craft long-term social ties in the borderlands that provide access to employment in both Mexico and the United States. The case of network formation at the borderlands illustrates the varied strategies people employ to find the contacts they need in a socially and economically diverse urban context.

As we have seen, the constant movement of people across the US-Mexico border means that Tijuanenses have access to information, ideas, and resources about US labor markets. Unlike their international migrant counterparts who depend primarily on ties to kin and friends from their hometowns, border residents are enmeshed in a broad network of people with varied labor market and migration histories that span both sides of the border. As a result, when internal migrants arrive at the border, they seek to craft ties to people with US experience. Rubén, as we saw, networked on a regular basis in his quest to join the ranks of the thousands of people who cross the border every day. This meant establishing ties to current and former migrants and even tourists through his place of employment. Although these ties were important in his incorporation to Tijuana, unfortunately they did not provide him with adequate information, knowledge, and assistance to allow him to obtain a BCC as he wanted. This illustrates that although Tijuanenses may have diverse network ties, we must not forget the limitations of human bonds in a region marked by intense border enforcement.

It is important to note, however, that not all ties in Tijuana were formed solely for the purpose of crossing the border. When men could no longer cross the border, they relied on women with more extensive Tijuana networks to create new relationships that would allow them to find employment on the Mexican side. Mustafa Emirbayer and Jeff Goodwin argue that social network studies have "yet to provide a fully adequate explanatory model for the actual formation, reproduction, and transformation of social networks."[24] In this chapter, I have shown how network members continually reconfigure their network ties through the course of daily interaction to increase access to goods and resources that allow them to seek livelihood strategies whether on one side of the border or another.

An interesting question that emerges from the case of Tijuana is why more people do not migrate or work in the United States, given the proximity of the border and the labor market information shared by residents. The narratives that I presented here provide some answers to this question. Networks are constrained by larger social forces, in particular the physical border and the immigration policies and laws that govern who can and cannot enter the United States. Unlike residents of the interior of Mexico, the Tijuanenses I studied were reminded of the power of the US-Mexico border every time they stepped outside of their homes and looked north. Only those with the means to cross the US-Mexico border—in most cases, those with a US passport, BCC, or Green Card—were able to benefit from the information and assistance that return migrants and border commuters brought back to Tijuana. Hence, while the narratives I have presented here illustrate how border residents challenge boundaries at the border, they also highlight the very real effects this physical and political boundary has had on people's movement. Ultimately, only a select few of Tijuana's population can cross the border to work or shop in the United States. As a result, we must not forget that people's creative agency to craft their livelihoods is shaped not just by how they utilize the resources at their disposal but also by political realities that block access to these resources or even snatch them away at a moment's notice.

CHAPTER 6 | Conclusion

| *Lessons from Tijuana*

TIJUANA, EL PASO, AND LAREDO are key hubs where millions of Mexicans and Central Americans have crossed to the United States over the course of more than a century. These border cities play an important role in the history of Mexico-US migration as a node of social networks and a "safe haven and staging area for crossing the border."[1] But these cities have grown beyond simple staging areas. Many return migrants now choose to settle in Mexican border cities like Tijuana rather than their place of birth.[2] This book uses historical and ethnographic methods to examine how different cohorts of migrants from Mexico's interior established roots in Tijuana and the strategies that they devised to lead social and economic lives that straddled the border. It also illustrates that while the border is a barrier to many livelihood options and lifestyle choices, it also provides opportunities for others. In response to this opportunity and constraint, individual human beings—despite or even because of their structural vulnerabilities—act within their social environment to enact livelihoods that are not perfectly contained by the boundaries of nation-states.

This final chapter addresses four major empirical and theoretical findings that emerged from this study of Tijuanenses: (1) individuals may combine migration and border commuting strategies across their life course; (2) labor market strategies sometimes transcend the border; (3) borderland residents employ diverse strategies to form useful social networks in a diverse urban context where knowledge can be applied to one side of the border or another; and (4) border crossers employ distinct strategies depending on the contemporary regulatory conditions and on personal circumstances. Together, these findings illustrate the unique experience of migrants who choose to establish roots in northern Mexico to build their lives as fronterizos.

These findings extend beyond Tijuana. They illustrate the generative potential of any region where two cities are divided by an international border that can be traversed by a binational labor market of workers. Similar circumstances exist in the European Union, Latin America, and other regions of the world. These findings also offer important lessons to sociologists regarding the interplay between structure and agency. Within the constraining social structure of the border, people agentically mined opportunities to construct their desired livelihoods through commuting, migrating, or some combination thereof: by working in the United States without authorization or purchasing goods with authorization and selling them in Mexico; by forming productive relationships in Tijuana, in the United States, and at the port of entry; and by converting US-based wages to sustain a Mexican lifestyle. Each one of these strategies was negotiated and renegotiated amid broad structural changes, such as the adoption of restrictive immigration policies and increased border enforcement that limited mobility across international borders. Despite facing considerable physical and political obstacles, border residents adapted to the dynamic social structure of the borderlands in their efforts to overcome disadvantage and inequality. However, some residents were more successful than others and even those who were successful relied on time and circumstance.

Ethnography at the Border

Historian George Sánchez writes that the border is "a social construct" and that the Mexican and US governments are actively involved in "creating" and "recreating" the border to suit the social and economic realities of the region.[3] Although Sánchez refers specifically to the first three decades of the twentieth century, his work applies to the contemporary context as well. One key theme of contemporary border studies is the contradiction between heightened border enforcement on the one hand and rapidly increasing global exchanges of money, ideas, and people on the other.[4] As suggested by Pablo Vila, instead of treating this contradiction as purely theoretical, it is important to delve ethnographically into the ways in which border residents, alongside state actors, participate in "recreating" the border as they negotiate this socially constructed barrier to mobility.[5]

In crafting my ethnographic study of the borderlands, I immersed myself in the lives of people who reside in one of the most highly policed areas along the US-Mexico border. I spent many days and nights visiting border residents in their homes and neighborhoods, and I observed their interactions as they crossed the port of entry. Ultimately, I produced an account showing that although the border constrains human mobility, it is also a place where people can creatively and strategically gain access to a binational livelihood. The lives of these border residents illustrate how "actors formulate new temporally constructed understandings of their own abilities to engage in individual and collective change, as well as how these micro level processes intersect with long-term social, political and economic trajectories."[6]

By focusing on shifts in border-crossing strategies over historical time and across individual life trajectories, I provide insight into how people alter their agentic activity to match the contemporary political economy.[7] One of my respondents once told me, "borders are not natural, they are made by man." As a Mexican citizen who observed physical changes in the border from her front door, this young woman was in a unique position to understand the divide between Tijuana and San Diego as a social and temporal construct. Despite the challenges the border presented to these residents, the stories I introduce in this book illustrate Tijuanenses' agentic potential to mobilize resources that broadened their economic opportunities in a constantly changing context. By studying the US-Mexico border at the ground level, I was able to understand border crossers' varied pathways to the US labor market. Ultimately, these choices were shaped by local political, economic, and social conditions that potential migrants and border crossers learned to negotiate by observing the experiences of other crossers and utilizing the networks they formed with coworkers, friends, and family. Through these relationships, border residents and migrants adapted to a rapidly changing world of global inequalities in which economic livelihoods were not restricted by national boundaries.

Although these border residents lacked political and economic power when compared to the employers and government officials who controlled their movement and labor, they found ways to overcome structural obstacles even if it was only short-lived. As men and women circulated across the border, they drew upon unique resources only available in the borderlands. The life stories that I gathered illustrate on-the-ground strategies for dealing with rising economic insecurity in a globalized world where workers must transition between formal and informal labor markets, urban and agricultural work, legal and extralegal employment strategies, and national boundaries between the United States and Mexico to provide for their families.

Migration and Border Commuting Strategies

In this book, I have shown that Tijuanenses employ a variety of labor migration and border commuting strategies to establish roots in the borderlands. Border residents engaged in internal, international, and border commuting to find jobs in the borderlands, build new networks, and earn income with the goal of living lives that capitalized on the best of both worlds through access to higher wages in the United States and the cultural comforts of living in Mexico. Theories of international migration, especially from Mexico, are primarily based on the experiences of rural migrants, though scholars have recently begun to document migration patterns stemming from cities.[8] These studies tend to focus primarily on long-distance migration from origin communities to US destinations.[9] Such research describes the process through which migrants eventually transition from "sojourner" to "settler," either adapting to and settling in the United States or returning to their community of origin.[10]

Through my ethnographic research, I identified four major south-north and north-south migration strategies that borderlanders employed at various points in their lives to gain access to the US labor market or to settle permanently in Tijuana. First, I found a group of domestic migrants who were drawn from their rural communities to Tijuana with the intention of moving on to the United States, only to settle permanently after developing roots in the borderlands. Second, I identified "return migrants" from the United States, who chose Tijuana as their preferred destination rather than their place of origin. Third, I identified "stepwise migrants"—international migrants who generally moved from rural areas in Mexico to Tijuana for a temporary stay before obtaining the necessary resources and legal documents to move on to the United States. Some of these migrants remained in the United States while others returned to Tijuana as a preferred destination to form the fourth group, which I called "stepwise return migrants."[11] The patterns that I identified here contribute scholarship on the multistage approach that migrants use to access the US labor market.[12] These migrants utilized different migration strategies in their efforts to seek new livelihood options and to obtain the necessary resources such as gaining access to Border Crossing Cards to eventually become part of cross-border labor force.

In addition, I found that Tijuanenses used border commuting as a strategy to access US labor market opportunities without migrating internationally. These border commuters crossed through the port of entry on a daily basis to work in the United States but returned home at the end of the working day. This population of border residents consisted of return migrants as well as people with no experience of living in the United States. In her study of Tijuana, Elizabeth Fussell argues that "Tijuana holds attraction for US-bound migrants, as both a home-base and a staging ground, but its binational economy deters migration overall."[13] Through my research, I offer a new explanation for the phenomenon of limited migration stemming from Tijuana: Tijuanenses substitute border commuting for international migration. Border commuting thus becomes a strategy that people employ to gain access to the US labor market without having to reside abroad on a permanent basis. These workers' daily lives straddled the border as their work, consumption, and living practices encompassed more than one country. Thus, though border cities may not be primary labor migrant sending regions, they contribute to the US economy by sending workers to perform labor on a daily basis.

Michael Burawoy once theorized that migrant labor forces are maintained at the destination and renewed at the origin; however, in binational economies like that of Tijuana, this separation is not clear-cut; rather, maintenance and renewal may involve both countries.[14] For example, a border commuter who works in the United States and lives in Mexico may actually turn back to the United States for his children's education and healthcare, social resources that are necessary for the renewal of the labor force. The case of border commuters also shows that the choice of country where one will work, live, shop, or obtain education or healthcare varies according to individual needs and life trajectories even as it is influenced by broader transnational social, economic, and political processes.

The case of Tijuana suggests that we must rethink the strategies that migrants and nonmigrants employ to gain access to the US labor market and live transnational lives on a daily basis. As previous studies have suggested, border cities like Tijuana have become popular return destinations for former international migrants.[15] Although Tijuana's place in Mexico-US migration continues to develop, scholars have yet to consider how the experiences of border residents differ from their international counterparts. The life histories and everyday lives of the borderlands residents I studied revealed that their labor and migration strategies changed across time to adapt to changing social, political, and economic realities.

Tijuanenses utilized a wide variety of migration and border-commuting strategies to overcome systemic inequalities by migrating to different labor markets. The Bracero Program, for example, created a demand for Mexican labor that led to large waves of migrant populations who dispersed throughout the American Southwest. After the program ended, US agricultural employers in the borderlands encouraged ex-braceros to settle in the region as part of a commuter population that lived in Tijuana but crossed the border on a daily basis to work in neighboring San Diego County. Ex-bracero commuters integrated their friends and family into the labor force, creating a vibrant cross-border labor force that saw this form of labor mobility as an alternative to international migration.

The next cohort of border commuters benefitted from another US policy, the Immigration Reform and Control Act of 1986, which created a larger group of Green Card commuters who could circulate across the border. The acquisition of legal permanent residency allowed previous international migrants to settle in the borderlands as part of a cross-border labor force. Jorge Durand and his colleagues note that IRCA created a geographically mobile population that could "seek to find a steady job and hold it, avoiding mobility to minimize the risk of detection, resulting in the dispersal of Mexican migration to new destinations including New Jersey, New York, and North Carolina."[16] In addition, my study shows that IRCA created a legalized labor force in the new destination of Tijuana, where Green Card holders were able to cross the border for the purposes of work and consumption while living in Mexico. What these experiences illustrate is that migrants enacted agency within a context of immigration policies that enabled them to participate in a cross-border labor force.

The third cohort of border crossers lacks access to a Bracero Program or to IRCA. These border residents find new ways to join a cross-border labor force through the acquisition of BCCs. Taken together, these three cohorts reflect the complex interplay between individual agentic strategies to access the transnational labor market and broad structural changes in border and immigration regulations that unfolded over time. The border-crossing strategies I describe provided border residents with the opportunity to enter the US labor market as immigrants who settled abroad, migrants who circulated on a seasonal basis, or border commuters who crossed on a daily basis. Ultimately, the options available to these actors were contingent upon their ability to cross the border based on either relaxed border enforcement or access to legal documents. Political policies and physical structures altered access to this ability over time, producing changes in border-crossing strategies and practices but never fully curtailing them.

Labor market Strategies

Most scholarship on Mexican immigrants' labor market experiences focuses primarily on issues related to job search techniques, wages, and occupational mobility in the United States.[17] This book demonstrates that border residents' labor market and livelihood strategies were not restricted solely to the United States or Mexico but rather involved both sides of the border. Border residents constantly altered their livelihood strategies, sometimes choosing to work in the United States and other times working in Mexico. Some ex-braceros continued to cross the border to work in the United States because their employer networks provided them with access to legal permanent residency in the years following the bracero program. These men labored in low-wage jobs that provided long-term stability and some limited occupational mobility. Another group of ex-braceros decided to forgo working in the United States and instead reinvented themselves as urban workers seeking to modernize the expanding Tijuana economy. Ex-braceros' choices regarding these distinct labor market strategies, which defined their settlement intentions in Tijuana and their occupational careers, depended on economic and noneconomic motives. The frames that these workers drew on to explain their choices did not favor laboring on one side of the border or the other but rather depended on a variety of structural and personal factors. Thus, ex-braceros' occupational choices were shaped by the resources available to them as former peasants and migrant farmworkers who relocated to the city at a particular historical moment, when Tijuana was expanding and there were still employment opportunities in agriculture in San Diego County.

Border residents did not view working in the United States and Mexico as mutually exclusive labor market strategies. Some worked in the two countries at different times in their labor history while others held jobs in both places simultaneously. Cesar is an example of one such respondent who combined employment in Mexico and the United States. In addition to his regular employment in the US construction industry, Cesar ran an informal bar on the weekends. Similarly, Julio worked in a factory in San Diego County but on the weekends held garage sales from his home in Tijuana to earn extra income. Households also combined employment activities in the United States and Mexico. Ramón's household, for example, included some members who worked in the United States while others worked in Mexico. These examples demonstrate that varied transnational practices were essential to the lives of fronterizos.

The Mexican labor market was essential to the making of a binational labor force. Border residents strategically pursued full-time jobs in the formal labor market in Mexico as a strategy to gain BCCs. Through their participation in the Mexican labor market, workers also developed interpersonal skills that helped them cross the US-Mexico border to work. Once respondents had obtained the prized BCCs, they were able to expand their livelihood strategies across international boundaries. Some people used these cards to enter the formal labor market in the United States as unauthorized workers. Others used the cards to purchase household items at garage sales or in US stores, which they then resold to Tijuanenses who could not cross the border. Thus, in Tijuana, border residents developed creative strategies to expand their economic livelihoods in ways that capitalized on the respective advantages that the US and Mexican economies had to offer. Although some residents were able to derive their economic livelihoods from both sides of the border, it is important to note that their strategies were shaped by regulations that controlled who could cross the border and who could not.

Strategies for Forming Social Ties

Border residents formed network ties that provided them with information and resources for crossing the border. Most studies on networks in migration address rural migrants' use of close-knit hometown ties to migrate to the United States. However, Rubén Hernández-León theorized that migration from urban settings is not sustained by family and friendship ties in the same manner as in rural communities.[18] Rural communities are organized around close family and lifelong friendship ties that act as resources for potential migrants. However, the complex division of labor and anonymous relationships that are common in urban settings mean that urban migrants depend on a more expansive network of friends, neighbors, and schoolmates to provide a link to US labor markets.

In the absence of hometown ties, I found that border residents drew on the support of family, friends, neighbors, workmates, acquaintances, crossers, Mexican and US employers, and even strangers to obtain information and resources to cross the border. The migration history of Ramón García illustrates the varied ties that Tijuanenses draw upon across time and space. When Ramón first migrated to Tijuana, his aunt provided him with shelter and a warm meal. Then, to help him obtain his BCC, Ramón's employer provided him with steady employment and a letter of recommendation. When he lost his job in Tijuana, Ramón's compadre Fidel encouraged him to migrate to Los Angeles, where he provided Ramón with housing and helped him find a job with a produce warehouse. Then, when Ramón finally decided to become a legal permanent resident, his US employer wrote him a letter of support. Finally, his wife and children convinced Ramón to return to Mexico. By the time he settled in Tijuana, he was a seasoned migrant, and rather than receiving help, he began to help others. I was there when he helped his sons and many other migrants obtain employment in the United States. When I stood in the long line at the port of entry, Ramón's story helped me better understand how the simple act of "waiting to cross" concealed the many relationships and structural obstacles that are in play when an individual commutes to work in the United States and returns home to Tijuana.

In this book, I have attempted to uncover the network ties among friends, family, and neighbors as well as the interactions between border crossers and state agents that ultimately determined who could and who could not stand in line to cross the border. The border is more than a physical structure or a set of immigration policies and laws. It is a construct produced in and through dynamic social interaction among the people who must navigate it on a regular basis. In turn, the border also exerts a strong influence on residents' ability to activate social networks. Although many border residents had friends with international migration experience, those ties did not always translate into US jobs or the ability to migrate to the United States. This is because the US-Mexico border stood as a major barrier between people who wanted to cross and those who could provide resources that would facilitate that move. Cross-border networks were selectively organized such that a person could join the regional labor market—for example, as part of a US-based landscaping or construction crew— only if he or she had access to legal documents to cross the border. Thus, in the borderlands, legal status provided access to the social networks that enabled workers to capitalize on the economic systems of both sides of the border.

The complex ways in which border residents utilized network ties throughout their life histories illustrate that in a binational economy what matters is not just "who you know" but also knowing "who can help." In general, I found that border residents were very strategic when it came to mobilizing social ties and knew which family, friends, schoolmates, workmates, and strangers could afford them the necessary resources to accomplish their short- and long-term goals. In this case study of Tijuana, the formation of network ties on a continual basis exemplifies how border residents enacted agency to live a transborder life.

Border-Crossing Strategies

The book also offers a window into the changing border-crossing strategies that migrants have employed when the physical and political border restricted movement across international territory. My interviews with border residents revealed that people have used multiple methods to cross the border at different historical moments and for different purposes. Strategies for crossing the border depended in part on boundary enforcement, which varied across time. For example, transient crossers who came to Tijuana in the pre-Gatekeeper era solely to gain access to labor markets in the interior of the United States attempted to evade inspection at all costs, either by outwitting immigration officials or hiring coyotes to smuggle them across the border. During that same period, daily crossers were an integral part of the regional economy of San Diego County agriculture and their crossing was encouraged by US growers and tolerated by Border Patrol agents. The need for agricultural workers in South San Diego created a reserve army of labor that was shuttled back and forth across the US-Mexico border. At the time of my study, however, the growers that encouraged this cross-border labor force were no longer operating in the region, and the border was closed due to policy changes in the United States, rerouting most clandestine crossings away from Tijuana to remote desert areas. These historical practices were firmly embedded in the political economy of the period and shaped how people crossed the border and the strategies that they employed.

Unlike the earlier cohorts of crossers whose goal was to evade inspection, the cohort that crossed after 1994 confronted a heavily guarded border that diverted commuters to the US labor market through the port of entry. Clandestine crossings through Tijuana are rare in the modern era, and most unauthorized migration involves the use of false or borrowed documents. In comparison to migrants from other urban and rural sending communities, border migrants are more likely to enter the United States with legal documents on their first trip. Some 55 percent of Tijuana's migrants entered the United States as either a legal resident or with a Tourist Card, in comparison with only 22 percent and 15 percent for urban and rural migrants, respectively.[19]

Though legal permanent residents are allowed to enter the United States to live and work, individuals with BCCs or Tourist Cards are allowed to cross to the United States only for the purposes of travel and consumption. In this book, I have shown the importance of these documents as a source of access to extralegal work. Border commuters had to employ a variety of border-crossing techniques to enter the US labor market in a legal context where Mexicans are embraced as consumers but shunned as workers. As such, border crossers concealed their affiliation to the US labor market from immigration officials. One strategy this group of crossers employed was creating what Josiah Heyman terms a "plausible story,"[20] to illustrate their place in the consumer class and demonstrate knowledge of their ostensible purpose for crossing. Thus, this book provides new insights on the crossing behaviors of authorized crossers but unauthorized workers.

In my interviews with Tijuanenses, I discovered that border residents had an extensive collection of stories that they carried with them when they crossed the border that they were able to recite on the fly when questioned by immigration officials. Border crossers attempted to align their appearance and narratives with acceptable roles such as consumers, romantic partners, or even bodybuilders, as in the case of Rodolfo, who pretended that he only crossed the border to visit a gym. Other strategies consisted of concealing occupational networks and taking on a presumed middle-class identity by carrying cash and credit cards. Crossers were careful to rehearse their stories to avoid raising red flags when crossing the border.

New concepts are needed to describe the strategies of border crossers who must maintain a certain relationship with immigration officials in order to gain and keep BCCs. In this book, I have drawn on Erving Goffman to discuss the self-presentation work that border commuters engage in at the port of entry. In *Border Games*, Peter Andreas suggests that state actors engage in "face work" and the "art of impression management" as they present the appearance of well-regulated boundaries to the world.[21] In my work, I argue that the border is not only a stage for state actors but also for border residents, who must employ "face work" to enter the United States. The border crossers I spoke with recognized that although Tijuana was one of the most highly policed areas on the US-Mexico border, there was still a strong demand for foreign labor on the US side, so workers could potentially cross if they were able to mobilize the correct resources. One key method to overcoming the limitations to geographical mobility imposed by the border was the use of "strategic friendliness" to win the trust of immigration officials and avoid detection.[22] Some of the border crossers I met had crossed for years without work authorization by blending into the local cross-border population. Their ability to participate in the US labor market was an outcome of both individual strategies and US capitalist demand for Mexican workers. Border commuters used Goffmanian strategies to negotiate passage through a port of entry that had clamped down on unauthorized guests over the years. Although these border residents enacted agency by outwitting immigration officials, it is important to note that there was very little room for error. Any mishap could result in the confiscation of a BCC for life which made the enactment of altered selves especially crucial for one's livelihood.

Throughout the book we have seen that the border has been reinvented time and time again. In parallel, people have adapted to the border by creating livelihood opportunities to fulfil their personal needs and desires. However, the border has become more restrictive, making it much more difficult to live transnational lives of the respondents that I present here. The border will continue to change so long as the policies that govern immigration change. Therefore, sociologist should continue to study this ever-changing landscape, and its effects on people's everyday lives.

Epilogue
Border Lives a Decade Later

ON OCTOBER 7, 2013, I revisited several key respondents to learn how their lives had changed over the course of almost a decade. I revisited some of the main characters in this book, including border commuters and childhood friends Julio, Cesar, and Jorge, who grew up together in Colonia Frontera, and Ramón García, who appears throughout the book. I also visited Aurelio and his sons, Rubén and Armando, who had moved to the border but were unsuccessful in obtaining BCCs that they planned to use to shop and work in the United States. In this epilogue, I describe the changes these central characters experienced in relation to three major themes: their legal status and migration intentions; their working lives; and their family lives. By revisiting these border residents almost a decade after my initial research, I was able to investigate longitudinally how the lives of respondents changed as they encountered new challenges across time. What I found was that people's agentic capacity depended on a variety of macrostructural processes, including the state of the US and Mexican economies and immigration and border-enforcement policies. Their actions were further influenced by the personal, micro-level factors that altered their aspirations for self and family, as well as their ability to achieve those aspirations. This epilogue is intended to document these changes in people's lives with special attention to their feelings, vulnerabilities, and strengths. The findings demonstrate that while the border may be both an opportunity and a constraint on livelihoods, it is essential to understand these processes longitudinally. They show that over the long run, it was difficult for these residents to sustain their border livelihoods given their marginal legal and economic status.

Legal Status and Migration Intentions

Many of the borderlands residents I interviewed for this book migrated to Tijuana with the intention of gaining access to legal documents to cross the border such as a BCC. Some were able to obtain these documents to craft transnational livelihoods, while others ultimately gave up this goal and instead sought upward mobility within Tijuana's urban labor market. On my revisit to Tijuana, I found that these legal statuses had shifted again as a result of personal choices and individual circumstances—some for better, and some for worse. As border enforcement has increased and the state is now scrutinizing BCC and Green Card applicants more closely, these respondents will likely have a much more difficult time reobtaining their crossing privileges.

Julio, Jorge, and Cesar

Julio was one of the few fronterizos I met who was born and raised in Tijuana. Since I last saw him, Julio had gained weight and lost much of his hair. He continued to live with his mother and extended family in a three-bedroom hilltop house with a clear view at night of the stadium lighting along the US side of the border. When I revisited Julio and asked if he was still crossing the border on a daily basis, he shook his head and said, "No, I let it [my Green Card] expire, but my brothers are going to help me get it back. It is going to cost me $450 to get my Green Card back!"

Julio's Green Card was revoked when immigration officials became aware that he was not residing in the United States and that he had not been consistently employed in the US formal labor market. Jorge and Cesar (his childhood friends) criticized Julio for losing such a valuable resource. Jorge believed that Julio was a "fuck-up" who had done nothing with his life and so deserved to lose his Green Card. In addition to losing his Green Card, by 2013, Julio's gambling problem had also worsened. He could not afford the $450 it would take to renew his expired documents because he had lost all of his money betting at the local Caliente Race and Sports book. Jorge stated, "Give him $20 dollars and he will spend all night trying to double or triple it. But he will end up losing it by the end of the night." Without the ability to cross, Julio depended on others to bring him garage sale items from the United States, which he then resold in Tijuana. In comparison to when he worked in the US formal labor market, Julio was barely making ends meet and depended on his family for support.

Although Jorge criticized Julio for losing his Green Card, he too had let his BCC expire, just over two years before. At the time, Jorge did not have enough money to pay the renewal fee and chose not to borrow money to pay it. When I first met him, he would get a rush out of crossing the border, getting great garage sale deals, and eating out at Denny's and Jack-in-the-Box. But over the years, he stopped feeling the same rush. As a result, he chose to not renew his BCC and instead was attending night school to become a full-time physical-education instructor.

The third of the three childhood friends, Cesar, was also no longer a border commuter. Jorge told me that Cesar, who liked to "live it up," had also "fucked up" by hanging out with the wrong crowd. Cesar loved driving nice cars and living in a nice home. However, his work in the US construction industry did not pay enough to buy expensive cars and keep up with his new wealthy fronterizo friends. To keep up with a high-cost lifestyle, Cesar tried to earn money illegally by crossing a vehicle with marijuana. He was immediately caught by Customs and Border Protection, jailed, and lost his Green Card most likely for life. In 2005, all three of these childhood friends crossed the border on a regular basis to work or buy groceries. In 2013, none could cross to take advantage of the benefits of living in the borderlands.

There are multiple ways to interpret this change in the lives of Julio, Jorge, and Cesar. One could explain the loss of their crossing documents as the product of "bad choices." Yet for each, the goals had changed over time, such that crossing the border to shop or to participate in the labor market was no longer a personal aspiration. In this sense, their choices were perhaps neither good nor bad but simply personal. In addition, regardless of how one interprets their motivations, their experiences and actions illustrate that Julio, Cesar, and Jorge were also in vulnerable positions within the transnational social structure. Just as Julio gambled with his money, all three men gambled with and lost their legal documents. There is no guarantee that any of these men will ever again be able to cross the border in the same way as when I first met them. Without the ability to cross, their economic options are now even more limited.

Rubén and Lupe, Armando and Christina

I also visited Rubén, who initially migrated to Tijuana with the intention of moving on to the United States. When I first met Rubén in 2004, he dreamed of obtaining a BCC to work in the United States or to buy US goods to resell in Mexico. Over the past decade, his desire to go to the United States had fluctuated based on his earnings in Mexico and his interest in trying a new occupation. By 2013, however, he was firm in his desire to migrate to the United States. At one point, Rubén was able to earn a good living as a taxi driver, due to the rapid growth of his neighborhood, but after more drivers entered the market he started to struggle economically. Despite having recently moved with his wife Lupe to a new home subsidized by the Mexican government, Rubén told me, "I now want to go to the US. I want to get my Visa so I can go work in the US."

Later that night, I spoke to Rubén's brother Armando, who told me that just a few months before, Rubén had raised the idea of crossing clandestinely to migrate to Los Angeles. Armando and his father were able to convince him to abandon the plan because crossing would both risk his life and involve leaving his wife and children behind. Another reason why Rubén decided to stay put in Tijuana—though he never admitted it—was that his wife, Lupe, had lost her BCC. She was therefore stuck in Mexico and waiting until she could reapply for a BCC. However, she would likely not be able to obtain one, because it was taken away for giving birth to her and Rubén's third child while in the United States.

Whereas residents like Julio, Cesar, Jorge, and Lupe had lost their crossing privileges, in 2013, Armando had finally been able to obtain a BCC, eight years after his first application. When I had last seen Armando, he had been disillusioned after three failed attempts at a BCC. On the last attempt, which coincided with a difficult romantic breakup, the US immigration official had asked Armando, "What is your hurry?" Armando had decided instead to put his energy into bodybuilding and finding alternative ways to generate additional income in Tijuana.

In December 2012, Armando tried again for a BCC and this time he was approved, along with his new girlfriend, Christina. Armando said he attributed their success to the fact that "my girlfriend and I got a really nice white American [immigration official]." Before going to their appointment at the US consulate, Armando recalled preparing himself by practicing what he would say to immigration officials. He spoke to several friends, gathering information about what techniques had worked for those who had got it and had failed for those who had not. He also hired a notary, who helped him fill out and organize his paperwork and who gave him advice. Armando said that his notary told him "to just say that we wanted to visit the US and nothing else." The notary continued, "You have to be stoic and answer questions honestly. You should not give them more information than what they ask you for."

"We memorized everything that was in our packet," recalled Armando and Christina. After their strategy had proved successful, Armando and Christina used their BCC to drive to Los Angeles. There they rekindled their relationship with Carmen (his brother Rubén's sister-in-law), who had used Tijuana as a stepping-stone to migration. By visiting Carmen and her husband in Los Angeles, Armando rekindled that connection which would serve as a resource he could draw on if he ever needed to work in the United States.

These updated life histories show that border residents' strategies change across the life course. Though these narratives illustrate different ways in which people enact agency, readers must not forget that the border in its physical and legal manifestations plays a powerful role in regulating who can cross the border and take advantage of resources in Mexico and the United States. For example, Armando's plans of moving to the United States were continually impeded by his legal status. While the decision to move to a new location to find a job is normally difficult, Armando's lack of a BCC gave him an additional set of obstacles to overcome. Only through persistence and careful planning was Armando finally able to obtain a BCC. Meanwhile, for Julio, Jorge, Cesar, and Lupe, their ability to cross was at the whim of the state, particularly in this historical period were mobility was increasingly restricted.

Working Lives in the Borderlands

People are structurally vulnerable due to their legal status and economic situation. Changes in the state of the Mexican and American economies and labor markets altered people's transnational livelihood strategies over the years. Obstacles to finding jobs presented themselves on both sides of the border, and, border residents attempted to enact strategies to overcome these obstacles. However, sometimes the obstacles proved insurmountable, especially for a population that lacked education, advanced training, and formal labor market experience. For some, age and health were also factors.

Julio and Jorge

After his Green Card expired, Julio began to search for employment in Mexico. Julio was notorious among his friends for his inability to hold onto a steady job. He did not like the structure of working eight-to-five because it conflicted with his enjoyment of the nightlife in bars and clubs or sports-betting facilities. As a result, he jumped from job to job. As of 2013, Julio worked as a delivery driver for a pharmacist, but the work was very sporadic.

Jorge let his BCC lapse after deciding to become a physical-education instructor. Yet at fifty-five years old, Jorge found it difficult to obtain full-time employment in Mexico, where employers prefer to hire younger workers. As a result, he struggled to make ends meet by teaching physical education part-time at a local school. He hoped that his enrollment in night school would help him find a full-time job, which he desperately needed now that he was unable to supplement his income by crossing the border to buy used goods for resale in Tijuana.

Armando and Rubén

In 2013, Armando was succeeding financially. He had purchased piece of land for $30,000 dollars and then spent an additional $50,000 to build a house and an automotive body shop, all of which he paid for with cash. He had entered into a business partnership with a Green Card holder, who grew tired of crossing the border and "wasting so much of his life" at the port of entry. Before becoming a body-shop mechanic, Armando had worked for a meat distribution center. He earned about $150 a week plus commission, and during the Christmas season he earned as much as $10,000 a month according to him. Yet at the body shop, he was able to more than double his income, which was already "not a bad wage for Mexico."

After obtaining his BCC, Armando regularly attended auctions to buy wrecked automobiles. When I visited him at his home, he showed me a 2011 Kia that he had purchased in San Diego for $2,200. After spending an additional $2,000 to fix it up, he believed that he could turn around and sell it back to a US buyer for $9,000, leaving him a $5,000 profit. He also showed me a Jeep Grand Cherokee that he had purchased for $3,700 and spent $2,000 rebuilding. He thought he needed to spend an additional $500 before he could sell it for $10,000. Armando and his father also now owned seven taxis, five more than the previous time I had visited. They charged drivers $33 a week to rent each taxi.

Armando and his girlfriend, Christina, had big plans for their BCCs. Both Christina and Armando planned to take English classes, and Christina planned to eventually enroll in a US college to become a veterinarian because she liked math and biology. Both were full of excitement; Armando told me that he had already gotten the most out of Mexico, and "now it's time to try new things in the US." Purchasing wrecked automobiles in the United States and reselling them to customers on both sides of the border was a first step toward these new experiences, but Armando felt that he currently had only one foot in the United States. Ideally, he would like to have both feet in the United States to capitalize fully on the possibilities that the US labor market had to offer. His goal was to someday become a legal permanent resident and work out of the United States rather than out of Mexico.

Armando had sold a taxi to Rubén for $3,500 dollars to replace his first one, which Rubén paid in weekly installments. Rubén also made extra money as an informal mechanic for taxi drivers and others on the weekends. He bought used automotive tools from his neighbor and compadre, who earned a living by regularly traveling to the United States to purchase used clothing that he then cleaned and resold in Tijuana swap meets. Though Armando succeeded financially, his brother Rubén continued to struggle as a taxi driver and mechanic in Tijuana's economy. Even for two brothers with similar levels of education, differences in their work ethic and starting positions in the labor market produced stark differences in their economic outcomes.

The narratives from these border crossers illustrate that some people were able to find their economic niche in Tijuana, others in the United States, and some in both. Over the course of almost a decade, these border residents exercised agency by combining formal and informal employment on both sides of the border. However, border residents occupied a precarious position in these labor markets. In response to precariousness, some were able to reinvent themselves, like the young and energetic Armando. Others, like Jorge, had to take extra steps in order to navigate a labor market that valued youth over age. In general, job prospects as a whole were dwindling due to bad choices, limited opportunities, and massive changes to the economy.

Family Life in the Borderlands

Individual aspirations and broad social-economic forces were not the only factors that influenced borderland residents' actions. These individuals were also embedded within families that constrained them from making certain choices and encouraged them to make others. Border and immigration policies may benefit some family members and exclude others, disrupting the flow of everyday life. The ability to cross the border creates a divide among families in which some people possess a BCC.

Armando and Christina

Although Armando and Christina were excited to obtain their BCC, the acquisition of the card also disrupted the normal pace of life for the young couple and their family. On weekends, it was customary for Armando and Christina to spend their time with his father and mother by taking a trip to a mall, to the beach in Tijuana or Rosarito, or to Mexicali to the homes of relatives. The BCC provided Armando and Christina with a range of new options for their weekend, allowing them to visit amusement parks, restaurants, and malls in Los Angeles and San Diego. Yet because his parents and brother Rubén could not cross, Armando had to sacrifice his time with his family when he and Christina chose to take advantage of these opportunities. When I spoke to Armando about this, he stated that he was sad but remained hopeful that his father and brother would someday be able to obtain a BCC. He worried, however, that this was unlikely because his father was once caught crossing the border without documents and a record of this violation was probably stored, along with his father's fingerprints, in a US government database.

Rubén and Lupe

Rubén and his wife, Lupe, had struggled in their marriage for a few years before I visited them again in 2013. Rubén initially attributed their difficulties to financial trouble. He thought that if he were a better provider and earned more money, then his marriage would be better off. But over the past few months, he had realized he would need to devote time to his wife and family to repair the marriage. His priorities shifted, and he stopped working on Sundays to spend time at home. Realizing that his immediate concern was his marriage, not money, Rubén decided to postpone his goal of crossing the border, to be closer to his wife.

The stories of Armando and Rubén show how family ties could be strained by the ability or inability to cross the border. Though Armando and Christina grew closer during their outings, Armando's relationship with his family suffered. Likewise, Rubén decided to prioritize his family over the financial advantage that came with crossing the border.

Ramón

At eighteen, to overcome rural poverty in Jalisco, Ramón migrated to Tijuana, where he was able to obtain employment as a construction worker and find a better future. When I first met him in 2004, he told me the story of using his first wages to buy a kilogram (2.2 pounds) of *carnitas* (fried pork), which according to him cured his childhood hunger. By moving to Tijuana, he was able to expand his livelihood options: first, by working in Tijuana, and then by joining the ranks of thousands of people who crossed the border on a daily basis to work in construction. Ramón found work in the urban labor market and eventually obtained a BCC. However, he lost his job after breaking his leg, which occurred at the same time as the peso devaluation. Nonetheless, he still had the BCC at his disposal, so he utilized it to migrate to Los Angeles, where he obtained work and eventually got his Green Card through IRCA.

He worked as a crew leader and earned as much as $1,800 dollars a week. He was able to employ his sons Ángel and Richard, and paid them $1,000 per week. By any measure, Ramón had achieved social mobility; he had even built a nine-bedroom house for his children. Yet one day it all came to an end. His former boss committed suicide, and the company closed. Ramón and his three children lost their jobs. All three found other employment, but soon both of Ramón's sons lost their BCCs—Ángel's to a dispute with a CBP agent, and Richard's as it fell from the back pocket of his jeans. Richard was unable to get a new BCC after the loss because he could not prove that he worked in Mexico. Still, Ramón continued to cross the border and continued to make the best of the opportunities he had. He was a man who never believed in giving up and was willing to do what it took to provide food for his family.

Almost a decade later in October 2014, I revisited Ramón. His physical change over the past ten years was dramatic: he had lost 15 pounds; his entire beard had greyed, and he had lost most of his hair; he was missing two teeth, had developed diabetes, and now wore glasses. Despite these signs of age on his body, he still had the energy of an eighteen-year-old. He awoke at 2:45 every morning and was out the door within ten minutes. After leaving his house, Ramón walked about a block down the hill to wait in the parking lot of a pharmacy for his taxi to the port of entry. With few taxi drivers working that early in the morning, Ramón depended on his personal relationship with his taxi driver, Filly, whom he knew by name. On their way to the port of entry, they usually talked about one another's children, soccer, and politics.

Once Ramón passed inspection at the port of entry, usually after 4:00 a.m., he bought a trolley ticket to ride to the Palomar station. From there, he walked about twenty minutes toward Broadway, arriving at a donut shop at around 5:00 a.m. He spent the next hour relaxing, reading the newspaper, eating donuts, and drinking coffee. Because his blood sugar level dropped easily, Ramón normally spent about $15–$20 a day eating out. By the time he started work at 6:00 a.m., he had already spent three hours on his commute. It took him another hour or so to return back home, adding an extra four and a half hours to his workday.

In the past, he used to drive his semi-new Honda Accord to the United States, but Ramón could not afford to buy a new car or fix the old one because he was unable to secure steady employment since the great recession of 2007–9. When I met him in 2004, Ramón had purchased three new cars, but because of the recession he had sold two of them. The third, the Honda Accord, could no longer be driven in the United States due to mechanical problems. There was a dent in the right side, and it would not pass a California smog test because the check-engine light came on. Not having a car to drive to San Diego County or beyond severely restricted Ramón's labor market mobility, resulting in the lengthy commute.

Ramón earned $12.00 per hour working in the United States for a labor contractor, but he could have earned more if he had a working car. The labor contractors often sought men for jobs up and down the state of California, but Ramón was unable to take advantage of these opportunities unless he could find a willing coworker to drive him. Furthermore, Ramón was unwilling to stay away from home for two weeks at a time. He had spent most of his life away from his family as a young man, and he refused to do that again.

He was deeply in love with his wife, Chelo, even after some forty years of marriage. I had never seen a man so in love with a women before. Ramón considered himself the luckiest man in the world. When talking about his wife he would often say "está retechula mi mujer" ("my wife is the most beautiful woman"). On their living room wall, Ramón and Chelo kept a photograph from their wedding in 1971. When Chelo first met Ramón, she knew that he was the one she wanted to spend the rest of her life with. Back then, Ramón was a journeyman on a construction crew. They married within a year of meeting, and within the next year, Chelo gave birth to their first daughter, who now lived in San Diego where she was awaiting her Green Card.

At the time of the revisit, I arrived at Ramón's house just as he returned from a twelve-hour workday tearing up a concrete floor in Chula Vista.

His blue jeans, long-sleeved sweater, and tennis shoes were saturated with cement dust. He also had a difficult time breathing and kept pulling out his handkerchief to blow his nose. When Ramón walked in the door, he shook my hand, and said, "Come here Sergio, and pick up my backpack!" I lifted the backpack and was surprised by the weight, which he told me was almost thirty pounds. Curious, I asked what was inside. Ramón reached down to open the backpack and out popped a bunch of copper wire that he had hauled from his demolition job in the United States to resell in Tijuana. He said that in the United States, copper was worth a little over $1.00 per pound, but in Mexico he sold it for about 60 pesos, or just over $5 dollars per pound. Once he sold the copper wire, he planned to "take Chelo out for a really nice dinner."

That night Ramón, Chelo, and I headed to their favorite hole-in-the-wall restaurant. Over dinner, Ramón described his history, explaining that he was the only one of his siblings who lived in Tijuana. In 1970, his father had driven him from Jalisco to Tijuana to stay with his aunt, and Ramón did not see his parents or siblings again until some two decades later. His only family now, he told me, was his wife and children. In fact, he liked to say that his life began in Tijuana, not in Jalisco. Even though for many Mexicans, it is common to claim direct or symbolic ties to one's place of birth, Ramón had none. Tijuana was the place where he lived his life.

Through the course of my research, I met many men and women who relocated to Tijuana to start a new life. These people told me that when they came to Tijuana, they knew no one, but over the course of many years, they established new ties in the borderlands. They do not claim to be unique; rather, their experiences are similar to those of many other fronterizos who arrived in Tijuana with the intention of crossing to the United States but stayed for one reason or another, or who crossed and then migrated back to Tijuana, or who simply came to take advantage of Tijuana's urban economic boom. Though Ramón broke off all ties with his birth family, he was able to create a new one, and thus new ties in Tijuana.

During our conversation, Ramón and Chelo updated me on family news. Their son Richard had divorced his wife, Maria. Chelo claims the divorce was precipitated by Richard's loss of his BCC; Maria ended up moving in with a man who was a legal permanent resident and could cross the border. Ángel, who had had his BCC confiscated, was making $350 a week but wanted to find a job that would pay $500 to reach the same wage level as a US worker. Ramón and Chelo advised him that he should be happy to have a well-paying job, particularly in Mexico. After the loss of the BCC, both Richard and Ángel moved in with their parents. Ramón and Chelo considered this a blessing. Years ago, when I first met Ramón, he told me that he was sad because he had built his house with so many rooms, yet none of his children lived in them. Today, three of his children resided at home: Esther, Richard, and Ángel. After dinner, Ramón and Chelo drove me to the bus station. On the way there, Ramón told me that although he was struggling economically, he was optimistic that the economy would get better. However, he was worried about Chelo because she was scheduled for open-heart surgery in a couple of weeks.

The Passing of Chelo

Approximately, three weeks after I left Tijuana after my final research trip, I learned that Ramón's worst fear had come true. Chelo had passed away during her open-heart surgery. Ramón was devastated by the loss. Throughout his life, Ramón had been able to overcome structural obstacles like poverty, discrimination, joblessness, and underemployment, but the one obstacle he was unable to recover from was the passing of the love of his life, "la mujer mas retechula."

Throughout this book, I drew on Ramón's life story in particular to illustrate the ways in which the border was both an opportunity and a barrier that borderlands residents negotiated time and again to earn a livelihood according to their own terms. It is only by studying people's everyday lives as they go about crossing the border, finding work, establishing families, making friendships, and finally, confronting loss, that we are able to uncover the true shape of the border as it enables or constrains each aspect of human life.

APPENDIX | Methodological Reflection

FROM THE START OF THE research to its eventual publication, this study took almost a decade to complete. In this chapter, I outline the project's evolution, the surprises I encountered in the field, and how these surprises helped me advance my research. I begin by talking about doing research in the context of a border city like Tijuana that has experienced rapid demographic change and economic development. Then, I discuss how I obtained participants using participant observation, key contacts, and snowball sampling to locate a diverse set of border residents. Finally, I talk about how I gathered, analyzed, and reanalyzed data in an iterative process. I write this methodological reflection to assist students of qualitative methods in developing their own research projects by explaining the lessons I learned through the challenges I faced in the field.[1] In particular, I stress that qualitative work does not simply involve informal conversations in the field but rather is developed in an ongoing process that involves systematic sampling and data-collection procedures.

Finding Participants in the City

To date, most scholars who study migration in Mexico have focused on rural communities, where social relations and interactions take place in small, intimate settings where everyone knows one other and are bonded through marriage and/or economic cooperation.[2] An advantage of conducting research in such a setting is that researchers come in contact with return migrants, would-be migrants, and nonmigrants on a regular basis by living with them and participating in their daily lives. This allows the researcher to become familiar with the research participants and for the participants to become familiar with the project. Moreover, in many of these communities, much of the male population may have previous international migration experience, making it relatively easy to locate participants.[3] Developing contacts to study border commuters in Tijuana proved far more difficult because this particular population was such a small proportion of the city residents. In addition, in the bustling urban context, it was not only challenging to find border commuters but also to develop rapport, because I simply did not run into the same people on a daily basis. Entering the field without any contacts, it was difficult to know where to begin. I clearly remember crossing the first day through the US-Mexico border turnstiles and feeling overwhelmed. I asked myself, "Where should I start? Who will I interview?"

To complete my research, I referred to the strategies used by other migration scholars who worked with hard-to-find unauthorized populations. To locate respondents, these scholars suggest establishing a rapport with key informants (e.g., teachers, members of nonprofit organizations and business owners) who can broker connections with the target population.[4] They also advise conducting observations in key places where migrants congregate (e.g., restaurants, supermarkets, worksites, and sports venues).[5] In this study, I sought the help of Aurelio, a business owner; Jorge, a physical-education teacher and well-known community member; and also participants at the port of entry, worksites, streets, and neighborhoods, which I discuss in further detail. I also followed the tried and true ethnographic recruitment method of snowball sampling to gain access to other participants.[6] I used these techniques together in a focused effort to access a diverse sample of respondents with regard to age, marital status, and migration and labor histories.

To immerse myself in the field, I decided to conduct observations at the port of entry, which I saw as the key site where I would find border commuters. I hoped to generate notes about what it was like to cross on a regular basis and to develop contacts with border commuters. My goal was to approach them and ask for their phone number. I would then contact them at a later date to schedule an interview. However, this approach did not work well; I did not see the same people every day, and most people were in a hurry to get to their jobs in the morning or their homes in the afternoons. On top of that, I did not have the confidence to recruit participants, and people likely picked up on this and declined to be interviewed. Whenever I tried to recruit people at the port of entry, they kindly responded, "Yes, of course. The next time I see you here, we can talk and you can ask me questions." Of course, I never saw them again, because thousands of people cross the border every day. On one occasion, I did manage to obtain the phone number of a commuter, but when I tried calling, the number did not exist. Thus, recruiting participants at the port of entry was not ideal because it was a setting where I was unable to develop trust or rapport with border crossers. I should not have been surprised; many commuters were likely using their BCCs to work in the United States and were fearful that by talking to me, they risked losing them.

Frustrated with my inability to recruit people at the port of entry, I decided to use the first few weeks of fieldwork to obtain detailed field notes on border life. This consisted of observing what it was like to take a taxi or bus to the port of entry; observing interactions between border crossers and immigration officials; and following workers as they boarded public transportation in the United States to their places of employment. This allowed me to understand what it was like to cross the border on a regular basis and to get a better sense of the people who crossed on a daily basis to work in San Diego. My field notes were filled with data on the physical and social environment of Tijuana, including what it was like to live in a neighborhood, people's consumption patterns in Mexico and the United States, and interactions in public spaces such as parks, taxis, restaurants, and so on. The goal of my field notes was to capture in detail what it was like to live a border life. The process went something like this. When I crossed the port of entry, I made mental notes of what was happening and what was said (or if I could write without disrupting patterns of interaction I took "jottings" in a small notebook). I wrote down these mental notes or expanded on my jottings in a larger notebook as soon as I found the time, and at night I typed up my field notes on my laptop computer.[7] Sometimes, the process of writing field notes extended into most of the next day as I seldom felt that I had enough time to write down everything I saw and heard. Even though I did not conduct interviews during the first few weeks of my study, my detailed notes on border interactions and daily life in Tijuana helped provide context for the lives of those whom I have written about in this book. These observations ultimately also helped me develop contacts in this Mexican border city.

Turning Contacts into Further Contacts

With time, I expanded my observations beyond the port of entry to other key public spaces in Tijuana. On one occasion, I stopped at an ice cream shop that belonged to Aurelio Nava, who worked alongside his son Rubén. They were chatty business owners who could converse endlessly about any topic for hours. At the time, I did not have very many contacts in Tijuana, so I became a regular at their ice cream shop once I had finished collecting field notes at the end of the day. My developing relationship with Aurelio and Rubén wound up helping me in ways I did not anticipate. After getting to know me, Aurelio and Rubén invited me to family events and weekend outings. They also encouraged me to spend more time at their business, where I could observe regulars who came to chat and eat ice cream. The shop's clientele included border commuters, migrants, deportees, and other fronterizos from all walks of life. Aurelio also introduced me to several friends who were ex-braceros and migrants. He encouraged me to talk to the former braceros who hung out there on a weekly basis, because he thought that they had played an integral part in the economies of the United States and Mexico. These former braceros became an invaluable connection, even though I did not originally conceive of them as being in my book. However, as I spoke with them, I came to realize that they had been agricultural commuters, and their stories helped shed light on how earlier cohorts of border residents navigated the border economy during the period of the Bracero Program (1942–64) and the open-border period (1965–85). Once he got to know me, Rubén also began to recommend contemporary border commuters to interview, such as his sister-in-law and brother-in-law. I interviewed both of them, but I wanted to avoid the problem of homophily—or the clustering of people who share similar experiences or attributes.[8] As a result, rather than remain within the comforts of Rubén's network, I sought out new "seeds" by reaching out to key informants and developing new contacts through my immersion in daily life in Tijuana.

To branch out beyond these initial seeds, I began to identify other commuters by turning to established connections that I had developed while living in a working-class neighborhood, and by meeting people at the port of entry and in public spaces. I then asked these contacts to refer me to additional border commuters they knew. Some scholars suggest that snowball sampling is biased because cases are not selected at random; however, I chose this method because I needed to develop trust with the community to get people to talk to me about sensitive issues like crossing the border without authorization. Mario Small argues that "[w]hat proponents of the random selection approach to small-n in-depth interviewing rarely mention is that many people who are cold-called will not agree to long, in-depth interviews on personal topics with a stranger."[9] Thus, for my study, I identified key informants who put me in contact with border commuters, who I then asked for further referrals of people to interview.

I made a daily requirement to introduce myself to a few people each day to expand my network connections and to develop confidence in approaching people to interview. I also spent a considerable amount of time talking to people and explaining my project with the hope that doing so would help me to locate border commuters. People were generally very excited to learn that I was writing a book about Tijuana, and as soon as they got to know me, they began to introduce me to their friends and family members. I also met people through daily life in my neighborhood and through the daily activities I participated in. For example, in an effort to make friends, I began to ride with a group of mountain bikers who rode on the mountains overlooking the Pacific Ocean and Playas de Tijuana. Through these excursions I met Jorge, the physical-education instructor, who became a close friend. When I needed to find border commuters, I turned to Jorge, who right away invited me to meet some of his neighborhood friends. He introduced me to Hugo, Cesar, Julio, Boris, Lemus, Lorenzo, and many other childhood friends, who were either current or previous border commuters and had begun to cross the border as commuters for the first time during the post-IRCA period (1987–93). He helped broker relationships with these men and also invited me to his neighborhood on a regular basis, where I was able to interview and observe commuters as they went about daily life. These border commuters provided me with rich interview and ethnographic data that I could not have obtained if I had recruited them as a stranger at the port of entry. I also met one of my key contacts, Ramón, through the woman who rented out a room to me, who was a relative of his. She helped me establish a relationship with him. As a result, Ramón introduced me to two of his friends and I ended up interviewing two of his sons as well. I branched out throughout Tijuana in hopes that I would identify border commuters from all over the city.

In 2010–11, after starting my new job as an assistant professor, I no longer had the same time that I had as a graduate student. I hired two undergraduate students to help me conduct further in-depth interviews with the younger generation of border crossers. Because they lived in Tijuana, had extensive research experience, and knew many people in the city, they helped to locate younger border crossers whose crossing experiences largely took place in the period after Operation Gatekeeper (from 1994) and female border crossers. To ensure appropriate data collection, we practiced the interview guide together, I accompanied them to several interviews, and we regularly spoke by phone about the findings. As a researcher, I tried to plant numerous seeds throughout Tijuana in an effort to avoid interviewing respondents who were all integrated into a single tightly knit community.

Recording People and Analyzing Data

With a few exceptions, I recorded all of my interviews, in an effort to capture what people said in their own words. While recording interviews allowed me to capture the exact words of my respondents, there were drawbacks to using this technique. For example, Ramón, a central character in this book, did not feel comfortable sitting down to be interviewed, much less being recorded. He felt most comfortable with normal conversation. Although he was normally a chatty, enthusiastic person, he did not have much to say the one time I did manage to convince him to be recorded. I also found that what Ramón said did not always align with his everyday behaviors.[10] For example, when I asked Ramón about his network connections during an interview, he mentioned having no friends or family outside of his household.[11] Yet by following him outside of his household, I found that Ramón had extensive networks; he had strong ties to friends, coworkers, and employers in Tijuana and in San Diego County that he drew on for support, and he helped them as well. However, in our interview he simply said that he considered himself a loner. By combining in-depth interviews and observations, I was able to compare what people said with what they did and to experience daily life in Tijuana by participating in activities such as crossing the border and shopping in both Mexico and the United States.

After interviews were conducted, I entered all of the basic demographic information into Excel, and then into a Microsoft Word document. Once basic information was entered, I took detailed field notes describing the person, the neighborhood they lived in, and things the respondent said after the recorder was turned off. I transcribed the majority of the first wave of interviews, but then hired Mexican undergraduate students to help with this time-consuming process. Once the interviews were transcribed, I reread each one numerous times until I became familiar with their contents. I also read and coded all of my field notes; these were coded by marking the margins of the text with key codes such as "crossing the border," "inspections by Customs and Border Protection," "social mobility discussion among braceros," "friendship moments," and so on. I analyzed the interview transcripts by creating several Microsoft Word documents organized according to theme, such as "crossing strategies," and pasting chunks of quotations into codes under that theme, such as "circumventing inspection," "drawing on social support," "gaining confidence," and "using local smugglers," which helped to organize the presentation of findings. Over the years, I returned to these documents time and time again, modifying them as the book went through major revisions. Nonetheless, my organization and ongoing analysis of the data meant that I never had to rely on memory to make decisions in the process of writing and analysis.

Revisiting the Field

I returned to the field on several occasions. As new themes emerged from my field notes and from the transcripts, I returned to the field to collect data to support arguments for which I thought that I did not have enough evidence. In the epilogue to *Street Corner Society*, William Foote Whyte talks about the challenges scholars face as they first enter the field and then later attempt to find patterns in the data, only to realize that they need to review the field notes and perhaps return to the field to gather more notes to "determine whether the pattern adequately represents the life we are observing or is simply a product of our imagination."[12] My most difficult struggle was that I had a difficult time believing what I wrote and wanted to talk to more people to validate my findings.

I first reentered the field to discuss with former braceros the conclusions I was coming to about why one group decided to work in Mexico while the other became daily crossers. I then returned to the field again in an effort to secure more interviews with the younger cohort of border crossers. I realized that I had enough information about the bracero commuters and the commuters who obtained their Green Cards through IRCA, but less about the cohort of contemporary border commuters who use BCCs to work without authorization. I returned to Tijuana with the goal of gathering more in-depth information about the strategies people employed to obtain the information they needed to acquire BCCs and the strategies they employed when crossing the border. This decision emerged from a back-and-forth process of conducting fieldwork, transcribing, and analyzing. If my process had been more linear, it might have been too late for me to return to the field to obtain further information by the time I realized that I needed to validate that the patterns I had observed were indeed a reflection of empirical reality. I also sought to add women's perspectives on this trip because my initial contacts and networks were with men. I wanted to make sure that I interviewed women to get a better sense of the ways in which they navigated border life and crossed the border. Finally, I returned to the field for the last time in late 2013 in an effort to understand the temporal nature of people's livelihood strategies along the US-Mexico border. As discussed in the epilogue, the revisits to respondents showed that livelihoods in the borderlands were difficult to maintain because they were economically vulnerable, in addition to their restrictive legal status.

How Many Interviews?

This book is based upon 158 interviews with border residents who came of age during different immigration and economic eras. For a qualitative study, I had a large sample. I interviewed this large number of respondents because as I conducted more interviews, new categories of crossers emerged, and I wanted to interview a number of people from each category to obtain a comprehensive view of border commuters from the post-bracero period to the present. Annette Lareau states that conducting thirty to forty interviews spread out over one or two settings can be enough to provide theoretically rich data about daily life that can help advance social theory.[13] However, border life was simply too diverse to restrict my sample to such a small size. That being said, I somewhat agree with Lareau that it is important to limit one's study to a more manageable sample and follow them over the course of the research, because the time and energy I dedicated to finding new respondents, setting up interviews, transcribing, and analyzing the interviews was taxing both physically and emotionally. However, each researcher needs to carefully consider their goals and the data needed to answer their research question. In my case, the more time I spent in the field, the more themes emerged that required further interviews to fully explore. I also needed to revisit respondents on numerous occasions to understand the changing situation in their border lives.

Study Recommendations

My time spent in the field in Tijuana provided many glimpses into interesting empirical realities in this border city. While I maintained my focus on my own research questions throughout the project, I kept these glimpses in mind as the seeds of future research projects that may be undertaken by scholars interested in doing ethnography in Tijuana or in another border community. First, women have different experiences than men of relocating to the border, attempting to find their niches in the Mexican side of the economy, obtaining border crossings cards, and developing social networks to cross. It would be exciting to read a study that delves into their experiences and studies how the practice of border crossing is gendered. Second, though my study examines the process of obtaining a BCC from the perspective of applicants, ethnographic research is needed to better understand how the legal ability to cross the border is constructed through interactions, by following respondents as they prepare their applications and undergo interviews and by conducting research with the US government officials who disburse these documents. Third, this study largely focused on the experiences of those who were able to turn the border into an advantage by working in the United States or Mexico. However, in recent years, the Obama administration has deported many unauthorized Mexicans to Mexican border cities, where they are cut off from their families in the United States. How these deportees find their niche in the Mexican economy and how the Mexican state facilitates or complicates their reentry are important empirical questions that remain to be answered. Fourth, scholars need to continue to study cohorts of border commuters in Tijuana. New developments since my research are likely to alter the experiences of border crossers now and into the future. The IRCA recipients are now slowly retiring from the labor force just as the US government has instituted new surveillance technologies to track individuals as they move back and forth across the port of entry. Potential new immigration-reform laws or shifts in US politics may lead to new regulations and policies that influence border crossing. These changes and their effects should be studied by new generations of border researchers.

Finally, the border is a fascinating location to study topics of interest to sociologists, such as labor markets, border and boundaries, and social networks. Yet the border is also a place of intense inequality, uneven urbanization, and gendered violence. Institutional support for border studies is needed to foster partnerships among Mexican and American scholars, not only to produce important sociological research, but also to address the social problems that are produced by and that manifest on both sides of the border.

NOTES

Chapter 1

1. All names are fictitious. To protect participants, I have used pseudonyms and changed information that I believed could potentially result in their identification.

2. See, for example, María Patricia Fernández-Kelly, *For We Are Sold, I and My People: Women and Industry in Mexico's Frontier* (Albany: State University of New York Press, 1983); Elizabeth Fussell, "Sources of Mexico's Migration Stream: Rural, Urban, and Border Migrants to the United States," *Social Forces* 82 (2004): 937–67; Oscar J. Martínez, *Border People: Life and Society in the U.S.-Mexico Borderlands* (Tucson and London: University of Arizona Press, 1994); Douglas S. Massey, Rafael Alarcón, Jorge Durand, and Humberto González, *Return to Aztlan: The Social Process of International Migration from Western Mexico* (Berkeley and Los Angeles: University of California Press, 1987). The Mexican Migration Project (MMP), which is often used by demographers and sociologists, surveyed residents of Tijuana but did not ask specific questions about border commuting practices even though this is a common form of crossing the border to work. The MMP specializes in long-distance domestic and international migration; thus, it fails to capture the labor market practices of border residents. See http://mmp.opr.princeton.edu/home-en.aspx for an overview of the MMP, which has surveyed Mexican households since 1982.

3. For a discussion of precarious work, see Arne L. Kalleberg, "Precarious Work, Insecure Workers: Employment Relations in Transition," *American Sociological Review* 74 (2009): 1–22.

4. Sharon Hays, "Structure and Agency and the Sticky Problem of Culture," *Sociological Theory* 12 (1994): 70.

5. Mustafa Emirbayer and Ann Mische, "What Is Agency?" *American Journal of Sociology* 103 (1998): 1011.

6. Anthony Giddens, *The Constitution of Society* (Berkeley and Los Angeles: University of California Press, 1984), 17.

7. William H. Sewell Jr., "A Theory of Structure: Duality, Agency, and Transformation," *American Journal of Sociology* 98 (1992): 1–29.

8. Thomas M. Wilson and Hastings Donnan, "Nation, State, and Identity in International Borders," in *Border Identities: Nation and State at International Frontiers*, ed. Thomas M. Wilson and Hastings Donnan (Cambridge: Cambridge University Press, 1998), 4.

9. George J. Sánchez. *Becoming Mexican American: Ethnicity, Culture, and Identity in Chicano Los Angeles, 1900–1945* (New York and Oxford: Oxford University Press, 1993), 39.

10. Peter Andreas, *Border Games: Policing the U.S.-Mexico Divide*, Cornell Studies in Political Economy (Ithaca, NY: Cornell University Press, 2000). 85.

11. John Torpey, *The Invention of the Passport: Surveillance, Citizenship, and the State* (Cambridge: Cambridge University Press, 2000), 166.

12. Max Weber, *Economy and Society: An Outline of Interpretive Sociology*, edited by Guenther Roth and Claus Wittich (Berkeley: University of California Press, [1922] 1978).

13. For an overview of how the sending state attempts to regulate the emigration of its population see David Fitzgerald, *A Nation of Emigrants: How Mexico Manages its Migration* (Berkeley and Los Angeles: University of California Press, 2009).

14. Martínez, *Border People*; Laura Velasco Ortiz and Oscar F. Contreras, *Mexican Voices of the Border Region* (Philadelphia, PA: Temple University Press, 2011).

15. David Ralph, " 'Always on the Move, but Going Nowhere Fast': Motivations for 'Euro-Commuting' between the Republic of Ireland and Other EU States," *Journal of Ethnic and Migration Studies* 41, no. 2 (2015): 176–95.

16. Ibid., 8.

17. Pew Hispanic Center, "Modes of Entry for the Unauthorized Migration Population, Fact Sheet"; http://pewhispanic.org/files/factsheets/19.pdf.

18. Daniel C. Levy and Kathleen Bruhn, *Mexico: The Struggle for Democratic Development* (Berkeley and Los Angeles: University of California Press, 2006).

19. Douglas S. Massey and Kristin E. Espinosa, "What's Driving Mexico-U.S. Migration? A Theoretical, Empirical, and Policy Analysis," *American Journal of Sociology* 102 (1997): 939–99.

20. Massey et al., *Return to Aztlan*; Tamar Diana Wilson, *Women's Migration Networks in Mexico and Beyond* (Albuquerque: University of New Mexico Press, 2009).

21. For an overview of changing border and immigration policies and their effects on migration patterns, see Douglas S. Massey, Jorge Durand, and Nolan J. Malone, *Beyond Smoke and Mirrors: Mexican Immigration in an Era of Free Trade* (New York: Russell Sage Foundation, 2002).

22. Fussell, "Sources of Mexico's Migration Stream"; Elizabeth Fussell and Douglas S. Massey. "The Limits to Cumulative Causation: International Migration from Mexican Urban Areas," *Demography* 41 (2004): 151–71.

23. Jorge Durand, Douglas S. Massey, and René M. Zenteno, "Mexican Immigration to the United States: Continuities and Changes," *Latin American Research Review* 36 (2001): 107–27; Fernando Lozano Ascenio, "Migration Strategies in Urban Contexts: Labor Migration from Mexico to the United States," *Migraciones Internacionales* 2 (2004): 34–59; Enrico A. Marcelli and Wayne A. Cornelius, "The Changing Profile of Mexican Migrants to the United States: New Evidence from California and Mexico," *Latin American Research Review* 36 (2001): 105–31.

24. Fussell, "Sources of Mexico's Migration Stream."

25. Rubén Hernández-León, *Metropolitan Migrants: The Migration of Urban Mexicans to the United States* (Berkeley: University of California Press, 2008).

26. Andrés Villarreal and Erin R. Hamilton, "Rush to the Border? Market Liberalization and Urban- and Rural-Origin Internal Migration in Mexico," *Social Science Research* 41 (2012): 1275–91.

27. Nina Glick Schiller, Linda Basch, and Cristina Szanton Blanc, "From Immigrant to Transmigrant: Theorizing Transnational Migration," *Anthropological Quarterly* 68 (1995): 48–63.

28. Glick Schiller, Basch, and Szanton Blanc, "From Immigrant to Transmigrant," 50.

29. Roger Waldinger, "Between 'Here' and 'There': Immigrant Cross-Border Activities and Loyalities," *International Migration Review* 42 (2008): 3–29.

30. See, for example, Luin Goldring, "Blurring Borders: Constructing Transnational Community in the Process of Mexico-U.S. Migration," *Research in Community Sociology* 6 (1996): 69–104; Roger Rouse, "Mexican Migration and the Social Space of Postmodernism," *Diaspora* 1 (1991): 8–23; Robert Smith, *Mexican New York: Transnational Lives of New Immigrants* (Berkeley: University of California Press, 2005); Peggy Levitt and Nadya B. Jaworsky, "Transnational Migration Studies: Past Developments and Future Trends," *Annual Review of Sociology* 33 (2007): 131.

31. Waldinger, "Between 'Here' and 'There,' " 24.

32. Anju Mary Paul, "Stepwise International Migration: A Multi-Stage Migration Pattern for the Aspiring Migrant," *American Journal of Sociology* 116 (2011): 1842–86.

33. Robert Alvarez, *Familia: Migration and Adaptation in Baja and Alta California, 1800–1975* (Berkeley: University of California Press, 1987); Carlos Vélez-Ibáñez, *Border Visions: Mexican Cultures of the Southwest United States* (Tucson: University of Arizona Press, 1996); Wilson, *Women's Migration Networks*.

34. Carol Zabin and Sallie Hughes, "Economic Integration and Labor Flows: Stage Migration in Farm Labor Markets in Mexico and the United States," *International Migration Review* 29 (1995): 395–422.

35. Josiah McC. Heyman, *Life and Labor on the Border: Working People of Northeastern Sonora, Mexico, 1886–1986* (Tucson: University of Arizona Press, 1991).

36. Velasco Ortiz and Contreras, *Mexican Voices*, 16.

37. Massey et al., *Return to Aztlan*; Richard Mines, *Developing a Community Tradition of Migration to the United States: A Field Study in Rural Zacatecas, Mexico, and California Settlement Areas*, Monographs in US-Mexican Studies 3 (La Jolla, CA: Program in United States-Mexican Studies, 1981).

38. Martínez, *Border People*, 25.

39. Chad Richardson and Michael J. Pisani, *The Informal and Underground Economy of the South Texas Border* (Austin: University of Texas Press, 2012).

40. Christina Mendoza, "Crossing Borders: Women, Migration, and Domestic Work at the Texas-Mexico Divide," PhD dissertation, University of Michigan, 2009.

41. Kathleen A. Staudt, *Free Trade? Informal Economies at the U.S.-Mexico Border* (Philadelphia, PA: Temple University Press, 1998); Velasco Ortiz and Contreras, *Mexican Voices*.

42. Fussell, "Sources of Mexico's Migration Stream."

43. Lawrence A. Herzog, *Where North Meets South: Cities, Space, and Politics on the U.S.-Mexico Border* (Austin: Center for Mexican American Studies, University of Texas at Austin, 1990).

44. Ibid., 140.

45. María Eugenia Anguiano Téllez and Maria Eugenia, "Cross Border Interactions: Population and Labor Market in Tijuana," in *The Ties That Bind Us: Mexican Migrants in San Diego County*, ed. Richard Kiy and Christopher Woodruff (San Diego, CA: Center for US-Mexican Studies, 2005), 128–29.

46. Ibid., 129–30.

47. Tito Alegría, "The Transborder Metropolis in Question: The Case of Tijuana and San Diego," in *Tijuana Dreaming: Life and Art at the Global Border*, ed. Josh Kun and Fiamma Montezemolo, 148–74 (Durham, NC, and London: Duke University Press, 2012).

48. Beatriz Acuña González, "Transmigración Legal en la Frontera México-Estados Unidos," *Revista Mexicana de Sociología* 50 (1988): 277–322; Tito Alegría, "Demand and supply of Mexican Cross-Border Workers," *Journal of Borderlands Studies* 17, no. 1 (2002): 37–55; Lawrence A. Herzog, "Border Commuter Workers and Transfrontier Metropolitan Structure along the United States-Mexico Border," *Journal of Borderlands Studies* 5, no. 2 (1990): 1–20.

49. Roger A. LaBrucherie, "Aliens in the Fields: The 'Green-Card Commuter' under the Immigration and Naturalization Laws," *Stanford Law Review* 21 (1969): 1750–76.

50. Juan Vicente Palerm, *Immigrant and Migrant Farm Workers in the Santa Maria Valley, California* (Washington, DC: Center for Survey Methods Research, Bureau of the Census, 1994).

51. Frank D. Bean, Roland Chanove, Robert G. Cushing, Rodolfo de la Garza, Gary P. Freeman, Charles W. Haynes, and David Spener, *Illegal Mexican Migration and the US/Mexico Border: The Effects of Operation Hold the Line in El Paso/Juarez* (Austin: University of Texas at Austin Population Research Center, 1994); Kathryn Kopinak and Rosa Maria Soriano Miras, "Types of Migration Enabled by Maquiladoras in Baja California, Mexico: The Importance of Commuting," *Journal of Borderland Studies* 28 (2013): 75–91.

52. Palerm, *Immigrant and Migrant Farm Workers*; Emily Young, "The Impact of IRCA on Settlement Patterns among Mixtec Migrants in Tijuana, Mexico," *Journal of Borderlands Studies* 9, no. 2 (1994): 109–28.

53. In border cities, residents have access to US tourist visas that can then be used to enter the United States to consume goods. For an account of how Mexican tourists obtain and cross the border using these documents, see Heidy Sarabia, "Global South Cosmopolitans: The Opening and Closing of the USA-Mexico Border for Mexican Tourists," *Ethnic and Racial Studies* 38 (2015): 227–42. This study does not highlight the experiences of border commuters but emphasizes the importance of these documents in the lives of Mexican residents.

54. Acuña González, "Transmigración Legal en la Frontera"; Herzog, "Border Commuter Workers"; Mendoza, "Crossing Borders."

55. See for example, Alegría, "Demand and Supply of Mexican Cross-Border Workers"; Hernández-León, *Metropolitan Migrants*; Fussell, "Sources of Mexico's Migration Stream." These studies provide an overview of current crossing dynamics in northern Mexican states.

56. Bean et al., *Illegal Mexican Migration*.

57. Elizabeth Fussell, "Tijuana's Place in the Mexican Migration Stream: Destination for Internal Migrants or Stepping Stone?" in *Crossing the Border: Research from the Mexican Migration Project*, ed. Jorge Durand and Doug Massey, 147–70 (New York: Russell Sage Foundation, 2004).

58. Acuña González, "Transmigración Legal en la Frontera."

59. Michael Burawoy, "The Functions and Reproduction of Migrant Labor: Comparative Material from Southern Africa and the United States," *American Journal of Sociology* 81 (1976): 1050–87.

60. Seth Holmes, *Fresh Fruit, Broken Bodies: Migrant Farmworkers in the United States* (Berkeley: University of California Press, 2013).

61. XII Censo general de población y vivienda, 2000. Instituto Nacional de Estadística Geografia e Informatica. Migración Por Lugar de Nacimiento; www.inegi.org.mx.

62. Alegría, "The Transborder Metropolis in Question," 166.

63. Ibid., 162–64.

64. Magalí Muriá Tuñón, "Enforcing Boundaries: Globalization, State Power and the Geography of Cross-Border Consumption in Tijuana, Mexico," PhD dissertation, University of California San Diego, 2010.

65. Alejandro Mungaray and Patricia Moctezuma, "El Mercado de la Frontera Norte y las Polítacas de Integración del Consume Fronterizo a la Producción Nacional," *Revista Mexicana de Sociología* 50 (1988): 235.

66. Antonio Bermúdez, *El Rescate del Mercado Fronterizo: Una Obra al Servicio de México* (Mexico, DF: Ediciones Eufesa, 1966); C. Daniel Dillman, "Urban Growth along Mexico's Northern Border and the Mexican National Border Program," *Journal of Developing Areas* 4 (1970): 487–508.

67. Dillman, "Urban Growth along Mexico's Northern Border."

68. Bermúdez, *El Rescate del Mercado Fronterizo*.

69. Elizabeth Fussell, "Making Labor Flexible: The Recomposition of Tijuana's Maquiladora Female Labor Force," *Feminist Economics* 6 (2000): 59–79.

70. John A. Price, *Tijuana: Urbanization of a Border Culture* (London: University of Notre Dame, 1973).

71. Ibid., 87.

72. Mungaray and Moctezuma, "El Mercado de la Frontera Norte," 235.

73. Alegría, "Demand and Supply of Mexican Cross-Border Workers."

74. Jane R. Rubin-Kurtzman, Roberto Ham-Chande, and Maurice D. Van Arsdol Jr., "Population in Trans-Border Regions: The Southern California-Baja California Urban System," *International Migration Review* 30 (1996): 1020–45.

75. Similar enforcement strategies were instituted in El Paso (1993) with Operation Hold-the-Line and Operation Safeguard in Arizona (1994, 1999), and Operation Rio Grande in South Texas (1997).

76. Andreas, *Border Games*; Wayne A. Cornelius, "Death at the Border: Efficacy and Unintended Consequences of US Immigration Control Policy," *Population and Development Review* 27 (2001): 661–85; David Spener, *Clandestine Crossings: Migrants and Coyotes on the Texas-Mexico Border* (Ithaca, NY: Cornell University Press, 2009).

77. Wendy Brown, *Walled States, Waning Sovereignty* (New York: Zone, 2010).

78. Claudia Masferrer and Bryan R. Roberts, "Going Back Home? Changing Demography and Geography of Mexican Return Migration," *Population Research and Policy Review* 31, no. 4 (2012): 465–96.

79. Ibid.

80. John F. Simanski, "Immigration Enforcement Actions: 2013" (Washington, DC: Department of Homeland Security, Office of Immigration Statistics, September 2014); http://www.dhs.gov/sites/default/files/publications/ois_enforcement_ar_2013.pdf.

81. See for example the work of Leo Ralph Chavez, *Shadowed Lives: Undocumented Immigrants in American Society* (Fort Worth, TX: Harcourt, Brace, Jovanovich College Publishers, 1998), and Ruth Gomberg-Muñoz, *Labor and Legality: An Ethnography of a Mexican Immigrant Network* (New York: Oxford University Press, 2011); Pierrette Hondagneu-Sotelo, *Gendered Transitions: Mexican Experiences of Immigration* (Berkeley and Los Angeles: University of California Press, 1994).

82. *Machismo* refers to men who embody the ideas of and who are, "sexually assertive, independent, and emotionally restrained, to wield absolute authority over the wives and children, and to serve as family breadwinners"; see Hondagneu-Sotelo, *Gendered Transitions*, 9.

83. Massey, Durand, and Malone, *Beyond Smoke and Mirrors*, 34–51. See also Fussell and Massey, "Limits to Cumulative Causation," for an application of period effect on migration-prevalence ratios in Mexico.

84. See Andreas, *Border Games*, 85–112, for an in-depth discussion of events in Tijuana after the establishment of Operation Gatekeeper.

85. Josh Reichert and Douglas S. Massey, "History and Trends in U.S. Bound Migration from a Mexican Town," *International Migration Review* 14 (1980): 475–91. These authors write that the Bracero Program, which brought temporary agricultural workers from Mexico to the United States, would eventually lead to large-scale undocumented migration, as growers turned to former braceros to help them recruit workers from Mexico.

86. Mario Luis Small, *Villa Victoria: The Transformation of Social Capital in a Boston Barrio* (Chicago: University of Chicago Press, 2004), 196.

87. Andreas, *Border Games*.

88. Robert R. Alvarez Jr., "The Mexican-US Border: The Making of an Anthropology of Borderlands." *Annual Review of Anthropology* 24 (1995): 447–70.

89. Emirbayer and Mische, "What Is Agency?"

Chapter 2

1. See for example the work of: Deborah Cohen, *Braceros: Migrant Citizens and Transnational Subject in the Postwar United States and Mexico* (Chapel Hill: University of North Carolina Chapel Hill, 2011); Massey et al., *Return to Aztlan*.

2. Vilan Francine Bashi, *Survival of the Knitted: Immigrant Social Networks in a Stratified World* (Stanford: Stanford University Press, 2007); Michael J. Piore, *Birds of Passage: Migrant Labor and Industrial Societies* (Cambridge: Cambridge University Press, 1979). Jacqueline Hagan, Nichola Lowe, and Christian Quingla, "Skills on the Move: Rethinking the Relationship between Human Capital and Immigrant Economic Mobility," *Work and Occupations* 38, no. 2 (2011): 149–78. Roger Waldinger and Michael I. Lichter, *How the Other Half Works: Immigration and the Social Organization of Labor* (Berkeley and Los Angeles: University of California Press, 2003).

3. Reichert and Massey, "History and Trends in U.S. Bound Migration."

4. Nestor Rodriguez, "'Workers Wanted' Employer Recruitment of Immigrant Labor," *Work and Occupations* 31 (2004): 453–73, see p. 458.

5. Kitty Calavita, *Inside the State: The Bracero Program, Immigration, and the I.N.S.* (New York: Routledge, 1992); Philip Martin, "Mexican Workers and U.S. Agriculture: The Revolving Door," *International Migration Review* 36, no. 4 (2002): 1124–42; Max, J. Pfeffer, "The Labor Process and Corporate Agriculture: Mexican Workers in California," *Insurgent Sociologist* 10, no. 2 (1980): 25–44.

6. See, for example, Calavita, *Inside the State*, 72; Pfeffer, "The Labor Process," 32.

7. Manuel García y Griego, "The Importation of Mexican Contract Laborers to the United States, 1942–64: Antecedents, Operation, and Legacy," in *The Border That Joins: Mexican Migrants and U.S. Responsibility*, ed. Peter G. Brown and Henry Shue, 49–98 (Totowa, NJ: Rowman and Littlefield, 1983); Martin, "Mexican Workers and U.S. Agriculture."

8. Cohen, *Braceros*.

9. David Lorey, *United States-Mexico Border Statistics since 1900* (Los Angeles, California: UCLA Latin American Center Publications, 1990).

10. Fernández-Kelly, *For We Are Sold*, 26.

11. Frank Meissner, "In-Bond Industries as Development Tools: A Mexican-American Example," *Third World Quarterly* 1 (1979): 141–47.

12. See the following studies: René Martín Zenteno, "Del Rancho de la Tia Juana a Tijuana: Una Breve Historia de Desarrollo y Población en la Frontera Norte de México," *Estudios Demográficos y Urbanos* 10 (1995): 105–32; María del Rosío Barajas Escamilla, "The Global Production Networks in an Electronics Industry: The Case of the Tijuana–San Diego Binational Region," PhD dissertation, University of California Irvine, 2000).

13. Fernández-Kelly, *For We Are Sold*, 45.

14. Jane Collins, *Threads: Gender, Labor, and Power in the Global Apparel Industry* (Chicago: University of Chicago Press, 2003), 13.

15. Michael Van Waas, "The Multinationals' Strategy for Labor: Foreign Assembly Plants in Mexico's Border Industrialization Program," PhD dissertation, Stanford University, 1981.

16. See Jacqueline Hagan, Rubén Hernández-León, and Jean-Luc Demonsant, *Skills of the "Unskilled": Work and Mobility among Mexican Migrants* (Berkeley: University of California Press, 2015), for an overview of how migrants transfer skills and retool themselves as they move back-and-forth between Mexico and the United States.

17. See Robert C. Tucker, *The Marx-Engels Reader* (New York: Norton, 1972) for a discussion of the concept of alienated labor.

18. In *Return to Aztlan*, Massey et al. mention taxi driving as one occupation that migrants worked in that helped consolidate their settlement in Tijuana.

19. Martin, "Mexican Workers and U.S. Agriculture."

20. Ibid., 1130.

21. Lamar Jones, "Alien Commuters in the United States Labor Markets," *International Migration Review* 4 (1970): 65–89. For further detail about the experience of agricultural commuters, see Frank Bardacke, *Trampling out of the Vintage: Cesar Chavez and the Two Souls of the United Farm Workers* (New York: Verso, 2012).

22. See Ernesto Galarza, *Merchants of Labor: The Mexican Bracero Story* (San Jose, CA: Rosicrucian, 1964).

23. Calavita, *Inside the State;* Pfeffer, "The Labor Process."

24. Erving Goffman, *Asylums: Essays on the Social Situation of Mental Patients and Other Inmates* (New York: Anchor, 1961). For a further discussion of the application of the concept of total institution to the Bracero Program, please see: Ronald Mize, "Power (in)-Action: State and Agribusiness in the Making of a Bracero Total Institution," *Berkeley Journal of Sociology* 50 (2006): 76–119.

25. Galarza, *Merchants of Labor*, 80.

26. Galarza, *Merchants of Labor*, 94.

27. See the work of Calavita, *Inside the State*; Jones, "Alien Commuters"; Palerm, *Immigrant and Migrant Farm Workers*, for an overview of agricultural commuters who lived in Mexico but crossed the border to work in the United States.

28. Fred Krissman, "Sin Coyote Ni Patrón: Why the 'Migrant Network' Fails to Explain International Migration," *International Migration Review* 39 (2005): 4–44, at p. 31.

29. Calavita, *Inside the State*; Joseph Nevins, *Operation Gatekeeper: The Rise of the "Illegal Alien" and the Making of the U.S.-Mexico Boundary* (New York and London: Routledge, 2002).

30. Julian Samora, *Los Mojados: The Wetback Story* (Notre Dame, IN, and London: University of Notre Dame Press, 1971), 40.

31. Burawoy, "Functions and Reproduction of Migrant Labor."

32. For a brief overview of the agricultural ladder see: Diane C. Bates and Thomas K. Rudel, "Climbing the 'Agricultural Ladder': Social Mobility and Migration in an Ecuadorian Colonist Community," *Rural Sociology* 69, no. 1 (2004): 59–75.

33. Young, "Impact of IRCA," 118. See also Herzog, "Border Commuter Workers."

34. Abel Valenzuela Jr., Lisa Schweitzer, and Adriele Robles, "Camionetas: Informal Travel among Immigrants," *Transportation Research* 39, no. 10 (2005): 895–911.

35. Velasco Ortiz and Contreras, *Mexican Voices.*

36. *Collective Agreement between Named Company and the United Farm Workers Association of America* (Publication location unknown, 1980). Unpublished document, available upon request from Sergio Chávez.

Chapter 3

1. Acuña Gonzalez, "Transmigración Legal"; Estrella Valenzuela, "Migración Internacional legal desde la Frontera Norte de México" *Estudios Demográficos y Urbanos* 8 (1993): 559–600

2. See, for example, the work of Herzog, "Border Commuter Workers."; Martínez, *Border People*; Young, "Impact of IRCA."

3. Herzog, *Where North Meets South.*

4. SANDAG, "San Diego-Baja California Ports of Entry Fact Sheet," July 2003; http://sandiegohealth.org/sandag/sandag_pubs_2009-7-25/publicationid_1184_5148.pdf.

5. Naoko Kada and Richard Kiy, eds., *Blurred Borders: Trans-Boundary Impacts and Solutions in the San Diego-Tijuana Border Region* (San Diego, CA: International Community Foundation, 2004), 1.

6. Ibid., 2.

7. Alegría, "Transborder Metropolis in Question."

8. Ibid.

9. For the California minimum wage, see http://www.dir.ca.gov/iwc/MinimumWage History.htm. For Baja, California's minimum wage, see http://www.wageindicator. org/main/salary/minimum-wage/mexico.

10. In "Transborder Metropolis in Question," Alegría finds that a 1 percent increase in wages between Tijuana and the United States translates into a 3 percent increase in the number of transmigrants who cross the border to work. Yet the only way to cross the border to gain access to employment is through BCCs.

11. Herzog "Border Commuter Workers"; Young, "Impact of IRCA."

12. For an overview of border commuter crossings along the US-Mexico border, see Roger A. LaBrucherie, "Aliens in the Fields." According to the US Citizenship and Immigration Services, a person may lose their permanent resident status if they intend to live in another country permanently, see http://www.uscis.gov/green-card/after-green-card-granted/maintaining-permanent-residence.

13. Muriá Tuñón, "Enforcing Boundaries."

14. See Andreas, *Border Games*, 89–103

15. Bean et al., *Illegal Mexican Migration*, 113.

16. David Spener, "Controlling the Border in El Paso Del Norte: Operation Blockade or Operation Charade?" in *Ethnography at the Border*, edited by Pablo Vila (Minneapolis: University of Minnesota Press, 2003), 182–98; Bean et al., *Illegal Mexican Migration*; Muriá Tuñón, "Enforcing Boundaries."

17. Torpey, *Invention of the Passport*, 7.

18. Martínez, *Border People*; Velasco Ortiz and Contreras, *Mexican Voices*.

19. Zabin and Hughes, "Economic Integration and Labor Flows." Paul, "Stepwise International Migration."

20. Katharine Donato, "U.S. Migration from Latin America: Gendered Patterns and Shifts," *Annals of the American Academy of Political and Social Science* 630 (2010): 78–92.

21. Paul, "Stepwise International Migration."

22. Ibid., 1844.

23. Alejandro Portes and Rubén G. Rumbaut, *Immigrant America: A Portrait* (Berkeley: University of California Press, 1990).

24. Green Cards give permanent residence to immigrants to reside in the United States. People can generally obtain Green Cards through family or employer sponsorship or by claiming refugee or asylum status. Applicants are generally placed in one of these categories, and their approval operates on a preference system. For family-based categories, preference is given to the adult unmarried sons and daughters of US citizens. For job-based applicants, primary preference is given to workers with extraordinary abilities, outstanding professors and researchers, and multinational executives and managers. See the US Citizenship and Immigration Services "Green Card Eligibility" at http://www.uscis.gov/green-card/green-card-processes-and-procedures/green-card-eligibility.

25. Giddens, *Constitution of Society*.

26. Torpey, *Invention of the Passport*.

27. Mendoza, "Crossing Borders"; Spener, "Controlling the Border." Fernández-Kelly, *For We Are Sold*.

28. Mendoza, "Crossing Borders."

29. Kathryn Kopinak, "How Maquiladora Industries Contribute to Mexico-U.S. Labor Migration," *Papers: Revista de Sociologia* 96, no. 3 (2011), 645.

30. Bean et al., *Illegal Mexican Migration*; Josiah McC. Heyman, "Ports of Entry as Nodes in the World System," *Identities: Global Studies in Culture and Power* 11 (2004): 303–27.

31. Bean et al., *Illegal Mexican Migration*.

32. Hernández-León, *Metropolitan Migrants*.

33. Spener, "Controlling the Border."

34. Bashi, *Survival of the Knitted*.

35. Wayne A. Cornelius, "Impacts of the 1986 US Immigration Law on Emigration from Rural Mexican Sending Communities," *Population and Development Review* 15 (1989): 689–705.

36. USDS, Nonimmigrant Visa Statistics; http://travel.state.gov/content/visas/english/law-and-policy/statistics/non-immigrant-visas.html. See also, http://travel.state.gov/content/dam/visas/Statistics/AnnualReports/FY2013AnnualReport/FY13AnnualReport-TableXIX.pdf.

Chapter 4

1. Josiah McC. Heyman, "Trust, Privilege, and Discretion in the Governance of the US Borderlands with Mexico," *Canadian Journal of Law and Society* 24, no. 3 (2009): 367–90. Sarabia, "Global South Cosmopolitans."

2. Héctor Antonio Padilla Delgado, *En el Puente con la Migra* (Ciudad Juárez: Universidad Autonoma de Ciudad Juárez, 2010), 61.

3. The Tijuana-based poet and novelist Heriberto Yepez outlined the following recommendations for crossing the border which include:

> Try to cross legally.
> Pick a time of day with little traffic.
> Before crossing, have a reason to tell the agent, a good reason, a true one, or at least a believable one.
> Drive a good car that looks classy or that says: I'm middle class.
> Drive a good car without provoking suspicions about where you got it from. If you are dark-skinned, drive a car that corresponds to your status.
> Cross by bike in the special line.
> Take a magazine when you cross on foot.
> Take two magazines when you cross on foot.
> Pick the line that is moving the fastest.
> Don't bring fruit or vegetables.

See Heriberto Yepez, "Tijuanalogies," in *Tijuana Dreaming: Life and Art at the Global Border*, ed. Josh Kun and Fiamma Montezemolo (Durham and London: Duke University Press, 2012), 68–69.

4. See the work of Erving Goffman, *The Presentation of Self in Everyday Life* (New York: Anchor, 1959).

5. Massey, Durand, and Malone, *Beyond Smoke and Mirrors*.

6. Cornelius, "Impacts of the 1986 US Immigration Law."

7. Chavez, *Shadowed Lives*.

8. Ibid., 50.

9. Ibid., 50.

10. Audrey Singer and Douglas S. Massey, "The Social Process of Undocumented Border Crossing among Mexican Migrants," *International Migration Review* 32 (1998): 561–92.

11. Christina Gathman, "Effects of Enforcement on Illegal Markets: Evidence from Migrant Smuggling along the Southwestern Border," *Journal of Public Economics* 92 (2008): 1926–41.

12. Katherine Donato et al., "The Cat and Mouse Game at the Mexico-U.S. Border: Gendered Patterns and Recent Shifts," *International Migration Review* 42 (2008): 330–59.

13. Andreas, *Border Games*, 14.

14. Jorge A. Bustamante, "Undocumented Migration from Mexico to the United States: Preliminary Findings of the Zapata Canyon Project," in *Unauthorized Migration to the United States: IRCA and the Experience of the 1980s*, edited by Frank D. Bean, Barry Edmonstron, and Jeffrey S. Passel (Santa Monica, CA: Rand Corporation, 1990), 215; Massey, Durand, and Malone, *Beyond Smoke and Mirrors*, 108.

15. Wayne A. Cornelius, "Controlling 'Unwanted' Immigration: Lessons from the United States, 1993–2004," *Journal of Ethnic and Migration Studies* 31 (2005): 775–94.

16. Massey, Durand, and Malone, *Beyond Smoke and Mirrors*; Spener, *Clandestine Crossings*.

17. Cornelius, "Controlling 'Unwanted' Immigration."

18. Karl Eschbach et al., "Death at the Border," *International Migration Review* 33 (1999): 430–54; Cornelius, "Controlling 'Unwanted' Immigration."

19. Massey, Durand, and Malone, *Beyond Smoke and Mirrors*.

20. Sarabia, "Global South Cosmpolitans."

21. See Mines, *Developing a Community Tradition of Migration*. The practice of families providing temporary refuge to crossers was more common that I expected. One day when I got home, I was surprised to find a total of three men and women in the home where I rented a room. At first, I thought that they were just friends of the landlady, but I later learned that she was providing shelter to US-bound migrants.

22. Spener, *Clandestine Crossings*.

23. Andreas, *Border Games*.

24. Goffman, *Presentation of Self*.

25. Price, *Tijuana*, 43.

26. Timothy J. Dunn, *The Militarization of the US-Mexican Border, 1978–1992: Low-Intensity Conflict Doctrine Comes Home* (Austin: Center for Mexican American Studies, University of Texas at Austin, 1996), 13.

27. Andreas, *Border Games*, 9.

28. All respondents knew that they were prohibited from working in the United States. However, they explained that they worked in the United States because it was the way things were in the borderlands. For decades, generations of border crossers had crossed the US-Mexico border to work in the United States. They saw this behavior as normal for borderland residents. However, it is important to note that the majority of Mexicans with border-crossing or tourist cards did not use them to work in the United States.

29. Padilla Delgado, *En el Puente con la Migra*; Sarabia, "Global South Cosmopolitans."

30. Padilla Delgado, *En el Puente con la Migra*.

31. Nevins, *Operation Gatekeeper*.

32. US Citizenship and Immigration Services, "Rights and Responsibilities of a Green Card Holder (Permanent Resident"; http://www.uscis.gov/green-card/after-green-card-granted/rights-and-responsibilities-permanent-resident/rights-and-responsibilities-green-card-holder-permanent-resident.

33. Heyman, "Trust, Privilege, and Discretion"; Padilla Delgado, *En el Puente con la Migra*.

34. Weber, *Economy and Society*.

35. Josiah McC. Heyman, "U.S. Immigration Officers of Mexican Ancestry as Mexican Americans, Citizens, and Immigration Police," *Current Anthropology* 43 (2002): 479–507.

36. Erving Goffman, *Interaction Ritual: Essays on Face-to-Face Behavior* (New York: Pantheon, 1967), 8.

37. Goffman, *Interaction Ritual*, 217.

38. Heyman, "Trust, Privilege, and Discretion."

39. Roger Rouse, "Making Sense of Settlement: Class, Transformation, Cultural Struggle, and Transnationalism among Mexican Migrants in the United States," in *Towards a Transnational Perspective on Migration: Race, Class, Ethnicity, and Nationalism Reconsidered*, ed. Nina Glick Schiller, Linda Basch, and Cristina Blanc-Szanton (New York: Annals of the New York Academy of Sciences, 1992), 32.

40. Kada and Kiy, *Blurred Borders*.

41. Ibid., A17.

42. Ibid.

43. Emirbayer and Mische, "What is Agency?"

44. Cornelius, "Controlling 'Unwanted' Immigration."

45. Massey et al., *Return to Aztlan*; Singer and Massey, "Social Process of Undocumented Border Crossing."

46. Spener, *Clandestine Crossings*.

47. Bean et al., *Illegal Mexican Migration*; Hernández-León, *Metropolitan Migrants*; Heyman, "Trust, Privilege, and Discretion."

48. Hernández-León, *Metropolitan Migrants*; Heyman, "Trust, Privilege, and Discretion."

Chapter 5

1. See Manuel Gamio's, *The Life Story of the Mexican Immigrant* (New York: Dover, 1971), 25–27. Gamio interviewed Bonifacio Ortega (age twenty-eight), who had been living in the United States a year and a half. At the time of the interview, Bonificio explained that while living in the United States, he had dislocated his shoulder and caught a fever, rendering him unable to work for three months. During this time, his paisanos gave him money and visited him in the hospital.

2. For an in-depth discussion of how social ties influence job earnings, see Michael B. Aguilera and Douglas S. Massey, "Social Capital and the Wages of Mexican Migrants: New Hypotheses and Tests," *Social Forces* 82 (2003): 671–701. Donato et al.,

"Cat and Mouse Game at the Mexico-U.S. Border," and Singer and Massey, "Social Process of Undocumented Border Crossing," highlight the role of family and friends in the border crossing experience.

3. Cecilia Menjivar, *Fragmented Ties: Salvadoran Immigrant Networks in America* (Berkeley and Los Angeles: University of California Press, 2000), 34 and 35.

4. Matthew Desmond, "Disposable Ties and the Urban Poor," *American Journal of Sociology* 117 (2012): 1295–335.

5. See Mark S. Granovetter, "The Strength of Weak Ties," *American Journal of Sociology* 78 (1973): 1360–80, at p. 1361.

6. In a review, Rubén Hernández-León finds that much of the literature shows that rural migrants draw on close-knit ties whereas urban residents draw on weak ties as a result of the occupational differentiation and anonymity that characterize the urban experience. Fred Krissman, "Sin Coyote Ni Patrón," similarly argues that the migration literature has focused more on strong ties and less on weak ties.

7. Gomberg-Muñoz, *Labor and Legality*; Waldinger and Lichter, *How the Other Half Works*.

8. Alvarez, *Familia*; Wilson, *Women's Migration Networks*.

9. Mario Luis Small, *Unanticipated Gains: Origins of Network Inequality in Everyday Life* (New York: Oxford University Press, 2010).

10. Sometimes Rubén and Aurelio would ask for my opinion on who was right. When that happened, I told them I could not get involved.

11. Louis Wirth, "Urbanism as a Way of Life," *American Journal of Sociology* 44 (1938): 12.

12. Ibid.

13. Fussell and Massey, "Limits to Cumulative Causation."

14. Georg Simmel, "The Stranger," in *George Simmel on Individuality and Social Forms*, ed. Donald N. Levine (Chicago: University of Chicago Press, [1908] 1971), 143.

15. Shortly after the terrorist attacks of September 11, 2001, the US government set up a special bike lane to allow commuters to cross the port of entry. This bike lane tended to move fastest during nonpeak working hours, when it could take less than ten minutes to cross. On several occasions, Aurelio, the ice cream shop owner, asked me to cross the border by bike and buy milk in the United States where it was less expensive. The special bike lane was closed five years after I left Tijuana after many Mexican vendors began to rent bicycles. Renting a bicycle cost $5–$10, depending on the wait time and supply and demand.

16. See Alejandro Portes, "Social Capital: Its Origins and Applications in Modern Sociology," *Annual Review of Sociology* 24 (1998): 16.

17. Hugo was knowledgeable about immigration issues. On one occasion, I spoke to Hugo about his process of applying for legal residence through IRCA. He explained that US employers at the time sold letters to undocumented immigrants regardless of whether they had actually worked in the United States. He explained that employers were strategic in doing so because it would create a pool of permanent and legal border crossers they could draw upon for their labor needs.

18. Hernández-León, *Metropolitan Migrants*.

19. Small, *Unanticipated Gains*, 177.

20. Secure Electronic Network for Travelers Rapid Inspection (SENTRI) is a US Customs and Border Protection program aimed at facilitating the crossing of low-risk travelers. Those who apply for SENTRI must undergo a thorough biographical background check to make sure they have no criminal offenses and have not violated any customs or immigration laws. Once approved, SENTRI crossers are able to use special lanes that allow people to enter the United States at a much faster pace.

21. Mitchell Duneier, *Slim's Table: Race, Respectability, and Masculinity* (Chicago and London: University of Chicago Press, 1992).

22. Javier Auyero, "Patients of the State: An Ethnographic Account of Poor People's Waiting," *Latin American Research Review* 46 (2011): 15.

23. Small, *Unanticipated Gains.*

24. Mustafa Emirbayer and Jeff Goodwin, "Network Analysis, Culture, and the Problem of Agency," *American Journal of Sociology* 99 (1994): 1413.

Chapter 6

1. Massey et al., *Return to Aztlan*, 56.

2. Masferrer and Roberts, "Going Back Home?," note that the top return locations for Mexican migrants are now Tijuana, Guadalajara's metropolitan area, Ciudad Juárez, and Mexicali.

3. Sánchez, 38–39.

4. Nevins, *Operation Gatekeeper*; Andreas, *Border Games*.

5. Pablo Vila, "The Limits of American Border Theory," in *Ethnography at the Border*, ed. Pablo Vila (Minneapolis: University of Minnesota Press, 2003), 309.

6. Emirbayer and Mische, "What Is Agency?," 1011.

7. Ibid.

8. See Erin R. Hamilton and Andrés Villarreal, "Development and the Urban and Rural Geography of Mexican Emigration to the United States," *Social Forces* 90 (2011), 661–83; and Elizabeth Fussell, "Sources of Mexico's Migration Stream," and Hernández-León, *Metropolitan Migrants*, as recent accounts for accounting for the distinctiveness of urban-based migration sources.

9. Durand, Massey, and Zenteno find that the average migrant originates from rural communities in the western Mexican states of Guanajuato, Jalisco, or Michoacán and who performed unskilled labor or agricultural work. See Durand, Massey, and Zenteno, "Mexican Immigration to the United States."

10. Wayne A. Cornelius, "From Sojourners to Settlers: The Changing Profile of Mexican Immigration to the United States," in *U.S.-Mexico Relations: Labor Market Interdependence*, ed. Jorge A. Bustamante, Clark W. Reynolds, and Raúl A. Hinojosa Ojeda, 155–95 (Stanford, CA: Stanford University Press, 1992); Massey et al., *Return to Aztlan*; Chavez, *Shadowed Lives*.

11. Masferrer and Roberts in "Going Back Home?" coined the term "stepwise" return migrants.

12. See the work of Paul, "Stepwise International Migration," Fussell, "Sources of Mexico's Migration Stream," and Zabin and Hughes, "Economic Integration and Labor Flows," as key examples illustrating the multistage approach to network studies.

13. Fussell, "Sources of Mexico's Migration Stream," 963.

14. Burawoy, "Functions and Reproduction of Migrant Labor."

15. Masferrer and Roberts, "Going Back Home?

16. Jorge Durand, Douglas S. Massey, and Chiara Capoferro, "The New Geography of Mexican Immigration," in *New Destinations: Mexican Immigration in the United States*, ed. Víctor Zúñiga and Rubén Hernández-León (New York: Russell Sage Foundation, 2005), 11.

17. See the work of Michael B. Aguilera, "The Impact of the Worker: How Social Capital and Human Capital Influence the Job Tenure of Formerly Undocumented Mexican Immigrants." *Sociological Inquiry* 73 (2003): 52–83, and Aguilera and Massey, "Social Capital and the Wages of Mexican Migrants."

18. Hernández-León, *Metropolitan Migrants*.

19. Fussell, "Tijuana's Place in the Mexican Migration Stream," 151.

20. See Heyman, "Ports of Entry as Nodes in the World System," and Josiah McC. Heyman, "Class and Classification at the U.S.-Mexico Border," *Human Organization* 60 (2001): 128–40.

21. Andreas, *Border Games*.

22. See Jennifer L. Pierce, *Gender Trials: Emotional Lives in Contemporary Law Firms* (Berkeley: University of California Press, 1995), 72. Here, Pierce develops the concept of "strategic friendliness" to refer to strategies which trial lawyers use to create particular impressions with witnesses and the jury. This includes "friendliness, politeness, and tact." Border crossers use strategic friendliness to avoid confrontation and extensive questioning when crossing the border. As one border crosser explained to me, "you have to get on their good side." This is important at the port of entry, where immigration officials have considerable discretion in revoking BCCs. Immigration officials are less likely to question extensively someone who appears to be of a higher social class and someone who engages them pleasantly.

Appendix

1. See William Foote Whyte, *Street Corner Society: The Social Structure of an Italian Slum* (Chicago: University of Chicago Press, 1943); Annette Lareau, *Unequal Childhoods: Class, Race, and Family Life* (Berkeley: University of California Press, 2011); Mitchell Duneier, *Sidewalk* (New York: Farrar, Straus, and Giroux, 1999); Matthew Desmond, *On the Fireline: Living and Dying with Wildland Firefighters* (Chicago: University of Chicago Press, 2007), as great key texts that exemplify what Annette Lareau terms the, "story behind the story."

2. Hernández-León, *Metropolitan Migrants*; Fussell, "Sources of Mexico's Migration Streams."

3. For an overview of the high rates of migration to the United States, see William Kandel and Douglas Massey, "The Culture of Mexican Migration: A Theoretical and Empirical Analysis," *Social Forces* 80 (2002): 981–1004.

4. Wayne A. Cornelius, "Interviewing Undocumented Immigrants: Methodological Reflections Based on Fieldwork in Mexico and the U.S." *International Migration Review* 16 (Summer 1982): 378–411; Holmes, *Fresh Fruit, Broken Bodies*; Chavez, *Shadowed Lives*.

5. Holmes, *Fresh Fruit, Broken Bodies*; Hernández-León, *Metropolitan Migrants*; Massey et al. *Return to Aztlan*; Gomberg-Muñoz, *Labor and Legality*.

6. See Cornelius, "Interviewing Undocumented Immigrants." Chavez, *Shadowed Lives*. Historically, snowball sampling has been used to investigate the structure of

networks and to study hard-to-find populations (such as drug users) for which there is no "sampling frame"; see Patrick Biernacki and Dan Waldorf, "Snowball Sampling: Problems and Techniques of Chain Referral Sampling," *Sociological Methods and Research* 10 (1981): 141–63.

7. See Robert M. Emerson, Rachel I. Fretz, and Linda L. Shaw, *Writing Ethnographic Fieldnotes* (Chicago: University of Chicago Press, 1995).

8. For an overview of the problem of homophily, see Miller McPherson, Lynn Smith-Lovin, and James M. Cook, "Birds of a Feather: Homophily in Social Networks," *Annual Review of Sociology* 27 (2001): 415–44. For an innovative approach to sampling hard-to-find populations, see Ted Mouw, Sergio Chávez, Heather Edelblute, and Ashton Verdery, "Binational Social Networks and Assimilation: A Test of the Important of Transnationalism," *Social Problems* 61 (2014): 329–59.

9. Mario Luis Small, " 'How Many Cases Do I Need?' On Science and Logic of Case Selection in Field-Based Research," *Ethnography* 10 (2009): 14.

10. For a discussion of the limitation of interview data, see Colin Jerolmack and Shamus Khan, "Talk is Cheap: Ethnography and the Attitudinal Fallacy," *Sociological Methods and Research* 43 (2014): 178–209.

11. In "Disposable Ties and the Urban Poor," 1303, Matthew Desmond writes that by studying eviction through ethnography rather than relying solely on interview data he was "able to compare what people said about the support they received from friends and family with support they actually received during that difficult hour."

12. Whyte, *Street Corner Society*, 280.

13. Annette Lareau, "Using the Terms *Hypothesis* and *Variable* for Qualitative Work: A Critical Reflection," *Journal of Marriage and Family* 74 (2012): 671–77.

INDEX

CPSIA information can be obtained
at www.ICGtesting.com
Printed in the USA
BVOW08s1712050917
494013BV00004B/4/P